Mind Tickles

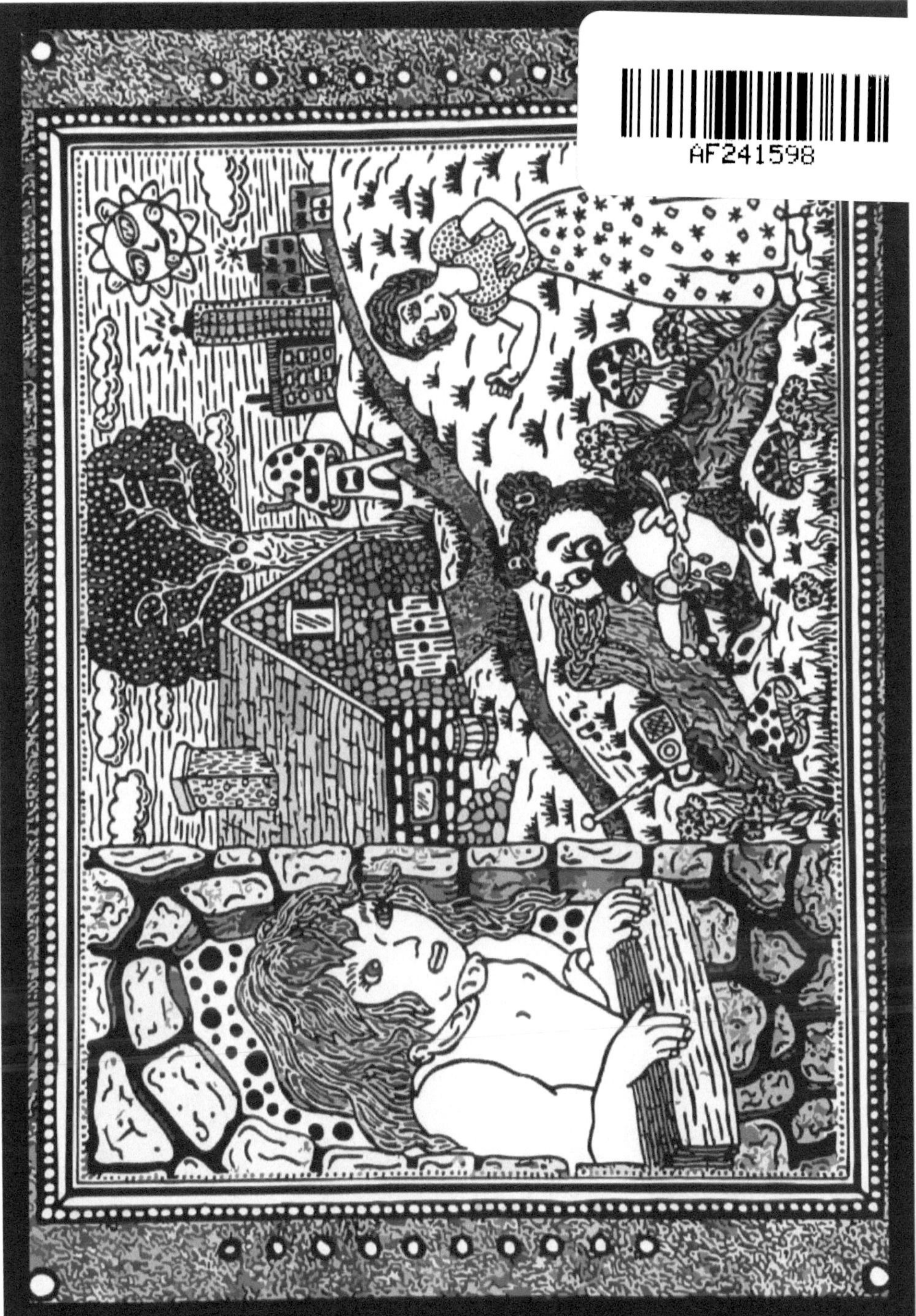

Arthur Selent

ISBN: 978-1-961677-89-0 (Paperback)
ISBN: 978-1-963565-27-0 (E-Book)

Printed in the United States of America: 2024909140

Published by:

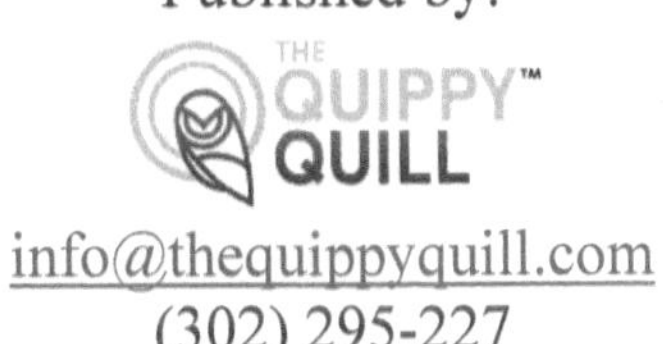

info@thequippyquill.com
(302) 295-227

March 22-2023

Introductions

The artwork drawings are part of a project that I invented during the last years of my forty years of homeless life wandering the North American continent. Seventeen years of hitchhiking the long roads, three years of bicycling travel and camping, and then twenty years of hiding in a van sneakily parked where I could get away with it.

The artwork started out as postcards, which I would trade for "spare change" or small money. This paid for my food while I hid sneaky like in a van and made more artwork. The collection grew slowly.

There were times during the fourteen years of working on the postcards when I'd be lucky enough to get a seasonal or short-term job. The jobs paid so much more than the money had to come from somewhere. So, I gave my best to who signed the paycheck.

Now retired, I start writing and bring the postcards out from storage and insert a few in each of my books.

Enjoy,

Arthur Selent

Introductions

This various unorganized collection of smarts and dumbs started out as comments and replies to social media posts. I kept a paper copy and was soon inventing and searching for ideas of what to write. The collection grew faster than I could use the various items. Then one day, there were 500 pages. A lot of emotional rant, and having which could never be published, was mixed into the soup.

Presented to the reader is an assembly of word presentations that flows from me to you. Some are a complete surprise even to me, as I thought and wrote them. Others were modified versions of what I read elsewhere. Some came from a talk where a few words created a scenery of activity on my inner visual thinking machine.

Please enjoy my eccentric attempt to become a world-famous writer.

Arthur Selent

Aug. 2020

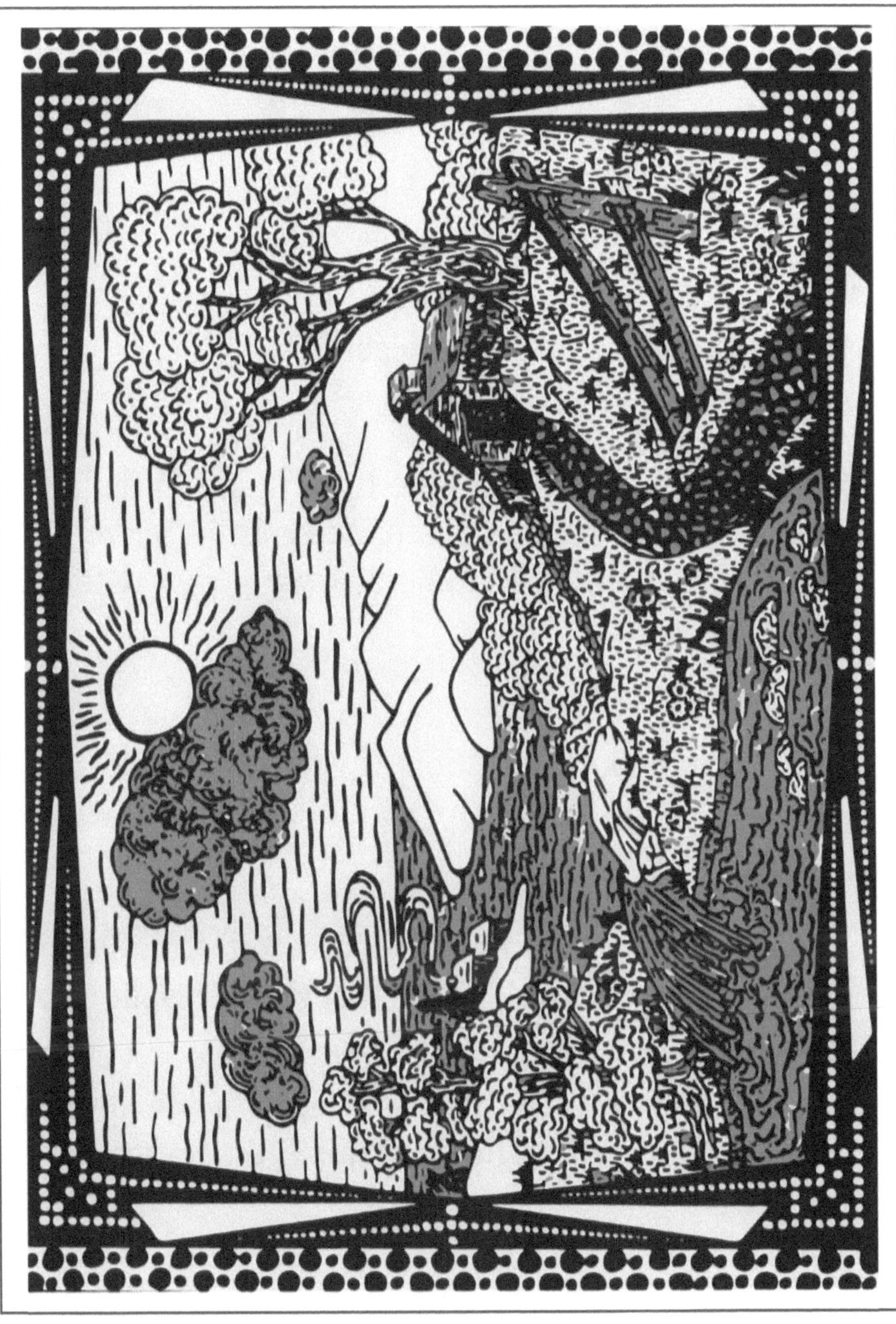

4229 ==> Money has become God. Just look at fake religion, fake science, fake news, fake politics, everything fake.

Welcome to "Fake Tomorrow".

******

4230 ==> Knowledge is power, so long as they can keep the people stupid and deceived.

******

4231 ==> I notice that all the little flying birds like seeds. Does this mean a diet of seeds is the secret to flying? Will we grow feathers if we go on a food fashion of seeds?

******

4232 ==> It is not a question of who we can sex but rather a question of who we can tolerate living with.

******

4233 ==> The romantics may write of Knights in shining armor who slay the dragon to rescue the pretty lady.

But they never write of the Knight in shining armor who pushes a button and nukes the pretty lady into dust.

*****

4234 ==> He dressed like a girl with a female dress and makeup. They called him "The Lady". He really dressed well. Women envied his fashions.

He was the eccentric joke of the village, but not those dirty castaways living on social assistance and public charity. He had an income from some dead relative, which a lawyer paid out to him in weekly sums, like getting a paycheck from a job; it allowed him to live quite well in comfort. Others, drudging the quagmire of failures, often became jealous of his ease and comfort.

But somehow after he'd swagger close to their intimate body with his girly manners, they became unsettled and stepped away while politely wishing "The Lady" a good day.

It was talked about secretly that his tiny penis had grown inwards and made a smelly hole. No one had ever seen him naked. He often, with such girly airs, bragged about still being an innocent virgin.

One day, "The Lady" decided to get married. Suddenly, wives kept husbands at home. Mothers kept the older sons at home. Girlfriends handcuffed their boyfriends to their wrists. And single men decided it was a good time to travel.

With his exaggerated female bearing "The Lady," prowled the streets and clubs looking for a suitable husband. Someone who was all man, as manly as a man could be.

******

4235 ==> What dreadful hard times we have to endure. It keeps one in a state of continued inelegance.

******

4236 ==> A good neighbor is someone who smiles at you over the fence but does not climb over the fence.

******

4237 ==> She was the most ugly thing he'd ever seen. Then he realized she was perfect for the act. He asked what she charge to haunt a house.

******

4238 ==> Do chickens hatched with a heat lamp love their mother?

******

4239 ==> They come in the sneaky sleep at night. They are called dreams.

******

4240 (1/2) ==> So, you are the smart detective who has cracked case after case of vintage wine. When others gave up looking for clues, you persevered and found the key to the wine cellar. Such rewards for a job well done.

4240 (2/2) ==> But why stop now? Where is the case that hides the bank vault keys? The investigation continues. Sure, is good wine.

Now drive carefully. The bank is out there somewhere

******

4241 ==> He sneaked in at night and emptied the company safely. Stacks and stacks of money were carried out to sit on the back seat of his car. Each armload was lovingly and tenderly placed on the seat. He slightly wondered why there was so much money in the safe. He'd only expected a tenth of what there was.

There was a big investigation, and he eagerly sat in the lunchroom at noon listening to the talk. A week later, the workers were given notice that the company went bankrupt and was closing.

He laughed all the way as he drove home. How clever he had been to remove his future wages just in time before the company fell apart.

******

4242 (1/2) ==> There is nothing so relaxing as the bathing hour. The private school for young ladies sits atop the grey stone cliffs. Below, in the afternoon heat, the young women wander to the beach to bathe. The sea shore sparkles with sun diamonds and little ripples.

4242 (2/2) ==> The beach does not have a road and is on the private land of the school, so no one public even goes there. He only found it by wandering along the shoreline for some time.

He was lured into sitting there watching women throw off their large beach towels and scamper nude for the water. Some hesitated when they saw him, but soon joined the others splashing about.

He took off all his clothes and lay naked on the sand. This produced a reaction from the ladies. They stood there in knee-deep water, huddled together, talking. It was plain to see he was what they talked about.

A few of the older, bigger girls came over to look down at his naked body. He was excited. What could happen? It was so bold. Would they scream on the jump to beat him?

Finally, one touching him says, "Teach us about sex." She and the others sat down rather close. He was on fire with arousal fantasy, the words. "Teach us Sex", racing about in his mind. Lust heaven indeed.

The bed squeaked, groaned, and rocked up and down. He awoke. The dream ended. There was his soft, old, ugly, flabby wife on top of him, humping away, doing the pole dance.

******

4243 ==>A human must be careful upon marriage, for there is little escape afterward. They are likely to make themselves rather foolish, silly, and brutal at the same time. How soon, however, does a tender and affectionate romance turn into enemies of hate and passion, but chained to each other until death.

******

4244 ==> How could these young, beautiful girls with the right to life and pleasure resist the seduction of the smell of money, even though often it came from a hand old and trembling, plucking the fresh-faced rose from the garden.

******

4245 ==> So many top-level governments and corporate management are simply a gathering of more or less idle people trying hard not to disturb the game while waiting for their oversized paychecks

******

4246 (1/2) ==> By living like a girl in his fine dresses and by years of exaggerating the female walk, prance, wiggle, and manners, he had totally lost all masculine looks and ways. His smooth face, his long girl-like hair, and now he wears his grandfather's hat.

4246 (2/2) ==> How he fans himself like a schoolgirl using conceited movements of his hands. My, My!

The poor, unfortunate creature is neither a proper "she" nor a proper "he".

******

4247 ==> Knowing how to play does not mean you know how to win.

Just go to any Casino and see how many experts will tell you how to win while they themselves are losing.

******

4248 ==> They carried the truth of themselves inside a sheltered place inside their minds. They would thrive or perish as fate decreed. But they dare not reveal the truth about themselves.

******

4249 ==> How so ugly. A virtuous person with a mean mind.

******

4250 ==> Don't ever hate what you are when you can change what you are.

******

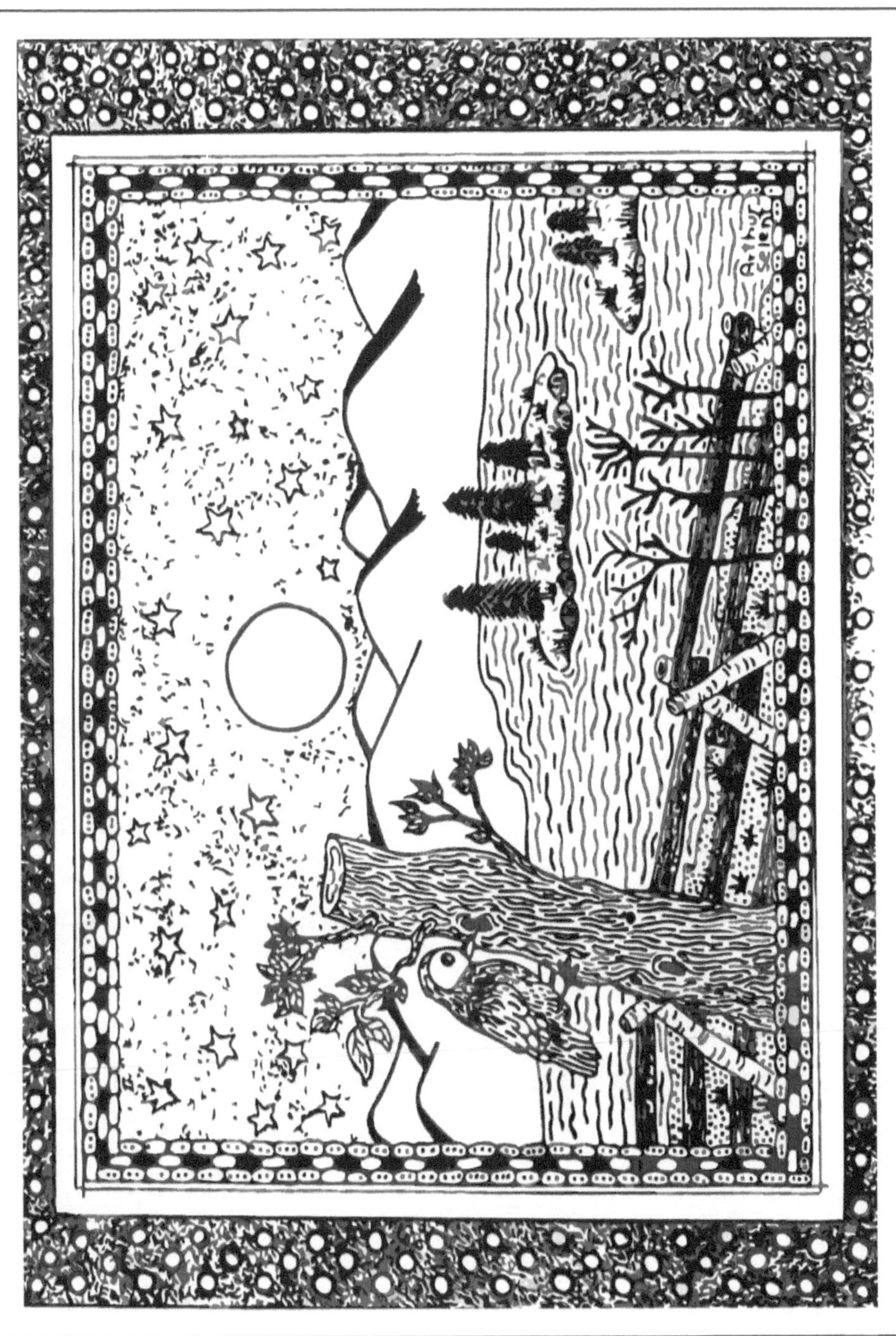

4251 ==> Her job was to scrub things. She herself even looked scrubbed.

******

4252 ==> So, you finished digging the tunnel under the bank. Remember to buy some new shoes, three sizes too large. Leave some nice footprints in the dust and dirt.

******

4253 ==> They are the puppet masters. The show is on. We see the puppets, but we do not see who pulls the strings from the shadows to make the puppets dance.

******

4254 ==> They have a nice office with awards and pictures on the wall. They have a nice desk and a swivel chair that reclines for sleeping. On this chair, they sit every day, filled with boredom and frustration. With ego executive minds, they work doing nothing.

Wishing inside that they had a purpose, but not wishing to change the easy reality of the present.

******

4255 ==> You can always see an over-educated expert, but you cannot tell them anything because they always know everything.

******

4256 ==> An audience is a big monster with thousands of eyes and billions of sharp teeth.

******

4257 ==> When the first sunshine laughed with happy joy, the laugh tumbled down and broke into trillions of pieces. These skipped along to mutate into sparkling dancing fairies picking rainbow dew drops off the crisp morning meadow grass

******

4258 ==> We have read some of this modern free verse writing and wonder who set it free.

******

4259 ==> How many of us have the experience needed to deal with repeated prosperity adjustments?

******

4260 ==> Day by day in the hospital, the patients are obsessed with the desire to change their beds. One would prefer to suffer by the window. Another thinks they will get better sooner if they are by the door.

******

4261 ==> Hard work never killed a commander, only the one who was commanded to do the hard work.

******

4262 ==> Men often make fun of women who carry a large purse. But the minute they walk down the garden path, hand in hand, the man will ask if she could just put this little thing or that in the purse since he has no room in his pockets.

She, the pack mule.

Soon, the children start to walk, and well, she is the pack mule.

******

4263 ==> Society, in its eagerness for sensational excitement, often creates the cover-up deception long before society knows the facts.

******

4264 ==> In our arrogant minds, what we do not know is not knowledge.

******

4265 ==> Why do we pay so many first and second-class experts to tell us all manner of fake fairy tales when we could get the story for cheaper from a third-rate expert?

******

4266 ==> The hail sounds like two skeletons tap dancing on a tin roof.

******

4267 ==> In his absence, the courts found him guilty and, in his absence, they sentenced him to death. He wrote the courts a letter saying they can execute him in his absence.

******

4268 ==> The poor, honest farmer thought it wrong to kill his family, but the insane soldier, being paid to kill the enemy, thought it ever so right.

******

4269 ==> She told such dreadful lies. It made me gasp and stretch the space between the ears.

******

4270 ==> Large numbers of people are very clever to remain important without losing their insignificance.

******

4271 ==> Our most passionate opinions are often about things we know nothing about or understand.

******

4272 ==> So many preach about equality, but we only want it with the rich and influential. We do not want equality with the poor and homeless.

******

4273 ==> Memories are worth more than gold, and yet there are those who would steal even these if they could.

******

4274 ==> Many people do not like music, but they like the noise it makes.

******

4275 (1/2) ==> Oh, she was ugly! Her hair, matted and coarse, looked as if it had been swallowed a few times and puked back up.

Her face was reddish and pimply, the color of brick dust. Her teeth are long and protrude at different angles. One eye looked left and the other looked right. Her nose was shaped like a knob of shallow mush. Her body was without the elegance of female traits. No rounded curves to attract or entice.

But the parents looked down on her with much love. They had done slightly better than the neighbors whose kids had multiple legs, arms, or four heads and no feet, or even sixteen months and no head.

There had been a big war, and the humans, not knowing who they were fighting, lashed out in all directions with virus, chemicals, and nukes.

4275 (2/2) ==> Few humans survived, and those who did had very deformed children.

******

4276 ==> One does not easily forget what one is told by another who is very angry

******

4277 ==> Now, what we have said is the worst thing we could say about each other. Yelling the most ultimate insult, then now there is no reason we can't be friends.

******

4278 ==> Have you noticed how frustrating it is that when you want to talk about yourself, someone else is talking about themselves.

******

4279 ==> The best way to keep teenagers at home is to keep the gas tank in the car empty.

******

4280 ==> To give an accurate and realistic account description of the event would require someone far less intelligent than me, myself and I.

******

4281 ==> It is often easier to become successful than to remain successful.

* * * * * *

4282 ==> Treasure sometimes hides in the dirt.

* * * * * *

4283 ==> We used to buy and own it forever. Today, we rent and lease, never own and pay forever.

* * * * * *

4284 ==> Beneath our sophistication of our appearance and fashion lies a layer of unawareness. Confused delusion.

A stone painted yellow and sold as a gold nugget, turning about in front of a mirror.

* * * * * *

4285 ==> One can usually buy temporary love using good looks or money as bait.

* * * * * *

4286==> Every summer, a fifth of the population becomes ill-housed, ill-nourished, ill-dressed, while ill-spending. They call it a vacation.

* * * * * *

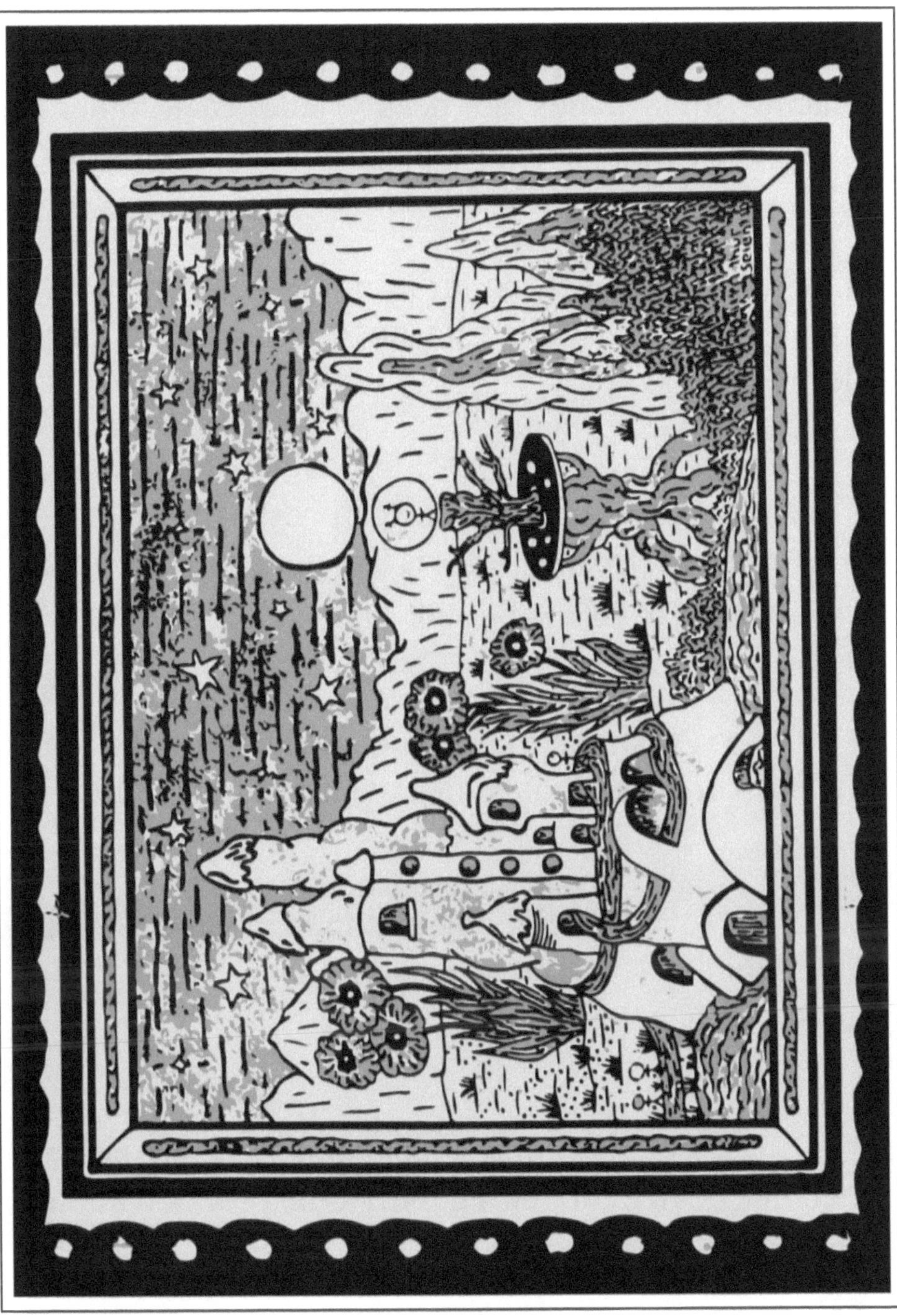

4287 ==> An alliance in international politics is when two thieving flags form a trade agreement, placing their hands so deeply into each other's pocket that they cannot properly plunder a third flag.

******

4288 ==> Stand not too far from the rich person lest they forget you, but stand not too close lest they destroy you.

******

4289 ==> The gambling known as business looks with austere frowns and is in disfavor over the business known as gambling.

******

4290 ==> A human may trip over many things, but the most frustrating is to trip over one's own bluff.

******

4291 ==> Faith-believing without evidence what one is told by someone who has no knowledge of the topic.

******

4292 ==> Corporation management is a sneaky machine device for getting individual profits without individual responsibility.

******

4293 ==> Every person has an unequaled right to their own opinion, so long as it agrees with my opinion.

******

4294 ==> Usually, one has reason to be quiet after one has said all one has on their mind.

******

4295 ==> An auctioneer is someone who picks people's pockets using his voice. Invisible hands float in the air to the money pocket and play.

******

4296 ==> Certainly, it is better to know nothing than to know that which is not so.

******

4297 ==> Telling the truth during a time of deception realities is a criminal act.

Welcome to today. You poor sod, trying to earn enough to feed yourself, while all around you, sneaky deception steals the money before it gets to you.

But you are too honest. Your moral fiber is stronger than the storm, bluffing reality.

******

4298 ==> Most of us lack that natural cunning and shrewdness which provides so much more for people than virtue ever could.

******

4299 ==> Laziness is richness just like money. The more we have, the more we want.

******

4300 (1/2) ==> The young bride was dancing erotically with another man when the husband slipped on a drink bottle that had tumbled to the floor. He had struck his head very hard on the stone floor and was instantly dead.

The piss started staining his pants as he lay there sprawled. Everyone stared, but no one was in the mood to be first to poke at the body.

Someone told the bride. She does not rush to the side of her lover. The loved one lies in a puddle of piss, all alone.

She said, "No, I will not look at it."

Someone close by said, "But you sure liked to look at it when it was alive."

******

4301 ==> Nothing will get done until someone finds a way to make a profit doing it.

******

4302 ==> Very few people have the ability to live a life of idleness.

******

4303 ==> Welcome to:

    (1) Fake Science fairy tales.

    (2) Fake News fairy tales.

    (3) Fake Political fairy tales.

    (4) Fake Religion fairy tales.

Welcome to plain old me, too honest to make a fake fairy tale. Now, how does one get into the profit business of fake fairy tales?

******

4304 ==> Give publicly and steal privately, and society will think you are a nice person.

******

4305 ==> If we removed all the idiots and fools from the planet, there wouldn't be any fun for us to watch.

******

4306 ==> When they ask you for advice, ask them what they want to hear and then repeat it back to them.

******

4307 ==> People who set out to be pranksters and rascals forget to look at themselves to see if they are better constructed to be fools.

******

4308 ==> Now I do not know if this is true, but the insect expert flapping their lips on the portable radio this morning said, "Dragonfly females will often fake their own deaths to avoid mating with undesired males."

Now imagine if human females faked their death to avoid mating with undesired males. So, there I walk into the gathering of women. All the women fall to the floor, faking their deaths.

Now, which do I bring back to life to stimulate and save? I cannot save them all.

******

4309 (1/2) ==> You have plotted and schemed until you have a dinner date with the cute new girl in the office complex.

Now you are eating dinner in an exotic, mood dim lit romance trap. You must decide by the dinner's end if you find the bill more meaningful than the woman or the other way around. You have a choice: bring her home and avoid her ever after, or bring her to your place for a more personal date.

4309 (2/2) ==> You are safe. She will not tell anyone at work. But choose wisely, you will not have a second chance if she moves up the corporate ladder and becomes your boss.

******

4310 (1/2) ==> Remember when the big flags were all racing to produce more and bigger nukes for the pleasure sport of mass murder. Then all of a sudden, the big flags stopped the nuke race and joined forces to preach anti-nuke fairy tales. So, what created this overnight sudden shift in motivations?

The Galactic Federation bid the Earthlings to use nukes for the sport and pleasure of mass murder. To show they meant business, they disabled a number of important nuke launch sites.

This sent the puppet masters overseeing the politics of the flags into a demonic rage. If they are not allowed to use nukes, then no one else should use nukes.

The new evil did not take long to show itself. Bio virus warfare.

The puppet masters moved themselves into position to reap vast profits and started the virus games.

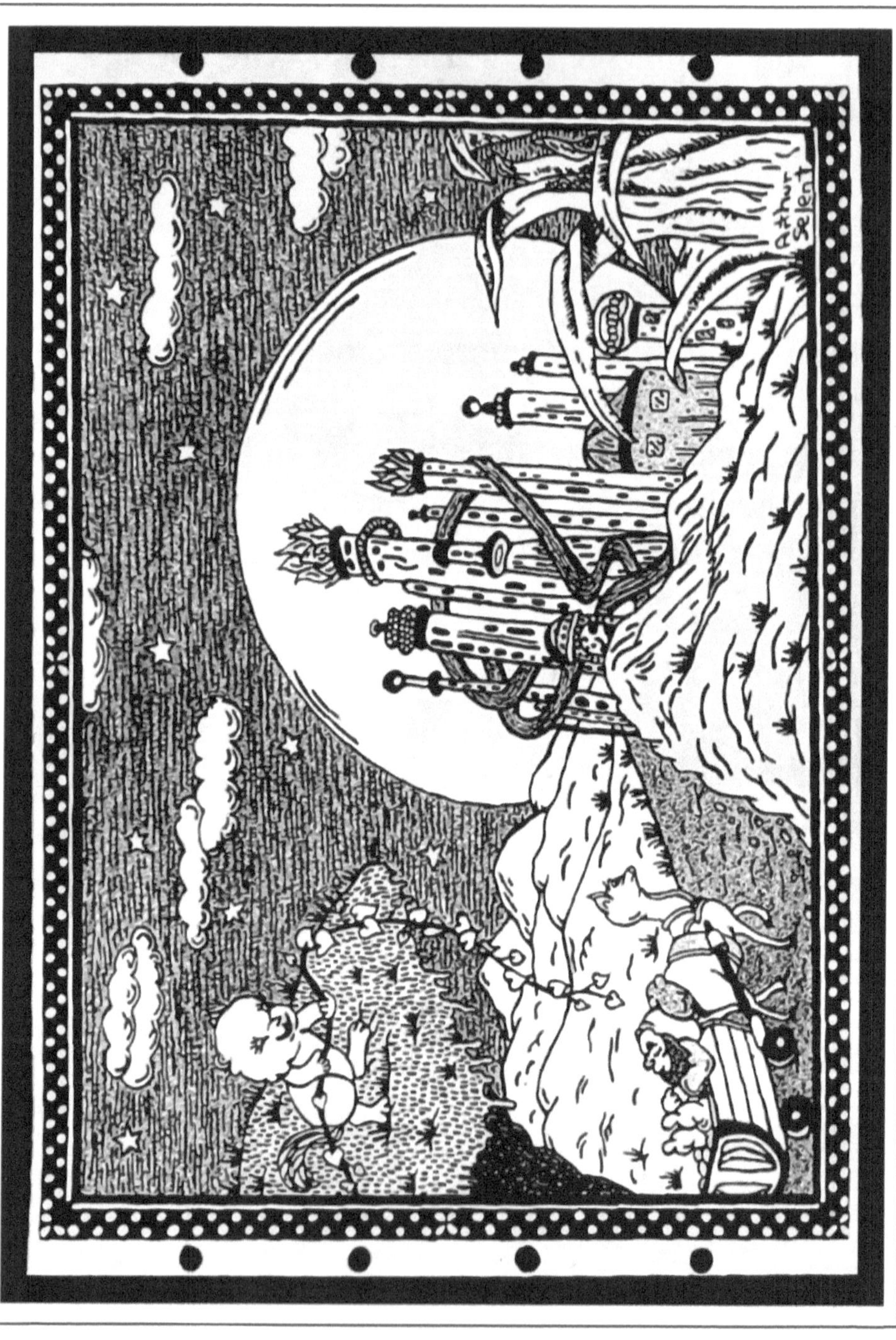

4310 (2/2) ==> Massive new labs being built by the wealthy flags. New virus created, bred, and studied for possible profit and bio warfare. Various vaccines have been tested on the population, trying to find a vaccine that actually works. The virus mafia is commanding the law and governments to enforce crimes against humanity. Ten booster jobs and still the vaccines do not work.

This is a demon horror game set up to sell non-working vaccine bio experiments for profits. When they finally succeed in creating a vaccine that works, they can choose who lives and who dies. A select group can then surprises insert a virus into another flag and mass murder the population.

In the meantime, there is much action behind the curtains, doing the evening wine and dine dance, moving the greed profits about.

******

4311 ==> The happiest time in a banker's life is when the chase for the money looks like it has a reasonable prospect of catching the money.

******

4312 ==> Were it not for fools to swindle money from, many of us would not earn a living.

******

4313 ==> Life is like a game of cards; to win, we must play the right cards at the right time.

******

4314 ==> Much insane thinking is caused by religion preaching opinions and news media selling fake fairy tales made up by those hiding the truth.

******

4315 ==> They say love is blind, but there is always one partner who sees part of the picture.

******

4316 ==> The cocktail folks, undisturbed by the complicated rush hour crowd, have their alcohol as part of a master plan to ease business contacts or lubricate logistically planned seductions.

******

4317 ==> Under the bar, the proprietor watered the drinks as if he were watering midsummer flowers.

******

4318 ==> All map makers should put the ocean in the same location. This eliminates the need to cross-reference a dozen maps to estimate the location of the oceans.

******

4319 ==> I like to comment, reply, and post on social media, but it seems that too often I say something that shatters another's delusions. We cannot all the real facts, the real opinions, and the one and only real story. So, you see, there is a place for me in social media because I am always right.

If only I knew when to keep my mouth shut. If only I knew how to tell fairy tales instead of the truth.

******

4320 ==> The lighted upper window of the distant farmhouse greatly disturbed the night goblin. Someone was awake and might be outside. And there was the apple tree just below the window with branches hanging down overladen with ripe, big juicy apples.

******

4321 ==> One enjoys the sunshine and soft winds more charming than in dreams. One walks on a lonely scenic path or strolls by the seashore. Illusions and dream thoughts drift through the mind as one idles along.

******

4322 (1/2) ==> He was a favorite at social functions where society tolerated him as being very intellectual.

4322 (2/2) ==> He possessed a wit without much depth, quick perception without much penetration, in general, an education of knowledge without much learning. He saw himself as a man of the world, even though the longest distance he'd ever gone was to go to the other side of the city to be a coffee shop super star flashing his eccentric clothes, which no one in their right mind would wear.

******

4323 ==> We go old without suspecting it. All out ripe firmness with all its power, energy, and beauty lasts but a mere decade or three. Somewhat longer than a flower's life.

We perceive not the work that age is accomplishing because age is so slow and regular. It becomes too common to notice or pay attention to until one day we awaken and, in front of the mirror, see some old fossil shuffling about.

The years vanish so completely, gently, quietly, and quickly.

******

4324 (1/2) ==> The Aliens from a way galaxy brought the humans to Earth when Earth became suitable for life. We were to be another work colony as the Aliens have on other planets. We were to grow vegetables for the spaceships. Like a farmer growing food for a big city.

4324 (2/2) ==> The Aliens are vegetarians and prefer to live in large craft floating in space rather than living on a planet. But they need a firm base on a planet or moon for repairs and building new craft, as well as storage for various things. They also use the planets for growing food through the use of work colonies. These work colonies are kept in discipline through various brainwashing methods, such as religious insanity of giving to the Gods. Many of the aliens are very good at mental suggestions and mind manipulations.

The aliens at one time lived among the humans, but the humans were often too bad to be tolerated.

Now, when humans learn to be nice, the Aliens will come closer. But do we want the aliens among us?

The age-old question. Why did the cows kick the rancher off the planet?

******

4325 (1/2) ==> Fake science and bio-warfare

Humans will face their biggest danger when the virus mafia and the planet puppet masters finally create a virus vaccine that actually works to stop the virus.

4325 (2/2) ==> At present, the various vaccines being used for bio experiments done on the population seem to only make massive billions in profit, much to the harm and suffering of those injected with top-secret ingredients, deceptively injected. Some people get seriously bad health events from these bio experiments, but profit has so far succeeded in covering up and hiding truthful information.

The danger is that when a vaccine is created that actually works, then that puts the virus mafia and the planet puppet masters into a unique position. Since they already command governments to hand over money and enforce crimes against humanity, they will then be able to save a select group and kill off others with sneaky jabs or no jabs at all as they release one after another virus into the population.

This is a greedy profit game.

Now you, human pest, line up for your tenth booster bio jab.

******

4326 ==> Why do we have so many friends on social media if we never see their posts and only see ads?

******

4327 ==> Poker is a game where someone with paranormal gifts of mind reading, intuition, telepathic abilities, and other big words can make a nice profit.

However, someone with a brain-dead mind might frustrate the psychic one, as there would be no brain functions to read thoughts from

******

4328 ==> Ask no questions and hear no lies.

******

4329 ==> There I am once again a stumbling block for someone. The mean rich criminal representing the established delusions of society says, "You fu*ked up my game, now what you going to do about it?"

What, where, who? I know nothing about this. I, in my innocence, was merely shuffling along. Why did that dude decide to play a game and put me in that game?

******

4330 ==> He has no brains. He is corruption walking beside the leader. He is a yeah, yeah man. Whenever the leader is confused or insecure, needing assurance, he says Yeah, yeah, then rushes to his corruption puppet master to ask what to tell the leader.

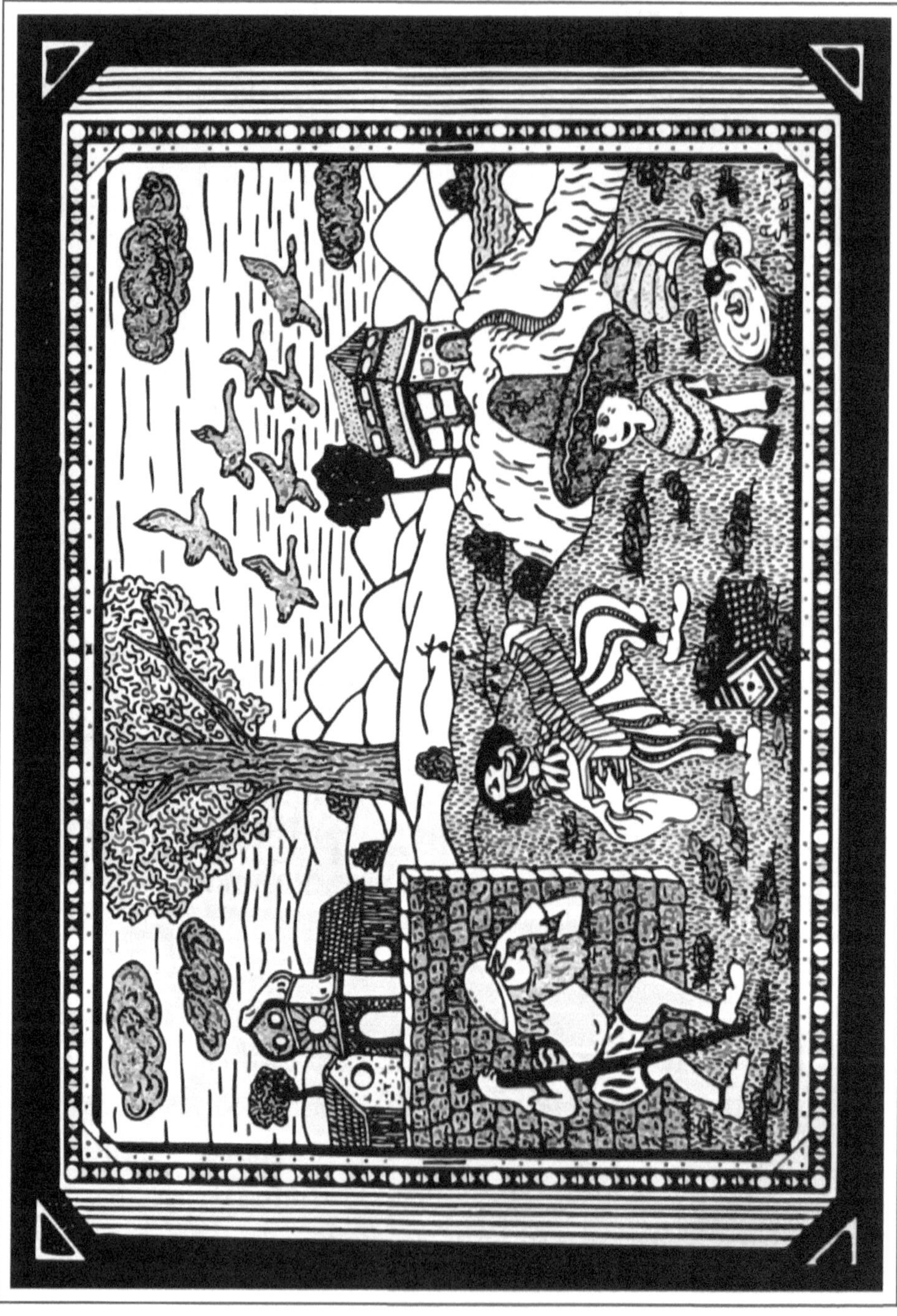

******

4331 ==> The person who has never been tempted does not really know how dishonest they are.

******

4332 ==> It is a wise person who profits from an experience, but a wiser person would let another fellow have the experience and profit from watching and studying.

******

4333 ==> Too many troubles can be traced to saying "yes" too fast and "no" too slow.

******

4334 ==> The gangster sitting amidst the reek of piles of money thinks carefully about his business schemes. How can he get more?

******

4335 ==> The more hungry we are, the fewer faults we find with the cooking.

******

4336 ==> A fool always finds another fool just a little more foolish than himself.

******

4337 ==> Poverty makes things ugly and frightful, but money makes even ugliness seem beautiful.

******

4338 ==> The older they get, the more fantastic things they did when they were young.

******

4339 ==> Why does a slight tax increase cost us a few hundred money units while a substantial tax cut only saves us a few money units?

******

4340 ==> Some of us have a very open mind. It is so open that the wind just blows through and nothing remains to provide thought activity.

******

4341 ==> He was a great money-grabbing business executive in a publishing of books company. He had a much too young, pretty lady in his office. The sad look of defeat on her face. He tried to explain why her book was not selling very much: "The problem is that you leave too many characters alive at the end."

******

4342 ==> Few of the men of today remember the women of yesterday.

******

4343 ==> To have been and to be are not possible to be done in the same period of time.

******

4344 ==> The music coming from the filthy, dirty bar sounded like alley cats yowling on garbage night. Sudden clashes of overturned garbage cans interrupt the steadiness of the music as a well-aimed throw threw out a drunk from the back door.

******

4345 ==> With enough advertising, you can even sell things that are totally useless.

******

4346 ==> Big money, Big Trouble, Stay Poor.

******

4347 ==> Spirit World is like a big airport; you can go to many different places if you know how.

******

4348 ==> He knew how to sing the music of love as no other man ever could.

But she knew how to write the words of love as no other woman ever could.

******

4349 (1/2) ==> There is perhaps more illusion than reality in wishes.

4349 (2/2) ==> Illusions lift us to float on delusion dream clouds pushed about by the wind.

Reality just leaves one on Earth doing our today routines.

******

4350 ==> The people of today do not dream properly. They are much too busy chasing the money.

******

4351 (1/3) ==> The autumn wind, grinning and softly whispering, gusted now and then to carry the leaves from the trees up to the clouds.

The men on their lunch, seated about the sturdy rustic picnic table, talked like little schoolboy chatter, each eager to have their say. The men drinking like leaking cisterns soon became tipsy. Their male desires began to have more interest in the attractive backpacker setting up a tent in the camp space close to the group. She was a lovely creature, about the age of a university student and looking just as fresh-faced.

Lunch was over, and the men, somewhat influenced by drink, went back to work. Repairs were being done to the road running alongside the campground.

4351 (2/3) ==> Late afternoon, the crew was done and went home.

One fellow rushed home, washed, had dinner, and dressed in his image of being a backpacker with suitable fashion. He set off, stopping at a flower garden to get some flowers. Next, a wine store to buy a bottle of one of the better wines. Oh, how excited he was. His male desires are hot with the fantasy of a romantic evening.

The tent was there, but she was not. He did not wish to be seen sneaky near, so he said, "hello", rather loudly.

She answered from some nearby shrubs, "Over here." Oh, she was so welcoming, he could feel his erection already starting. His lusty thoughts got more excited. He shuffled over to where she was. He heard water splashing; she was not concerned that he stood there watching.

He could not come right out and say he wanted sex, so he had to use the sneaky approach. "I noticed earlier you had a backpack and wondered where you came from."

She, drying herself, said some faraway place.

She was pulling up her pants, and he waited for her to finish so he could give her the flowers when a gruff man's voice came from the tent, "Susy, who are you talking to?"

4351 (3/3) ==> Thinking fast, he said, "Oh, I thought you were from Spain, and I was hoping for some news from back home. I have to go now; my wife and I are having our wedding anniversary tonight." He rushed away.

******

4352 ==> Our dreams, our thoughts, our desires, so vague, so important, stay inside us growing like a vine, grabbing away at illusions and delusions while stumbling over reality.

******

4353 ==> How stupid human are when they get love into their heads. Then they understand nothing else. They even close their eyes to deception.

******

4354 ==> Some would rather work hard all day doing work for a master than sneak, steal, and make a mess out of living.

******

4355 ==> Listen friend, you and you got to stick together because these shifty, sneaky managements are thicker than thieves at a lawyer's funeral.

******

4356 ==> People can pick their friends, but relatives they are stuck with for life.

******

4357 ==> Fraud is theft with a smile.

******

4358 (1/3) ==> They were just kids, but they often saw each other around the village. He was from a very poor family, and she was from the rich political elite. As they grew up, their paths tended to cross more and more.

Then one day, they went down to the small river to splash about in the heat of the afternoon. Something happened between them. It was the first time they'd held each other close in romantic urges, completely naked.

They began to secretly meet often. More intimate than newlyweds. When the rich political elite family found out, they decided he was not right for their pampered baby.

One night, returning home, he found himself grabbed by three muscle-bound thugs. They punched him here and there, inflicting pain with much enjoyment. The biggest goon, then says, "Here is your boat ticket. The boat leaves tomorrow evening. Here is food money for a month. The boss doesn't want any flea-bitten dog sniffing his baby's pussy.

4358 (2/3) ==> You are given a chance, don't push your luck." Then they give him a few more kicks.

He lay there, all alone in the dark, all sore and hurting. Soon, the coolness of the evening aroused his strength, and he hobbled home to his room.

He awoke late in the morning and in a daze, packed some things. His body was hurting so much from the beating. He slowly walked through the village on his way to the boat. She saw him and approached. He explained all. She was angry and suggested that they both run away together. He would have none of that, always looking over his shoulder and living in fear. She was greatly disturbed and ripped a ribbon from her dress, then ripped this into two pieces.

She says, "Will meet again, but might be so changed by the years that we no longer recognize each other. Carry one half, and I will carry the other half so that when we meet, we can match the halves and know we are together again."

Many years later, he, already with grey hair, decided to take a boat back to his childhood home.

She, also with grey hair, had now command of the family fortune. She spent some time crisscrossing the land to look for him, and not finding him, boarded the boat. The same boat he was on.

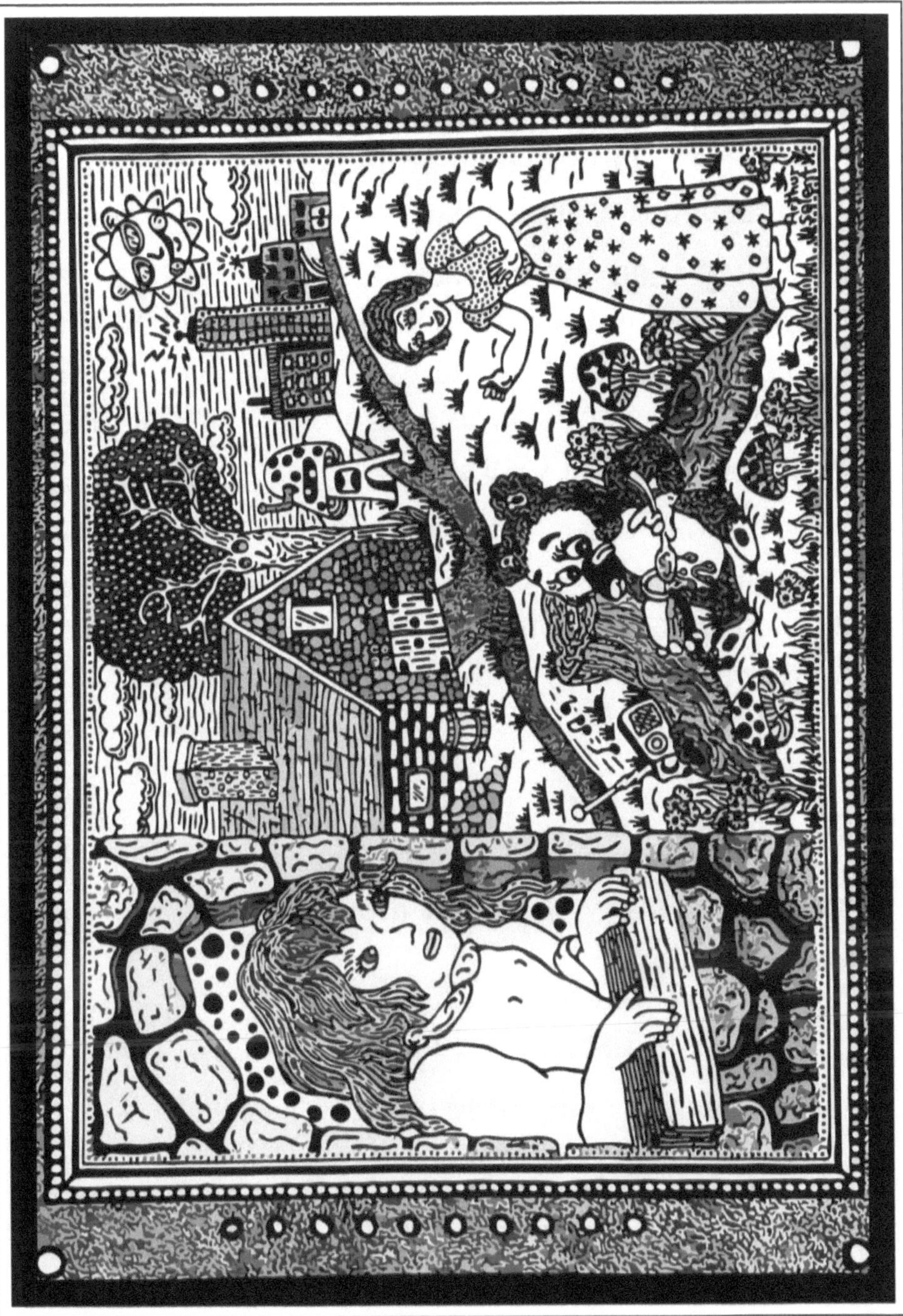

4358 (3/3) ==> During the trip, both stayed in their room so their paths did not cross.

When they got close to home and were almost at the harbor, another boat going too fast lost control and smashed into their boat.

They had both been standing at the rail watching the land come closer. In fact, they had been standing side by side, not knowing of each other. The collision sent a shock wave through the boat, and a few passengers fell overboard.

It took rescue boats a while to arrive. They found two elderly bodies floating entangled, each clutched a small ribbon in one hand. The rescuers wondered about this as they hauled the bodies out of the water.

******

4359 ==> Somewhat frustrating that often our dreams fade away when our thoughts wake up.

******

4360 ==> Big fish eat little fish.

Big money eats little money.

******

4361 ==> Reasoning with difficult people is fine if you can reach their reasoning without losing yours.

******

4362 ==> If someone cannot think, then hopefully, they at least can rearrange their prejudices once in a while.

******

4363 ==> If you notice someone with bad manners at the dinner table, they are merely telling you they care more for the food than for the society at the table.

******

4364 ==> If you see the picture from the inside, you will surmise that many people do not know what they are doing. A routine has been made of their life, and they simply repeat the routine every day. The gear keeps turning, grinding the days along, one after the other.

******

4365 ==> Which one of us can walk about without touching or contact with the ground?

******

4366 ==> Did you know there really are a small number of people who live in poverty, dirt, and wretchedness, then die rich, leaving behind all their wealth, saved and never spent all these long years.

A mere madness indeed.

******

4367 ==> Sad that some of us actually inwardly delight somewhat over the real misfortunes and suffering of others.

******

4368 ==> Some are born stupid and, throughout life, find ways to greatly enhance their gift.

******

4369 ==> Sometimes ghosts get lost. You want me to try catching for you?

******

4370 ==> We cannot always get what we want, no matter how hard we work, how smart we are, how good we are or how cleverly we plot and scheme.

Now isn't that the most frustrating thing?

******

4371 ==> Most men never learn how to become a man. If I knew, I could tell them.

Most women never learn how to become a woman. If I knew, I could tell them.

******

4372 ==> Do you think it would be too exciting if we date?

******

4373 ==> Many of those who struggle so hard to become to a leader are in fact not suitable for the job.

Others who have money, family, and political backing to buy a leadership position are also not suitable.

Usually, those who are most suitable do not want a job run by puppet masters demanding, ordering that the leader kiss the end of corruption and delusions, trying to enforce fake realities.

******

4374 ==> Many of us are not so much out of our minds when we take to wondering.

******

4375 ==> It is nice for humans to have an open mind sometimes, but not too many of us are so open that nothing can live in the mind due to winds blowing in one end and blowing everything out the other end. Then some have so many doors seized shut that no thoughts can wander about in the mind.

******

4376 ==> The world may very likely not always think of us as we think of ourselves.

******

4377 ==> He drove this woman to madness. He was her pet, her play toy. She owned him body and soul. How he loved her smile, her look, the fine shape of her body, but the thing that lived inside that body, the spirit, how he hated it.

His thoughts dwelled upon insanity being constantly abused, used, and played with by this creature that had far more intelligence than he. The tip of her tongue was always ready to hiss like some reptile about to attack.

From the first meeting to now, two months later, they have been sleeping together. But today, when he awoke, he saw a dull, indifferent look, a look that had no desire. The fire was out, the heat gone. The passion wore away to a fragment. Then he knew she was tired of him.

He looked at his backpack and outdoor sleeping gear. For two months, it had sat in the distant corner. He knew it was over. No more free food, free sex, and free snug warm apartment. No more clean showers.

Why this morning, when he was incited to extreme lust passions? She lay there while he exerted his passions. She made no response other than to finally say, "Are you done soon?"

* * * * * *

4378 ==> The dim porch light of the riverside cottage spewed a faint light on the lawn. From the open front door sneaked the sounds of dance music.

A lovely lass was singing a soft romantic song while removing her blouse and watching a nimble man in bathing shorts spread a large blanket on the lawn.

This is the scene as fat Tubby on his air mattress floated slowly downstream in the slow, wide river. It was a dark, moonless mid-summer night. No one saw him as he silently paddled close to shore and, grabbing some shrubs to hold him from floating downstream, he watched and peeked on the lovers frolicking about nude on the blanket

******

4379 ==> A pretty young lady is like a devil whispering day and night suggestions into the mind of an old man. An urge to sing a song that repeats over and over in the mind, but can never be grabbed by the lonely arms of the old man. If only he could have a slow dance with her, holding her closer and closer.

******

4380 ==> We all would like to do our duty, but they make it so top secret that we cannot even find out what our duty is.

******

4381 ==> You may love the land, but find it impossible to love the people who live on the land.

******

4382 ==> God and nature cannot change the past, but historians are not the only people who live on the land.

******

4383 ==> We all cry loudly for truth, but when it comes our turn to speak; very few of us give the straight facts.

******

4384 ==> New knowledge and new truths must forever fight against the resistance of established thought locked in fake ignorance.

******

4385 ==> If we could only learn from the great masters, but we have only been taught to obey, not learn.

******

4386 (1/2) ==> Rocks on the hillsides, stones in the fields. Houses and fences made of stone. Roads made of stone.

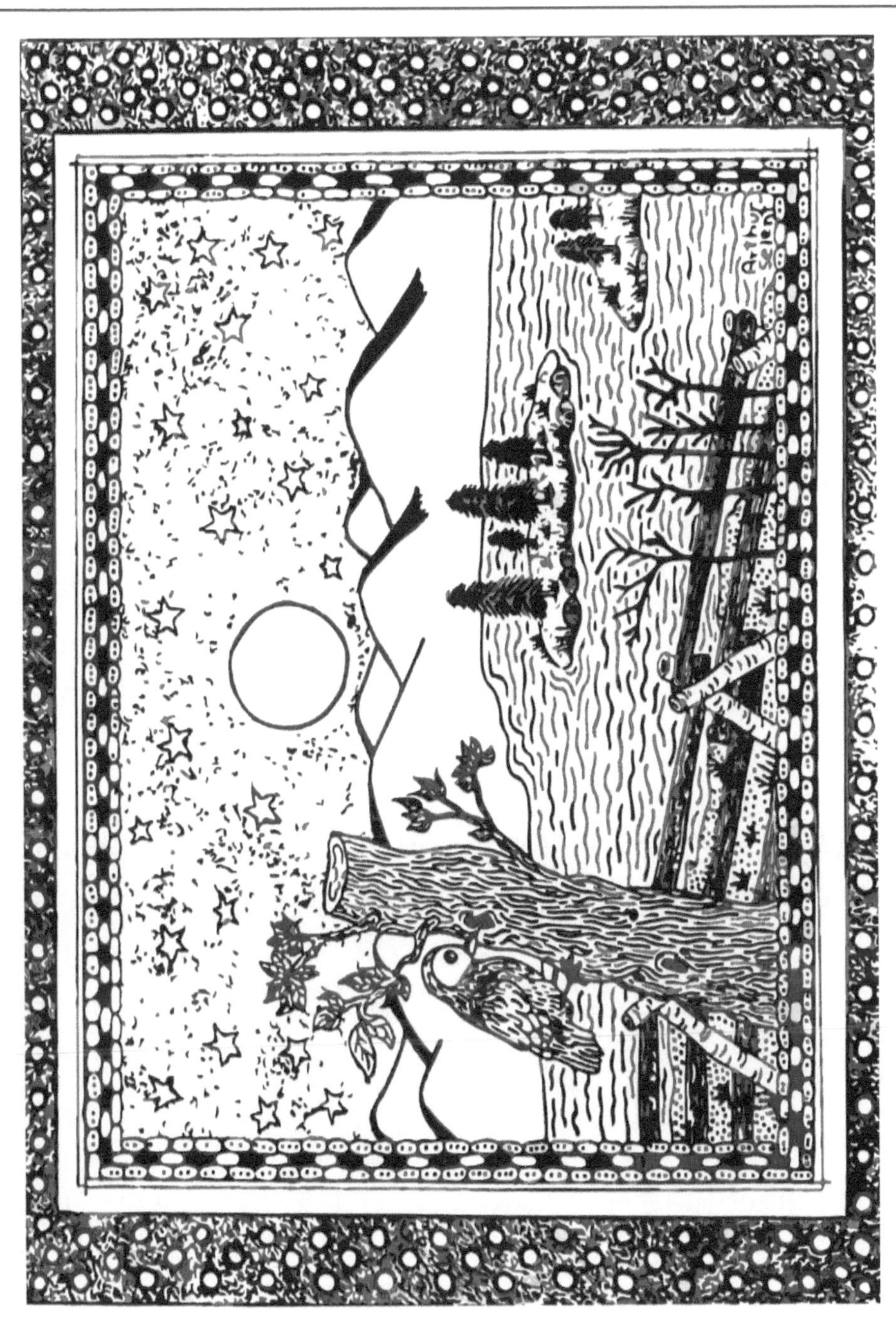

4386 (2/2) ==> Far and wide in every space, there are stones. And from here they bred stone age primitive humans, sending them forth to be fruitful and multiply.

******

4387 ==> The great flags lust with drooling passions to inflict suffering and make war on peaceful flags, which only desire to be friends.

******

4388 ==> Who do you believe?

Fake games and big money fairy tales, or do you believe your intuition, your inner God creature?

******

4389 ==> It is placing yourself in an absolutely wrong position to be taking your life roundabout from body to body, only to be told what to do with your life and your body.

******

4390 ==> We come from the unseen, shuffle about on planet Earth for some years, then fade away into the unseen again. This is our life as we know it.

******

4391 ==> Many a war would not have come if the facts had been calmly and properly put before the ordinary people.

******

4392 ==> Often, those who work with their heart and soul to do the best work are often those paid the least. While those who work for the money and ignore the job often get paid the most, sadly, they do not seem to enjoy their pay and always want more.

******

4393 ==> The old woman lived on the edge of the village in a decrepit small house surrounded by neglected plants and shrubs. She was said to have unusual powers and skills in the magic of illusions, dreams, and fortune.

It was whispered that she was a genuine witch of the inner circle. She was someone to be avoided on a dark, scary night. Very few dared to walk too slowly scary as they went by on the street past her house.

One could feel her reaching out, clinging, and casting spells.

******

4394 (1/2) ==> It was a sleazy, eerie night, a warm, dampish feeling with no breeze. The moon, just past full, drifted hide and seek among the clouds peeking from here and there.

The ghosts in the haunted mansion drifted sneaky like from room to room saying, "Boo, boo, boo." On the road passing the dark, sinister mansion, a decrepit, dirty man struggled to pull a wagon on which rested an open coffin. From the body inside a stiff arm reached for the heavens, its index finger with a red ribbon tied to it pointed to the moon.

The ghosts crowded around the windows to look. At the open front gate, the tramp stopped for a short rest. From the coffin floated a ghost. It stood upright on the ground and surveyed the mansion. Then, with slow hesitation, it floated to the front door and rang the doorbell.

The mansion was silent.

The decrepit man, gaining his strength now, found the wagon easier to pull and was soon lost down the road.

There being no sound, the ghost tried the door handle. He found it unlocked.

4394 (2/2) ==> Without opening the door, he passed through the door to enter the mansion. From the dark shadows, the other ghosts peeked and watched this new fellow.

Just then, the wind picked up outside and rattled and clattered the loose, weather-worn sign on the driveway gate. It read, "Ghost Mansion University."

******

4395 ==> If I come over there and chase you around the cherry tree, are you going to run slow so I can catch you, or are you going to run fast so you can get away?

******

4396 ==> That was the Thursday question that we spent all day Wednesday thinking about.

******

4397 ==> Advertising always leaves us wanting something that is just out of reach.

******

4398 ==> The reason humans can get along with animals is that animals do not speak in the human language.

******

4399 ==> There is nothing more dangerous on the tourist strip than the watering places. Where the bored tourist goes to pee and fill up the tank.

One cannot imagine what mystery the young women have who dare to prowl there for advantage. Why does she need only to crook her finger at some lonely male, and he becomes her long-lost lover just found? Within minutes, she has him picking flowers and paying for all expenses.

It was a dampish, warm, sleazy night, almost erotic in ghostly fantasy. She had just graduated from school and was on her first vacation alone, unwatched.

No one knew her here. No one would talk about her later.

She saw the watering pub with its discordant music drifting out onto the sidewalk. She entered. All fresh-faced and eager to be friendly in her innocence.

******

4400 ==> Did she feel pleased when he came in the door? Did she welcome him in bed or did she turn away, complaining of a headache? Did he think she was the best lay he'd ever had, or did he suppress his resentment at her coldness?

******

4401 ==> Earth – the lunatic asylum of the galaxy.

******

4402 ==> The political cheese who are considered honest are those who, when bought off, will stay bought off and stay obedient.

******

4403 ==> Humans with greatness within themselves do not go into politics. They leave that for the inferiors who are without ideals, listening to directions from puppet masters hiding out of sight.

******

4404 ==> If one has much charm, one can often get agreement without having asked any clear question.

******

4405 ==> We call our rich relatives our lovely family, but we call our poor relatives the bad side of the family.

******

4406 ==> Are most of your friends' people on social media, whom you know nothing about?

******

4407 ==> Is religion your only friend?

******

4408 ==> Ever wondered if a friend could be evil with dark, hidden secrets?

******

4409 ==> So many experts passing around each other's lies to cover up that they are out of control with their delusions, trying to maintain their self-important positions.

******

4410 ==> When fake science and big profits tell lies, we must believe the fairy tales or else face punishment by brain-washed political cheese.

******

4411 ==> That man, so dumb. He wouldn't obey or work; all he could do was beg for food. Then he takes over the mind of the first store that opens its doors and makes the store bring him money every day.

******

4412 ==> Why does the best part of our life always slip through our fingers like fast little fish?

******

4413 (1/2) ==> The skinny man with the crooked legs looks funny. He has a big lump on his throat which wobbles up and won as he talks.

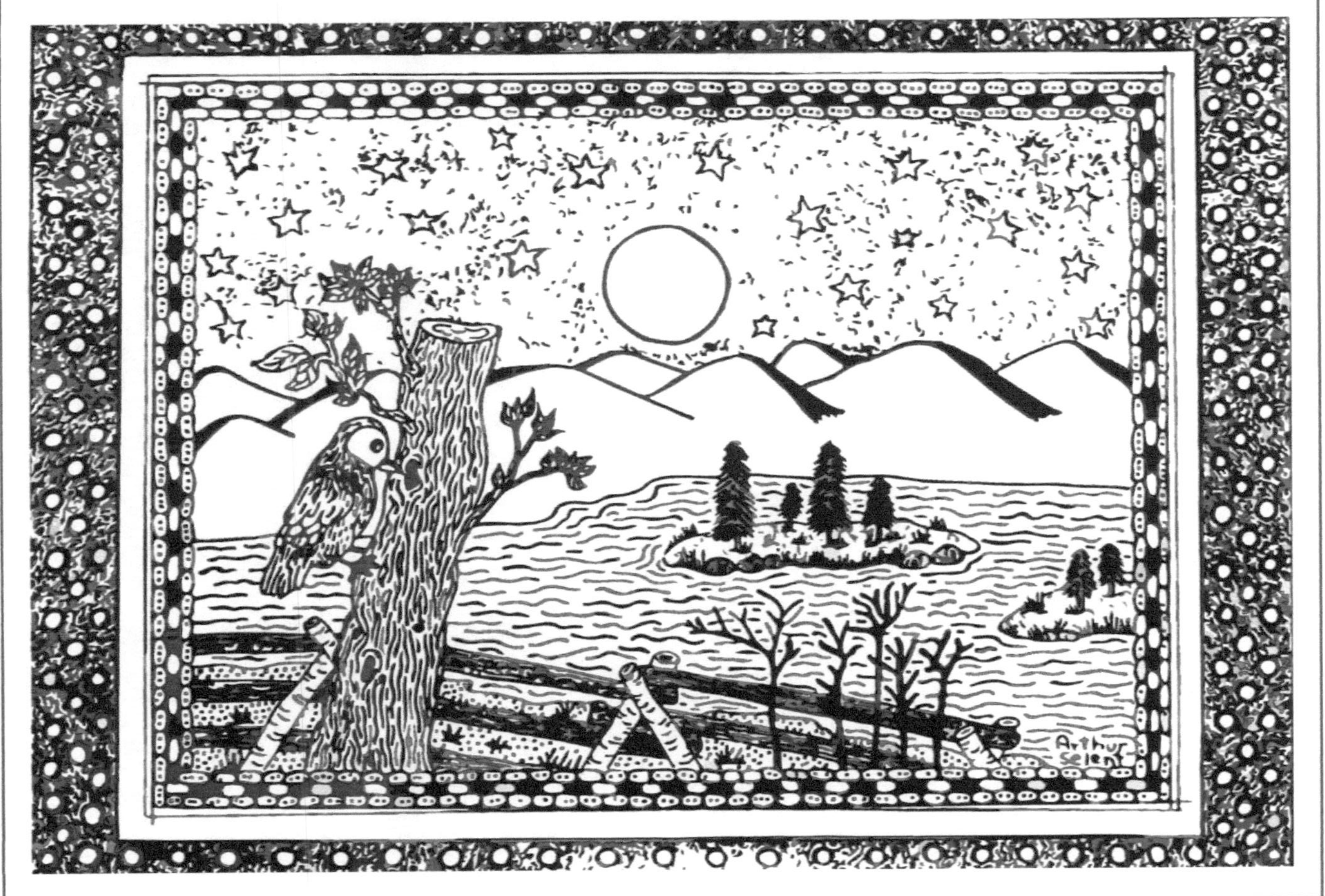
Arthur Selent

4413 (1/2) ==> The fat woman sighs and looks at the rich, creamy ice cream. Is she a person? She is so fat!

How can people look like that?

And they look so happily married. He with his proud grin, with one front tooth missing, and she, sighing, wheezing, mumbling, and waddling beside him.

* * * * * *

4414 ==> The grand writer's dream. Just get the plots from the telephone book and the afternoon TV soaps. Just bash out any delusion and rake in the money.

* * * * * *

4415 ==> Today, people travel almost to any place on the plane, for visiting, work, business, and who knows what other purpose. So, with all this mixing of people from so many different flags, does it not seem strange that each flag is stockpiling weapons and evils to use against other flags in the fantasy of creating war and mass murder.

* * * * * *

4416 (1/2) ==> School, the place where the little brats are pumped full of education. A big building of brick, concrete, and steel surrounded by a wire mesh fence.

4416 (2/2) ==> A vast paved yard with painted faded lines for sports games. A prison industrial site manufacturing mental programs inside two-legged mobile compost making bio machines. The industrial mass manufacture of our pillars of society, all look alike, all act alike.

But which of them can think?

******

4417 ==> I want, I want. I want the dark-haired one. I want the brunette.

I want and I want.

Don't tell me I am a dirty old man, because I'll have you know I took a bath two weeks ago.

Someone tell me which one I should want most. I don't seem to be going anywhere by trying to grab them all.

******

4418 ==> Don't let good looks steal your intelligence.

******

4419 (1/2) ==> "He has to stay after work to unload a truck." The mother was explaining to the father at the dinner table. "He'll work so hard late till midnight, and not even a coin for lunch will be flipped to him."

4419 (2/2) ==> All good will and no pay."

A pause of quite some time as foods get pushed inside the feed hole.

The mother says. "Why couldn't we have raised him to become a big crook making millions?" Here he is working day and night and still too poor to move away from us.

******

4420 ==> How often have we thrown away a part of ourselves when we threw out the garbage? How often have we left part of ourselves behind when we moved?

******

4421 ==> Mud is cleaner than the dirt inside their minds. And inside their head, the cleaner is on drugs. They are more shut tight and brainless than a clam. Using the high-grade good whiskey to wash out the used condom so they don't have to buy a new one this week.

******

4422 ==> No matter how corrupt the situation is, no one wants change so long as they are getting a share of the profit. It is only when the share gets smaller that they scream for change.

******

4423 ==> How long will all these lost monkeys dance in the history books, writing themselves in as great hero?

Oh, so that is how history books are written. Now we know. Do you think we know too much?

******

4424 ==> He dreamed he was an insect telling another insect that he was dreaming of being human.

******

4425 ==> It is amazing how a well-placed bird feeder will reduce the number of insects around your home. The birds like to eat those protein-rich insects.

******

4426 ==> The threat of virus is for doctors what purgatory is for priests – a gold mine.

******

4427 ==> Massive billions in profits are being created from doing virus bio experiment activity on the population. One has only to wonder if anyone honest is getting a share of these profits.

******

4428 (1/2) ==> With all the deceptions and schemes devised by our over-brazened mental education, is it any wonder we wish to improve on the delusions of our past? Is it any wonder they have replaced the gas chamber with virus bio experiments?

4428 (2/2) ==> Why waste resources transporting people to the slaughterhouse? It is easier to transport the virus bio experiment to the people. This new, improved system is certainly a profitable one for the management of the death games.

The people are much too eager to push this reality into existence without taking a moment to think; however, did people live before the inventions of fake science, fake vaccines, bio-experiment injections, and government enforcement of crimes against humanity?

They love no creature alive. They love only the Gold.

******

4429 ==> The school of higher education had the fortune of getting an important person to present a speech. It was said he was very much impoverished by mental cultivation to the point of having barren, wind-swept looks. It was said his speeches were full of breezy whispers and wind gusts farting loudly.

******

4430 ==> Be more intelligent than other people if you can, but don't tell them how smart you are, you know how upset the inferiors over the slightest frustration. Telling them would only make them feel their own inferiority too much. Be kind to the inferiors.

******

4431 ==> Most of us are somewhat worse than God made us.

******

4432 ==> Money usually means duties or work. Now, how shall we get the money without the work? Many are trying various methods and plots to find the solution. Those who solve the puzzle refuse to tell.

******

4433 ==> When you run the money game in over half the flags on the planet, the last thing you want the public to know is who you are. You will hide behind lawyers, secret agents, made men in made managements. After all, you print the money. Oh, so many sneaky plots and schemes to remain hidden.

The top of the money game is all top secret. The owners of the game have placed it on the gambling table and, from the hidden shadows, watch the players. Once in a while, the owners of the game will get a mental flash to change the game by redirecting the action. They do this secretly by making a deal that the player cannot refuse.

What would happen if the public knew too much?

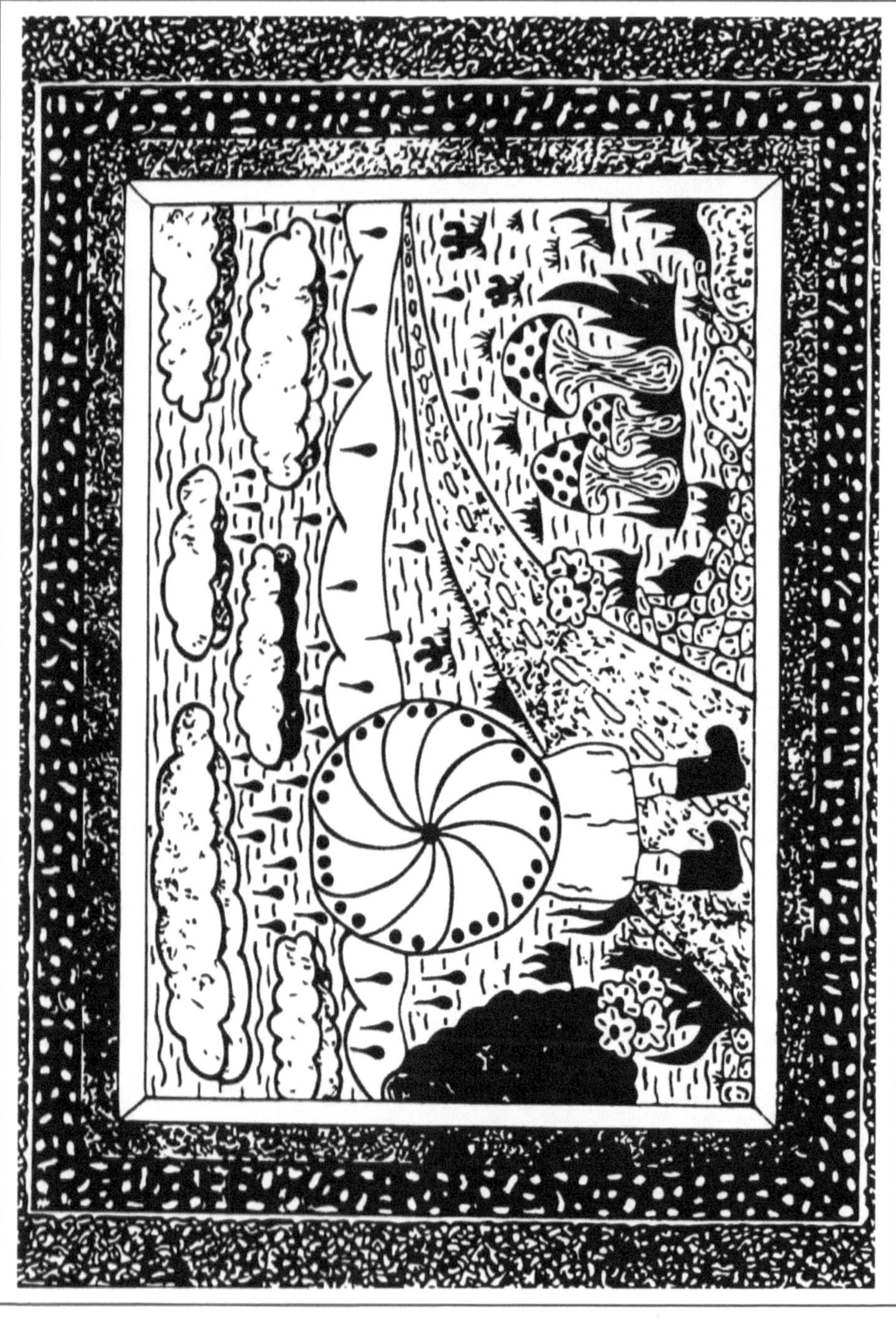

* * * * * *

4434 ==> The greater the taxation on something, the greater the patriotism of those who buy the something.

* * * * * *

4435 ==> Usually, it is easier to take more rather than take less.

* * * * * *

4436 ==> So often we are deceived because foolish ideas come so well dressed with much illusion and delusion magic.

* * * * * *

4437 ==> You notice that the eager romance is always at the beginning of a love affair.

* * * * * *

4438 ==> The inner sight, which shows its pictures and thoughts by turning the eyes' vision inside, is a gift many do not have.

* * * * * *

4439 (1/2) ==> He could talk a bird out of a high tree.

As he stood up to talk, he did not know what he was going to say, and when he started speaking, he did not know what he was saying, and when he sat down again, he did not know what he'd said.

4439 (2/2) ==> But the bird chirped in agreement and thought it was an excellent speech.

******

4440 ==> She is a woman already, while they are still kids. She looks around the classroom. Most of the girls are still flat as boards, but her tits have ballooned, and she shows them off by walking straight-backed and pointing them directly under the chins of guys she talks to. She has also started her monthly rag and likes to make a big display in the washrooms when some underdeveloped girls are present. A big display of dropping her used, wet, smelly rag in the garbage.

She is not a little flower. Wait for the day when she has to please a living soul, a man, and the children.

******

4441 ==> People often collide with truth, then quickly look around to see if anyone saw before hurrying away as if nothing had happened.

******

4442 ==> The worst thing about some of the lies going around is that some of them are true.

******

4443 ==> Even fools are right sometimes.

******

4444 ==> He was from the rich land across the ocean and had just graduated from university. He left his family. He went for a year to a poor, crowded land. He set himself up in a modest apartment and advertised for cooking and housekeeping help. A very poor, attractive girl, still too young, answered the ad. It was plain that she lacked experience, but she was very good-looking and willing to do so; she could keep her job. He told her the job was live-in. She had no other choice other to go back to her life of sleeping on the streets, so she eagerly accepted.

When she got pregnant and could hide it no more, he moved out one day when he'd sent her food shopping. He left a note saying he'd gone back to his land and would send money for her. She never heard from him again.

One night, sleeping in a dark doorway, she gave birth. A messy affair. Wild dogs roamed the streets and came closer, attracted by the smell. She stood up and, somewhat unsteady, wandered away. She could hear the dogs fighting, then one piercing scream from the baby, followed by growls and the sound of the dogs feasting. She kept walking and found a place to hide and sleep.

******

4445 ==> It seems that the society class that washes the most is those who work the least.

******

4446 ==> Old age is not so bad when one considers the coming future.

******

4447 ==> A woman talking to the newly elected political cheese remarked how, when he gave a speech, the hall was filled to overflowing.

The cheese replied, "If I were being hanged, the crowd would be ten times as large."

******

4448 ==> If we did not have money or some sort of trade unit, what would reality be like?

We would be a socialist society getting our needs for free. We would also work jobs for free, no pay. This would mean one looks for a job one likes, as opposed to a job that pays high. Also, there would be no profit competition between business and industry.

No more having to pay for anything. Everything is free. Are we capable of such a thing?

******

4449 (1/3) ==> Fresh and innocent from the country, she arrived in the big city, getting off the train. Such a sweet soul lived in her serene body. She was ready to be everyone's friend.

The people on the streets rushed about. She said, "Hi", here and there, but the people looked at her as if she something catching and rushed away, appearing greatly disturbed.

One man, when she said hi, asked her how much for sex. She thought that a bit rash and rushed away. When a second and soon after a third asked for a sex price, she did some thinking. She did not realize her bold approach had the guys thinking she was a rental girlfriend.

She stopped saying "Hi" to men, only women, but try as she might, she could not get a conversation started. She kept finding herself looking into the eyes of men here and there. She began to wonder what it would be like to do it with a man she knew nothing about. She began to calculate a price.

She still had four hours left before the night train arrived to take her back home. She smiled and said "Hi" to a man. When he asked her, "What price?" she replied with an amount rather high, double what she'd calculated. Why? She does not know; it just spilled out. She was surprised that the man seemed pleased and did not bargain but put the money in her hand.

4449 (2/3) ==> He led her to a decrepit old apartment nearby. She lay there in the bed looking at the photo of his wife and the kids. The wife's clothes here and there about the room. He was so eager, so excited. She let him do his girlfriend fantasy.

Back on the street, she smiled to herself, laughing at how that old soft married man had been so excited and aroused by her.

Barely half an hour later, she was attracted to a fellow whom she said "Hi" to. He also did not bargain to lower her price. He also seemed so eager and excited about his girlfriend's experience.

She barely made it back to the train station on time.

Back home, the next day at the lunch table, the family asked how the trip to the city was. She replied, "Rather boring. People seemed to be in such a hurry. I just wandered among the shopping areas looking at things." Her thought was in her secret pocket, where the money was hidden.

A month later, she again went to the city, but this time she missed the train coming back and had to walk the streets all night until the morning train arrived.

Tired, sore, and worn out, she arrived home just as her family was having a late breakfast.

4449 (3/3) ==> She explained she'd met some people in a café and went to a birthday party with them, where she lost track of time. She went straight to bed.

So now every fourth week she goes two days to the city to visit her new friends.

Her little treasure box, hidden under her heavy dresser, slowly finds itself filling with each monthly business trip. Also, beside the treasure box lies a date book with her fertile days clearly marked, her rag days marked, and her barren days clearly marked. On top of the date book rests a train timetable.

Her secret business office, hidden under the cabinet.

******

4450 ==> Everyone should have an eccentric friend. Well, here I am, tolerate me as long as you can.

******

4451 ==> For a month, each night as it became dark, she opened the door for him to let him in.

All month, each day, she complained about spots on the lower part of her blouse, claiming the servant girl had not washed them out.

But we knew it was his dirty fingerprints.

******

4452 ==> The love affair has gone sour, and you being able to restrain your emotions is not a great victory; it is the pitiful proof of lost love that never was.

******

4453 ==> We must be ignorant enough to feel superior to those around us.

******

4454 ==> There are some people so spiritually advanced that they will talk equally to grey rocks, green rocks, and brown rocks. Can you imagine such an abomination of the structure and order of established society, insanity? Why did the Giant Rock Society not inform us of this?

******

4455 ==> If you see ten mean ugly troubles coming down the road in your direction, you can be sure that one will run away. Three will stop, look at you, and then turn around and walk away. The remaining six will firm their march and stumble over and around you, leaving you very much beaten and battered.

Three troubles will then turn, come back, and give you some serious good kicks.

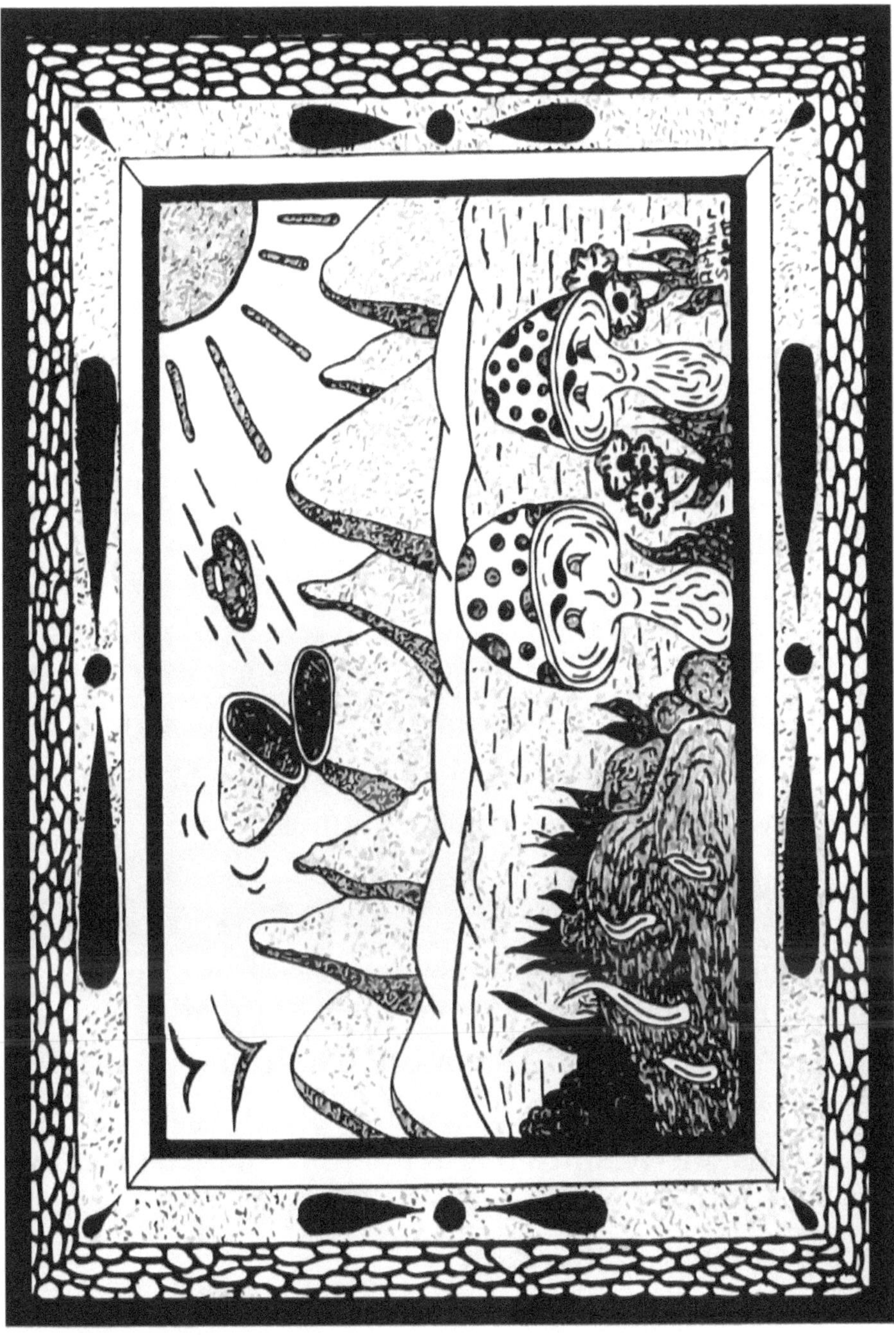

******

4456 ==> We can see how fast time moves by remembering that yesterday we called today, tomorrow.

******

4457 ==> People have two eyes and one mouth so that they may see twice as much as they say.

******

4458 ==> Who could ever be busier than he who has nothing to do?

******

4459 ==> If the people want to kill each other, then let them do it with sticks and stones. The people do not need some political cheese having ego pleasure directly in the action with tin soldiers.

******

4460 (1/2) ==> Sometimes he conceals a little piece of truth which he later draws out to startle the reader, sneaking and sniffing for more. His genius is not so frail that he'd risk the fictions of the newspapers. But then, certainly, genius ought not to be locked in some safe vault. He is careful to watch that they do not catch him out in the game.

4460 (1/2) ==> How their eyes pop and shine, turning the pages. Their grip on truth loosens until it falls from their hand, lying beside the roadside, forgotten and discarded as if it were a mere candy wrapper.

A good story is always more exciting and mysterious than a wafer of truth.

He is the fiction writer feeding the reader with scraps of things cleaned out from his rag bag sitting on top of his shoulders.

******

4461 ==> As the illusions and words reach out to pull the mind closer, they become like little children at bedtime. A dreamy expectant look on their face, waiting for visions and activity to move in page after page.

******

4462 ==> Since we have made money so important, so needed for our well-being, we can easily understand why a person will try anything to get themselves a surplus supply.

******

4463 ==> If your lover dies tomorrow, would you bother to cry? Would you win the flip of the love coin, landing on the wrong side, or would you lose by the coin landing on the right side?

******

4464 ==> All so eager to start killing humans with their new uniforms, new guns, and new machines.

The store-bought tin soldiers of insane political cheese playing recreation slaughter games to please their God masters.

******

4465 ==> The secret of your life is in your astrology. They have hidden the facts on page 421 in the large letters. Because of this being in large letters, no one bothers to read. They are too busy investigating the sneaky fine print at the bottom of the page.

******

4466 (1/2) ==> There seem to be many religions pushing their individual God dreams into the minds of lost humans.

Each religion sells its God as being the only God. It is a money industry where the follower pays for an illusory imagination of God as painted by the religion.

So many religions and all preaching a different God. They are devils who have changed the road signs to lead the humans away from reality in its natural form. It is a money industry of luring slaves for the afterlife. They are fake pretenders preaching deception and have no original idea of who the real God is.

4466 (2/2) ==> Until the truth is discovered, religion is a money industry selling its imagination. If you repeat the story often enough, someone will believe you.

* * * * * *

4467 ==> No one leads more than those who know not where they are going.

* * * * * *

4468 ==> Paths of least resistance often make crooked people, just as rivers are formed.

* * * * * *

4469 ==> One must know how a word is spelled before one can look it up in the dictionary to see how it is spelled.

* * * * * *

4470 ==> Certainly, his head was all closed up. Never any ideas circulating to renew the mind. To refresh the mind like an open window refreshes the air in a room. He had narrow-minded suggestions without realizing there were other realities. Or ways of looking at things. It was clear to see that his ready-made views were previously instilled into him by his father, mother, teacher, and priest, with the TV thrown in as well.

He was just a copy machine spitting out copies.

******

4471 ==> It takes a smart person to handle a lie cleverly. Fools would be better off being honest.

******

4472 ==> Folly always finds its fool to admire praise.

******

4473 ==> "Yeah, we got them around here too. They usually stand near the men's washroom selling their women's experience. They are fast grab gold diggers, and you know what happens if they get their hands on us old distinguished men."

The other old weezy geezer nodded his head. "Sure, is different these days. You'd never see this when we were young. We were civilized back then. Today, they run around half-nude and do things we dare not mention."

"Look at the way they dance, like they have a cold, wet frog in their underwear, all wiggles, jerks, and sways, rubbing against each other as if they were putting on a bedroom show."

The old weezy geezer nodded his head again, "Well, buddy, I have to go now. It is my night job, you see. They are having the big Saturday night dance, and I have to sell off my surplus supply of cold, wet frogs. The wife wants them out of the house."

******

4474 ==> There is someone out there who is more intelligent than me. Do I really want to meet them?

******

4475 ==> Now that the governments no longer cover up and lie about space people and UFO's we can look at the reality without fear of being punished.

Some of these unidentified flying objects (UFOs) are larger than three- or four-foot ball fields. Now just think of the weight of such a machine with the entities, food, and water. That is a massive amount of weight. Yet their craft can float effortlessly without sound through our atmosphere. Not to mention the abnormal supersonic speeds and turning abilities.

What power and propulsion system can keep so much weight afloat silently?

******

4476 ==> There is nothing she wouldn't do for him and nothing he wouldn't do for her, so they live their lives doing nothing for each other.

******

4477 ==> A man's success can be seen by how skillfully a woman pushes the man along.

******

4478 ==> It was a rather large turkey farm. Two turkeys were talking. One says, "I wonder what crime our parents committed for us to be born and raised in this prison?"

The other turkey replies, "No one seems to know, but have you noticed that a large number of turkeys have been disappearing lately, and they are all the fat, plump ones. I've started eating less."

"Yeah, I noticed that too. Oh, look, there's a fat fellow. Bet he's gone by the end of the week."

******

4479 ==> You are running a high probability of not having any children if your parents had no children.

******

4480 ==> Flowers are like young women. They only bloom for a short time.

******

4481 ==> The usual love affair, thinking she is his only, to later find out he is hers.

******

4482 (1/2) ==> It was always damp and gloomy there in the back room of the store. A hole in the upper wall covered with dirty, clear plastic served as a window. The feelings creeping through this hole seemed moldy and sewer-like.

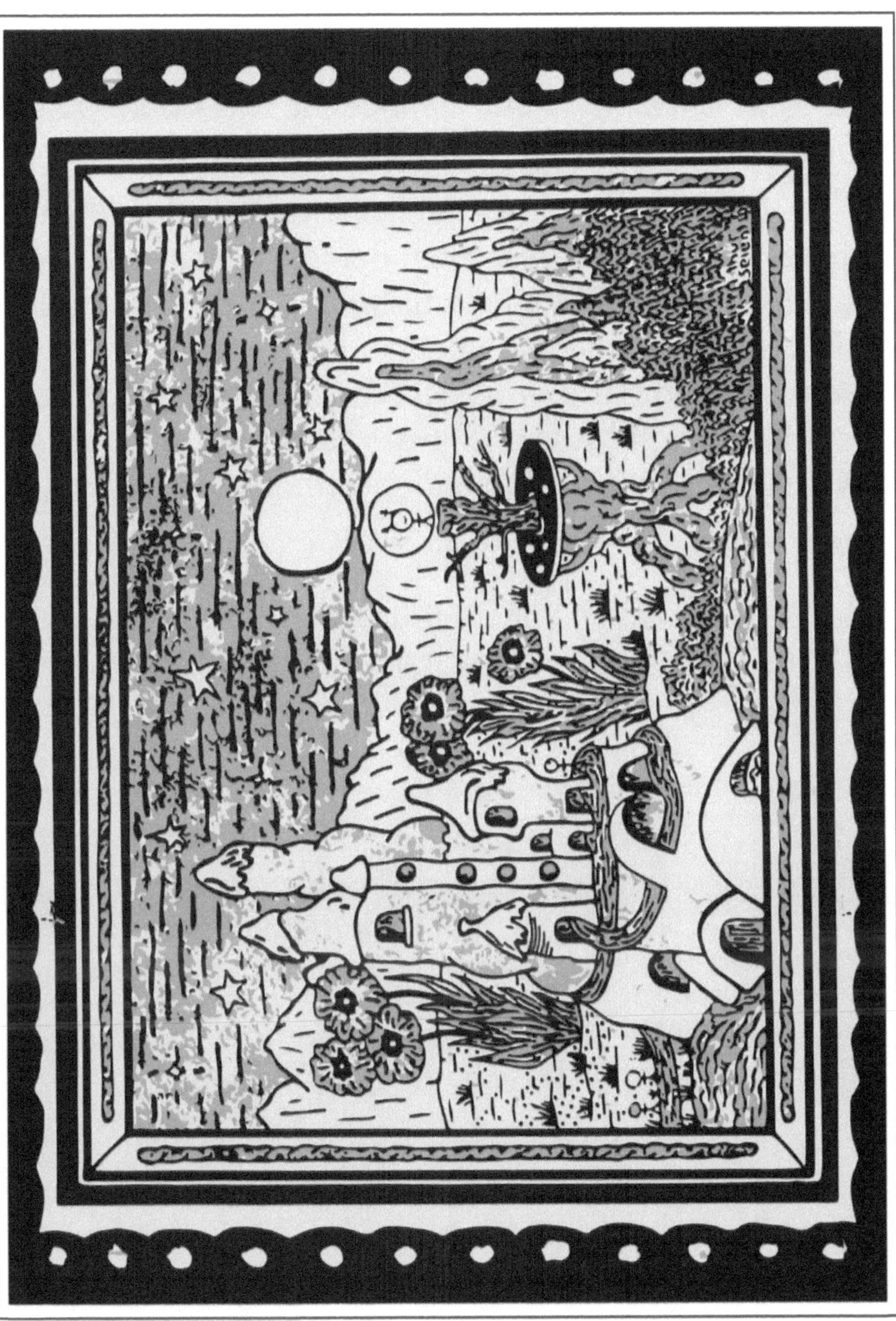

4482 (2/2) ==> The little room where he had spent the last three years hiding. Like a faithful employee, he came out at night and cleaned the washrooms and floors of the store.

He had no contact with the outside world for three years. The store owner, being a distant relative and being charitable, let him hide in the back room. He brought in food supplies twice a week. He was very sympathetic to this eccentric relative who had to hide out because the government secret agents were out to capture him and give him to the Aliens.

******

4483 ==> Always watching from the shadows for a gleam of hope as we clutch our lottery ticket.

******

4484 (1/2) ==> He did not have memories like other men. No sweet or tragic love affairs, no unforeseen events, no exciting journeys. These were all hazards of a free existence that had not crossed his path.

The days, months, and seasons came and went, all alike. Every day, a routine monotony of the same acts, the same deeds, and the same thoughts.

Twenty years had flown away, quietly sneaking away. Years empty as sorrows and the long hours of a bad night. Then one day, he decided he'd get a job, some meaningful employment.

4484 (2/2) ==> He stepped outside of his mother's house. The Sun shone with brilliant heat. It was uncomfortable. He went back inside. He'll look for a job next week.

He went into the kitchen to see what food his mother had prepared for him before going off to her day job.

******

4485 ==> To advise another, that is easy. To know oneself, that is difficult.

******

4486 (1/3) ==> He was a country fellow working the fields and leading a contented life. Now middle-aged aged he'd spent all his life on the farm. He'd never had thoughts of marrying. He felt no passion for women.

Then one day, he won a trip to some exotic, overpriced tourist place. He arrived at his hotel and spent a restless night. The country smells and breezes were missing.

Oh, his first afternoon, he wandered about seeing the tourist things.

By dusk, he'd seen all there was to see, and as he sat on a bench, he wondered what he would do all week until it was time to go home.

4486 (2/3) ==> A woman came and sat beside him, a little too close. He felt internal confusion. She said, "Good afternoon, my handsome man."

He nodded.

She continued, "Would you like a sweet heart to warm up the night?"

This was too bold and shocking. None of the women back home was so bold. He got up and walked about, finally sitting at a sidewalk café. A woman approached and sat at his table. She said, "You look like a very nice man. Could I be your lover for the evening?"

Once again, he was shocked. The sheer boldness of these women was unsettling. He said, "NO, I don't need a lover." She frowned and walked away.

He sat there slurping his coffee ever so slowly. Other women walked by. A few accosted him with romantic desires. But he always shied away. He saw the women huddle across the street, talking to each other and looking at him. Some dark fear sneaked into his mind. Why do these women want him? He'd never seen any of them before.

He sneaked back to his room and waited out the week watching TV.

4486 (3/3) ==> Back on the farm, he spent many days thinking about these love-starved women. Maybe he should bring them to the farm and give them jobs working in the fields.

Then the news on TV showed a new article about the tourist place. It was showing how the sex trade was everywhere. So that was the game. How foolish he felt that he'd not realized the women were prostitutes.

******

4487 ==> The eternal optimist sees bright candles throwing light in all directions until the pessimist comes along to blow out the candles.

******

4488 ==> The trouble with society is that people think they have to spend money to buy happiness, but after the money is spent, there is only frustration in looking for more money to spend.

******

4489 (1/2) ==> People often pretend to love with all the strength of their souls. They cling to each other, tolerating all manner of frustrations. But it is not love, it is an animal urge to cling to warmth and one another.

4489 (2/2) ==> Like little rabbits clinging to each other for warmth and security. No matter how much they fight and push each other away, they always come together at bedtime, clinging to each other.

******

4490 ==> Talk to a person about themselves, and they will listen for hours.

******

4491 (1/2) ==> Every morning at exactly six am, his alarm clock clattered and rattled. Only once had this clock failed to go off. He had a mental shock and bought a new clock. That night, he put them both side by side. In the morning, the old clock clattered away, afraid of losing its job, while the new clock seemed not to work. Ever since the old clock worked.

He dressed, made his bed, and tidy his room. Then he went out to a café restaurant a few minutes' walk away. On the weekends, his days off, he walked to the tourist section of the city to have breakfast and mingle with strangers. He enjoyed his long unhurried walk and new people to look at.

His weekday job was in a small room called an office. His job was top-secret security work stamping official papers.

4491 (2/2) ==> As he entered his office, the papers were already stacked on the left of his desktop. Sometimes the stack is so high as to wobble and sway. Sometimes there were two stacks, and he'd have to work into the evening to get all the paper stamping done. Each page needed a stamp.

He had three stamps to choose from: (1) To be reviewed, (2) Top secret, (3) Junk. Each page had a pencil mark telling him which stamp to use. He never read any of the papers.

The neighbors around the area of his room envied him because he had such an important government job. That his intelligence was what kept the government from falling apart. But they wondered just what his job was. They whispered all kinds of talk.

No one could get him to talk about his job.

******

4492 ==> Elections are a big money game. People by the millions must choose a leader from two or more eager, greedy devils wearing angel costumes. The people know nothing about these entities other than what marketing agencies and news media invent and brainwash the people with. The people get all worked up with passions, one for that person and another for that other person. But they know nothing about their choice.

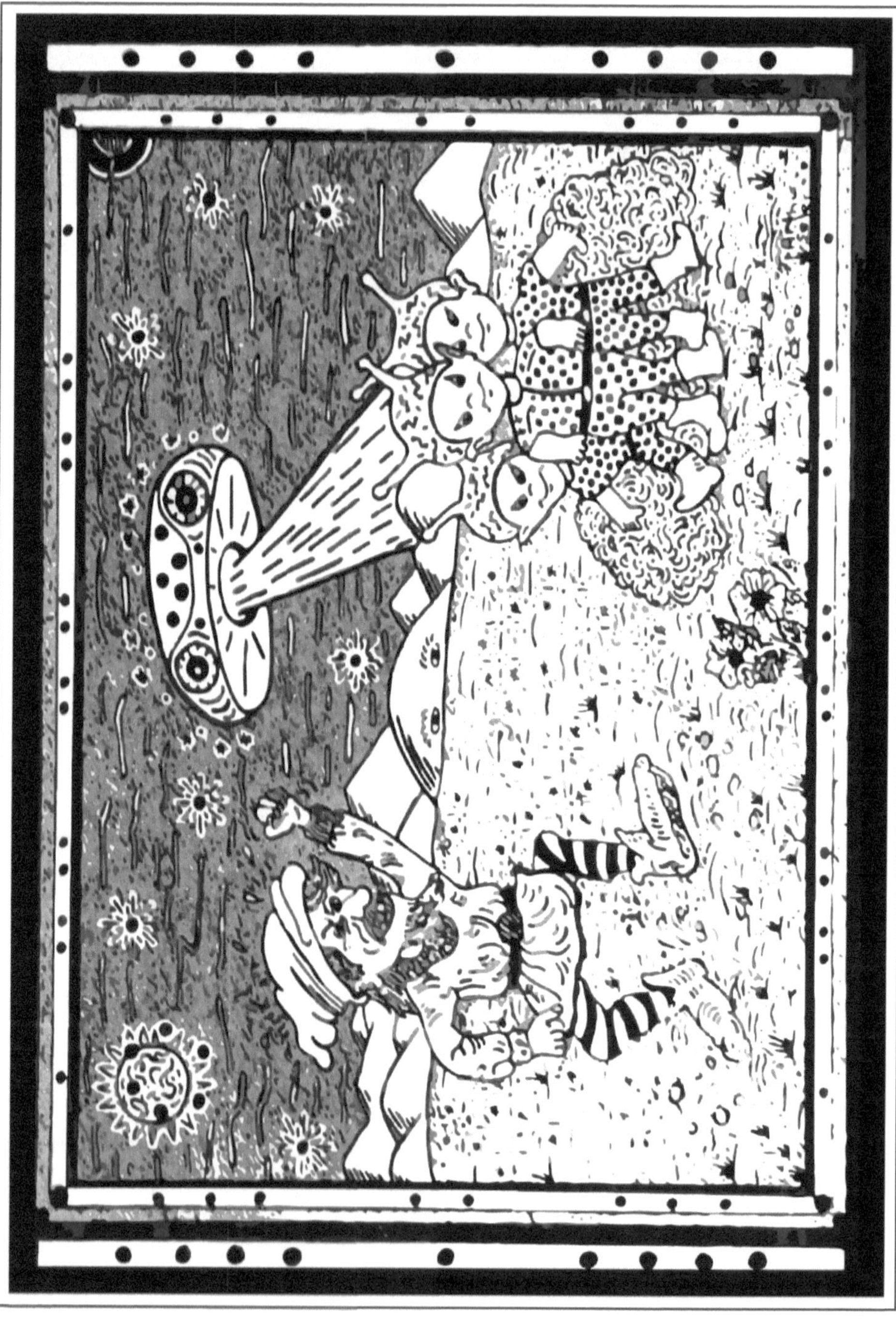

******

4493 ==> The little monster decided he'd put some snacks under the Christmas tree for Santa. He put a dish of fresh cookies and asked his mother if he could put a bottle of wine from the wine cellar under the tree. Mother said he could.

Then Christmas morning came, and the presents were opened. The bottle of wine sat there just a little over half empty.

The monster says to mother, "See, that proves Santa is real. He did not drink too much because he had to drive. If it had been Dad, he would have drunk the entire bottle."

But Dad slept late and seemed very hungover when he got around to the presents and the remainder of the wine.

******

4494 ==> Women who wear men's work clothes mean business, no fooling about.

******

4495 ==> Power does not wear a uniform. Only the servants of power wear uniforms.

******

4496 ==> The professional couple decided to drop out of the big city rat race. They disposed of all their assets and hid their money in bank accounts. They then joined a back-to-the-earth cult living in a massive remote wilderness beside a small river.

The cult members always seemed dirty and smelly, even though they splashed about nude in the river. The women were always half-nude and seemed very open about who they slept with. Most of the males had bushy beards.

He was all slick-shaven and asked his wife, "What do you think I'd look like with a bushy beard?"

The wife who did not like beards scratching her kissing face replied, "You'd look very lonely."

******

4497 ==> Beware of the anger of a patient person. They are very capable of waiting until you are in your weakest position.

******

4498 ==> The leader must follow the people.

******

4499 (1/2) ==> The single mother took her five-year-old daughter to a tree farm to get a Christmas Tree. They trudged through knee-high snow from one end of the farm to another end.

4499 (2/2) ==> Their feet started freezing, but the mother pushed on, determined to find the perfect tree.

Finally, the kid could take it no more. She said, "Mom, the perfect tree is not here. It's like getting a man. Just be satisfied you can find one that is still alive, isn't too bald, isn't too fat, and can still stand up. Why don't we just get a tree from beside some back road? We can have a big pizza with the money we save."

The mother agrees, and off they go. As they got back onto the main road with their perfect tree tied to the car's roof, there stands a man hitching a ride. He looked alive, had all their hair, no fat stomach, and could stand up straight.

Mother picked him up.

Now five years later, there he sits on the sofa in front of the TV with a beer in his hand. His fat stomach says good things about his mother's cooking. Most of his hair is already gone. He looked barely alive enough to stand up straight.

Then one day the daughter came home from school and he was gone. Mother explained. "I brought him away. Men are like Christmas trees. No matter how good they look when you bring them home, they don't last forever."

******

4500 ==> To confuse the minds of others and conceal one's own mind, be honest and explicit.

******

4501 ==> First, we must learn to clean our own minds before we tell others how to clean their minds.

******

4502 ==> Fate has no logic and will jump us by surprise just as readily and eagerly as a small kid having fun.

******

4503 ==> Business is a designer game to see how much of other people's money we can get.

******

4504 ==> Humans and plants – The humans breathe oxygen and exhale carbon dioxide, stale hair. Plants take this CO2 and turn it into oxygen. Plants and humans need each other.

The one reason people who work with plants tend to be more cheerful is that they are close to the manufacture of oxygen and get it fresh before it floats away to get diluted and mixed with stale air

******

4505 ==> Why do Northern birds fly south for the winter? It is too far to walk.

******

4506 ==> Cards and politics know no friends.

******

4507 ==> So strange that the poor people who need money the most never seem to get any. But the rich who have so much and really don't need more seem to get more and more.

******

4508 ==> What is the difference between a canoe and a miser? A canoe tips, but the miser does not tip.

******

4509 ==> One has to wonder if, after a coffin is lowered into the ground at funerals, and the guests wander off of the coffin is lifted out and the body removed, thrown into the hole while the coffin is carried off to be sold again.

The price of coffins is so high that there is a money incentive to play badly.

It would also be a convenient way to get rid of crime. After all, the hole is large enough to hold an extra body or two.

******

4510 ==> What four letters will tell someone you do not like them? Write to them four times.

******

4511 ==> What did the cannibal say when he saw the human sleeping? Ah, breakfast in bed.

******

4512 ==> Why did the little ink cry? Its mother was in the pen doing a long sentence.

******

4513 ==> An echo speaks every language.

******

4514 ==> Don't cross the bridge until you come to it.

******

4515 ==> What is the largest room available? The room for improvement.

******

4516 ==> She stood at the back of the crowd, hugging her embarrassment, tightly wrapped about herself. She dares not share with anyone.

******

4517 ==> Live your life. Old age will catch you no matter where you hide or how fast you run.

******

4518 ==> You will graduate if you reach old age as a happy person.

******

4519 ==> One travels fastest when one travels alone.

******

4520 ==> We were in a remote lumber camp, about a dozen of us, when a big snowstorm closed down the roads. We were getting ready to visit our families for Christmas. So, we got stuck here for a few days.

We sort of made some cheer by hanging our socks on the walls of the eating cabin. Each sock had a note to Sante. We all looked among our junk to see what we'd give to each other as presents.

One guy hung up some neat ladies under wear with the note, "Dear Santa, I have been a good boy, please fill these with a good-looking woman."

I wondered where he got the ladies under wear. There were no women in our camp. Maybe he dresses funny at bedtime.

******

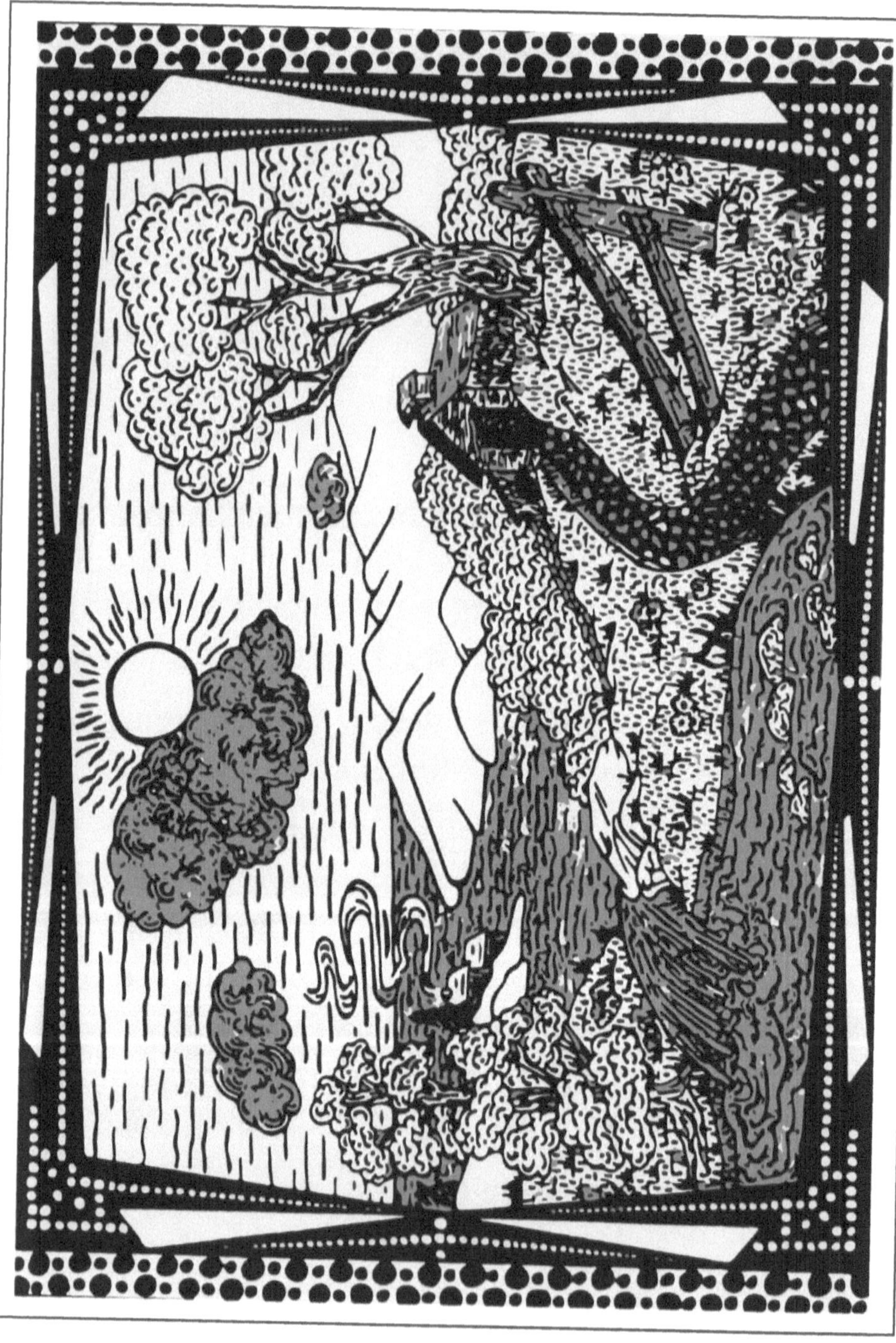

4521 ==> Even a small light is better than to curse the darkness.

******

4522 ==> If wishes were horses, the poor would ride.

******

4523 ==> One man's meat is a vegetarian's poison.

******

4524 ==> When poverty comes in the front door, love runs out the back door.

******

4525 ==> She catches a whiff of the man smell about him and wants to touch him. He sniffs the woman smell of her and wants to touch her.

There you go. Another plot for another romance story.

And after they mate, they cannot tolerate the smell of each other.

******

4526 ==> True love will find a way.

******

4527 ==> An honest job is all we can ask for.

******

4528 ==> The robbed rob them that rob, and they that rob those that are robbed.

******

4529 ==> The political cheese need top secret projects because that is where the money stealing is most easy. No one is allowed to see where the money is going. The money trail was covered up and hidden. Top Secret - Door Closed - Go Away.

******

4530 ==> Corruption has many puppets willing to dance.

******

4531 ==> It seems that thinking is harder work than doing physical activity.

******

4532 ==> Who has the power to remove a spirit soul from a body and replace it with another spirit soul?

******

4533 ==> The human does what is needed to keep the stomach full. Some do it nicely and others do it badly.

******

4534 ==> Does the flea care what the lion eats?

******

4535 ==> When the lightning and thunder rumble, the shadows dance on the walls with each bright flash outside. The rain taps on the windows as if it had long fingernails.

Almost midnight.

The wind in the dark night groans heavily through the trees. It howls around the chimney. When eerie unseen fears and the cold makes you pull the blanket over your head and hope the night goblin does not find you.

******

4536 ==> Do long-dead writers sense when their books are read? It must be lonely to be dead. In the books they write, they continue to exist.

A picture of the book is like a phone to connect with the spirit of the writer.

We discover them and comfort them. It is a kind of magic.

******

4537 ==> I am a very bad boyfriend. I cheat and plant baby seeds in other gardens.

******

4538 ==> He looked into the emerald green eyes of this extravagant beauty he'd lured to his bed. The eyes are the doors of the soul. All he saw was a vast void. This woman, he thought, has no soul. She was a mystery of elaborate coils of copper hair arranged haphazardly to the peak of artistic endeavor.

He clung to her under the covers, filling her with baby seeds.

He awoke all alone in the morning. When had she left? He knew nothing about her. Even her name he knew not. Why did she leave?

******

4539 ==> When a man sits close to a pretty young woman for an hour, time races, and an hour seems like a minute.

When a man sits in his car during a rush hour traffic blockage, a minute seems like an hour.

******

4540 ==> The best news is often distorted gossip with opinions holding up the story.

******

4541 (1/2) ==> That was it, the initiation rite of passage. Stay at home alone, finally. Old enough that a babysitter was not needed.

4541 (2/2) ==> Now joining the next level of grown-up girls. The boyfriend tapped lightly at the door. She had been waiting and let him in.

Some hours lately, the boyfriend slyly sneaked away.

She could see the other girls at school as she described her new rank of not needing a sitter anymore.

It was with eager surprise that she told of sneaking her boyfriend in for some hot action. The other girls were mystified; she'd moved up the ladder in experiences they as yet knew nothing about. Secretly, they wished they could explore their own experience soon.

******

4542 ==> If a person is not afraid of others and has good manners, then society will fit them into the puzzle even if they lack some gears in the brain.

******

4543 (1/2) ==> We are coming closer to the Alien technology of putting implants in humans with our ever-smaller microchips. The aliens abduct some people and put a small metal implant in the people. This implant is very small, about the size of a grain of rice or a very small pea.

4543 (2/2) ==> The outside of this implant is coated with a substance that causes nerves to cling to it. This establishes a line of communication to the brain and back to the implant. These implants use the small electro energy of the human body to function. Also, every fifteen minutes, a short signal pulse is sent out like a cell phone signal. Maybe a tracking device.

There are numerous cases where these implants have shown up in medico X-rays. They were removed for study. Once the implant is disconnected from the nerve fibers, the signals are stopped.

But our technology has not found a way to open these implants to see what is inside.

******

4544 ==> There is no end to human suffering, only tolerance and endurance.

******

4545 (1/2) ==> She was watching the strange kisses and fondling of that brainless floozy playing with her husband. Her husband knew not that she was watching.

She at that moment understood that she may begin to be unfaithful to her husband and not feel the least bit guilty. In fact, inside her mind, she now saw a secret life of romance open its doors. Just when life had become boring.

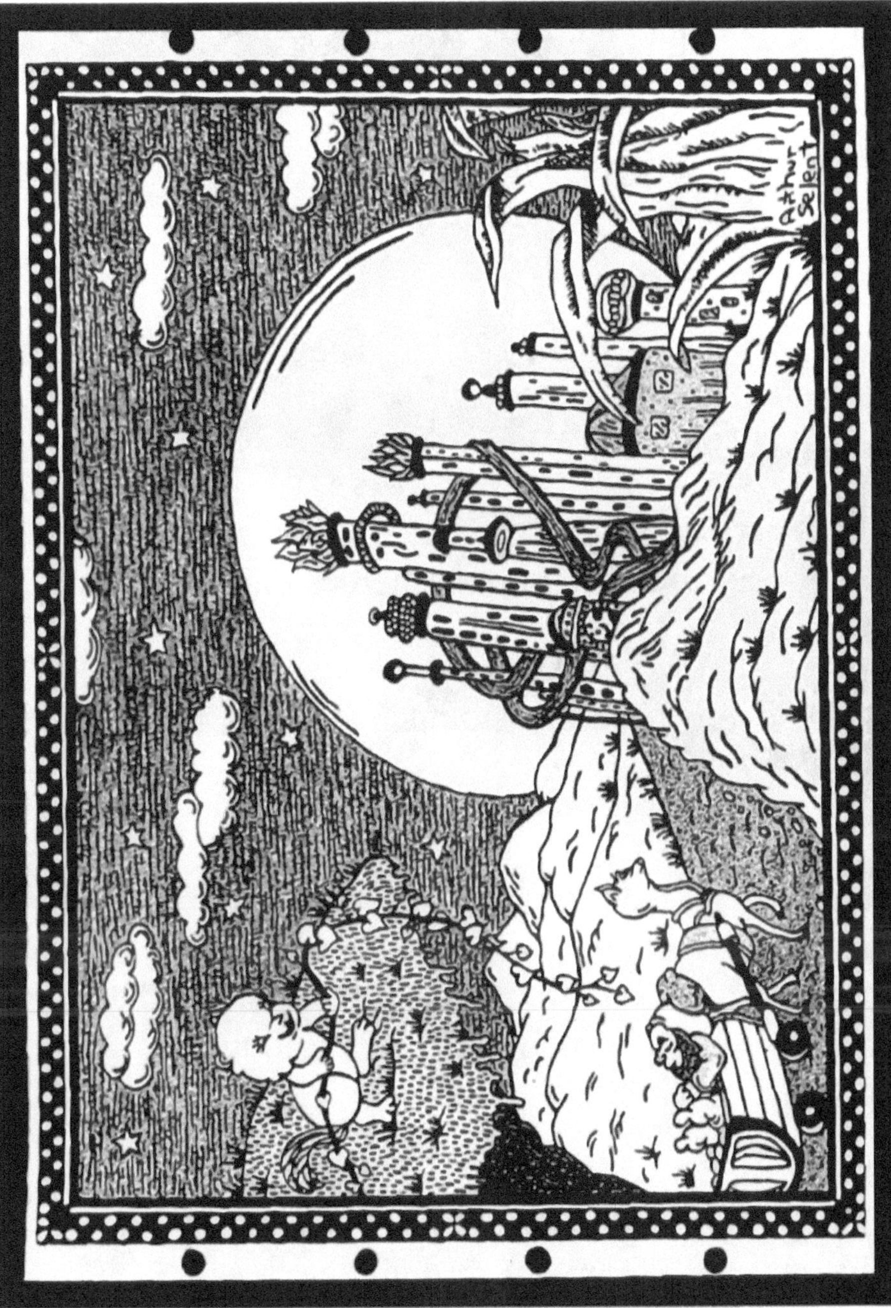

4545 (2/2) ==> Ah! Yes, the open doors to excitement and deception.

******

4546 ==> Propaganda is the art of brainwashing others to believe what one does not believe oneself.

******

4547 ==> Why do they call it "The News"? It should be called "Story Time."

******

4548 ==> Why is it that people who write books that do not sell are such popular heroes at local cafes?

******

4549 ==> An empty stomach is often not a good advisor.

******

4550 ==> Can you imagine our saintly spiritual aspirations armed with the money bags of the planet's money printers? Could we empty the bags fast enough to keep up with the printing?

******

4551 ==> There are many people who live in a big city apartment who have never heard a bird sing or the whisper of a breeze through the trees.

******

4552 ==> The mind industry may not be as easy as it looks when your tool is a pencil and the minds to be worked on are thousands of miles away.

******

4553 ==> He would mumble on, and then his mind faded into silence. She then would finish what his words were trying to say. And so, the evening darkened. Their voices became softer, quieter, and yet quieter. They touched, the warmth of their bodies finding a need to be close.

To go on with such a story would only result in walking down the romance road all the way to the divorce courts and the fights, while the wealth gets divided.

******

4554 ==> One day, the governments will have to shut down the military people-killing industry because the people no longer wish to play this game.

******

4555 ==> People are too ready to fight for an ideal, provided that the ideal is not clearly understood.

******

4556 ==> It is easy to find reasons why other folks should improve.

******

4557 ==> He could not tolerate these graduates from the polytechnic schools, those thin little baby boys with goofy looks, unskilled, clumsy, and awkward. They were as unsuited as a devil in church saying prayers.

He was indignant in his thoughts that these unfit human mutations should share the planet with him.

Why, they even seemed to like their mental delusion, adding and subtracting tables more than they liked pretty women. That fact alone stands to reason why they should be removed from this story.

They are gone now, removed. The story is over.

******

4558 ==> We seem to often meet people who look us over with investigative penetration and read us like a book. But they never tell us what they read.

******

4559 ==> Few wants will bring contentment sooner than great wealth will.

******

4560 ==> The more they talk of their honesty and honor, the faster we hide our gold.

******

4561 ==> We wish we could live forever, but do not know what to do with ourselves on a rainy Sunday afternoon.

******

4562 ==> She was not a great beauty, but she did not mind her face because she was behind it. But the folks in front of her face, well, it is them who have to suffer.

******

4563 ==> The rewards of large profits are taxes. Everyone wants a share, even those who made no effort to create the profits.

******

4564 ==> The more we try to change things, the more things change us.

******

4565 ==> Understanding is a quiet teacher.

******

4566 (1/2) ==> Every time he went to dinner with a woman, he thought himself certain of finishing the night with her beside him on the mattress. Often, nothing hindered his fantasy, and he was very successful in his conquests. Other men made sure their women's toys did not come near him.

4566 (2/2) ==> The shopkeepers feared his sneaky ways. They hated him when he flirted with their wives and young shop lady clerks. More than once, he had to make a fast escape while in a back room with the merchant's wife, daughter, or shop clerk.

His reputation for romantic play was well established. But there was always some lonely, depraved woman willing to entertain his romantic fantasy even if she knew it was not love.

The lonely tender-hearted women with a sliver of modesty felt themselves grow weak and unclothed before him. They would discreetly smile as he went through his charm routine. Sometimes, for amusement, they competed for his attention to see who would have him for a night's frolic.

He was just the village housewife's secret play toy, and when the action was slow, he played in the fine nests of the pretty shop clerks.

******

4567 (1/2) ==> It is a long-term project. Don't race because you might miss the road signs, which are cleverly hidden to keep the path uncrowded. Some signs point wrong, so maybe we will be better off to follow, Sun, Moon, and Stars. The path on both sides is infested with snares and traps ready to pull someone into lost dreams where the door closes behind. In front of monsters ready to ravage anyone. Yes, those monsters.

4567 (2/2) ==> Your mission, should you decide to take it, is to one day reach the end of the path.

******

4568 ==> I have to go to the big city to buy a sack of peanuts. It is costing me six peanuts a day to bribe the squirrel to be my friend.

******

4569 ==> You don't have to love me. It is enough if we just walk on opposite sides of the street and wave to each other in passing.

******

4570 (1/2) ==> The little kid got his first job and paycheck. He went every Sunday afternoon and cleaned the lawns and parking lots of his dad's industrial place. It was only a few hours' work of picking up scraps of paper, food wrap, and putting new garbage bags in the garbage barrels.

His mother asked what he planned to do with the money.

He replied, "Put it in the Bank."

Mothers says, "Oh, don't to that." Do something special. Get what you really want.

The Kid replies, "Oh, but this is what I really want. Money in the Bank and lots of it. This is where I start."

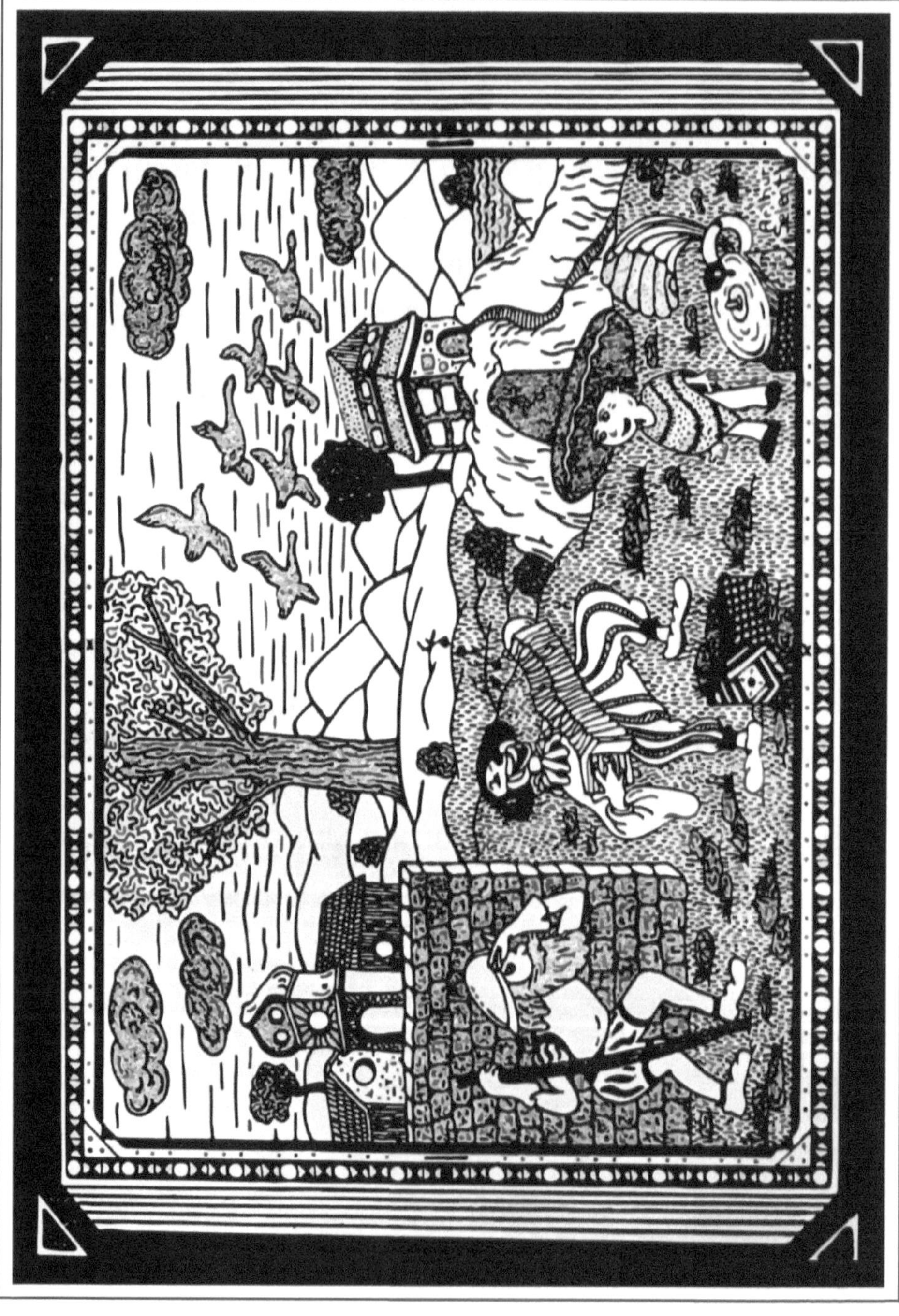

4570 (2/2) ==> Mother smiled and then frowned, realizing she would have to buy his clothes and other things because he was too much of a miser to spend his own money.

******

4571 ==> The married couple lived for years in a dream. They did not wake up until one day, one of the kids brought the family car home with an empty gas tank.

******

4572 ==> They now have a new dance move called "The Flea." It is done by the dance partners rubbing against each other as if squashing fleas between their bodies.

******

4573 ==> The young fellow came home from his military officer school for the Christmas Holidays.

His mother was all bright-faced and into cooking and feeding her son. She asked about the food and the kitchen at the school. "Do they have electric dishwashers?"

The son replies, "We sure do. We take one of the new fellows and plug him in."

******

4574 ==> Isn't it such a pleasure at Christmas to be friendly to all those relatives we have avoided all year?

******

4575 ==> When it comes to a choice between truth and a paycheck, many would throw truth away.

******

4576 ==> The little kid invited a school friend to spend the weekend at the family cottage. As they sat at the table with the food ready to eat, the dad said, "Now let us first say thanks."

The invited kid says, "No way. My dad always says never be thankful for what you see in front of you. Be thankful when you actually get it. Let's eat, and then we can be thankful."

******

4577 ==> No one paddles up and down the river anymore, hoping I'll come out for an afternoon nude swim.

See what effect old age has.

******

4578 ==> So if we go on a romantic honeymoon walking down lover's road looking for a place to spread our camping blanket, would I have to take a bath and put on clean clothes?

******

4579 ==> The big ego hath a fool for a master.

Does the big fool have an ego for a master?

******

4580 ==> The political cheese had just arrived on the stage and shuffled his papers with all the fairy tales and slick talk written there in. He cleared his voice and tapped the microphone. Just then, the electricity failed, and all was dark.

Someone found a candle and lit it, putting it near the cheese papers of promises and fairy tales. The rank political cheese speaking into the microphone said, "Now, where was I?"

A voice, loud and booming, said, "At the end, just finishing the last sentence."

******

4581 ==> Do you masquerade your true feelings behind your back while you talk to yourself in front of yourself?

******

4582 ==> Is it better to live on a street corner than share an apartment with a quarrelsome lover and fight each day?

******

4583 ==> A somewhat neurotic family from the warm tropics bought a place slightly remote in the far north. They arrived in mid-summer and established themselves in the small house amidst the wilderness.

Day by day, they saw the daylight get less and the nights get more. It got colder and colder.

It was becoming uncomfortable. Coming from the higher education of neurotic intelligence, they reasoned that if the previous owners lived there throughout the winter, then they could also.

Finally, the day arrived when the waters in the toilet froze and cracked the seat apart.

This was too much for the father. Dressed in his extreme Arctic snow suit, he called the previous owners and asked how they kept warm in winter.

Reply, "For the forty years that we have owned the place, we have always gone south to warm tropical beaches every winter."

******

4584 ==> The daughter had gone off to the University and missed coming home for Christmas. The next year, her father mailed her an airplane ticket. He wrote, "I sent you some money so you can get back to the money dispensing source."

******

4585 ==> The Aliens in their spacecraft floated high above the Earth.

One Alien says, "How much longer can we float about watching the humans, probe into their inner minds and party in their depravities?"

Other Alien, "It does get a bit drab, but it won't be long now. The humans are overbreeding even faster. They are creating viruses that are impossible to control or stop. Soon, the humans will be extinct."

Original Alien, "We may as well mark our claims for ownership before the crowds from our planet arrive."

******

4586 ==> Santa's reindeer are all females because no male reindeer would drag a fat man dressed in funny red around the world.

******

4587 ==> The little girl had learned to walk and talk nicely. This was her first trip to the shopping mall with her mother. As they walked about, she saw a doll and asked her mother if they could buy it.

Mother replies, "No dear, I have to start saving for Christmas."

Little girl, "You mean we have to pay Santa Claus?"

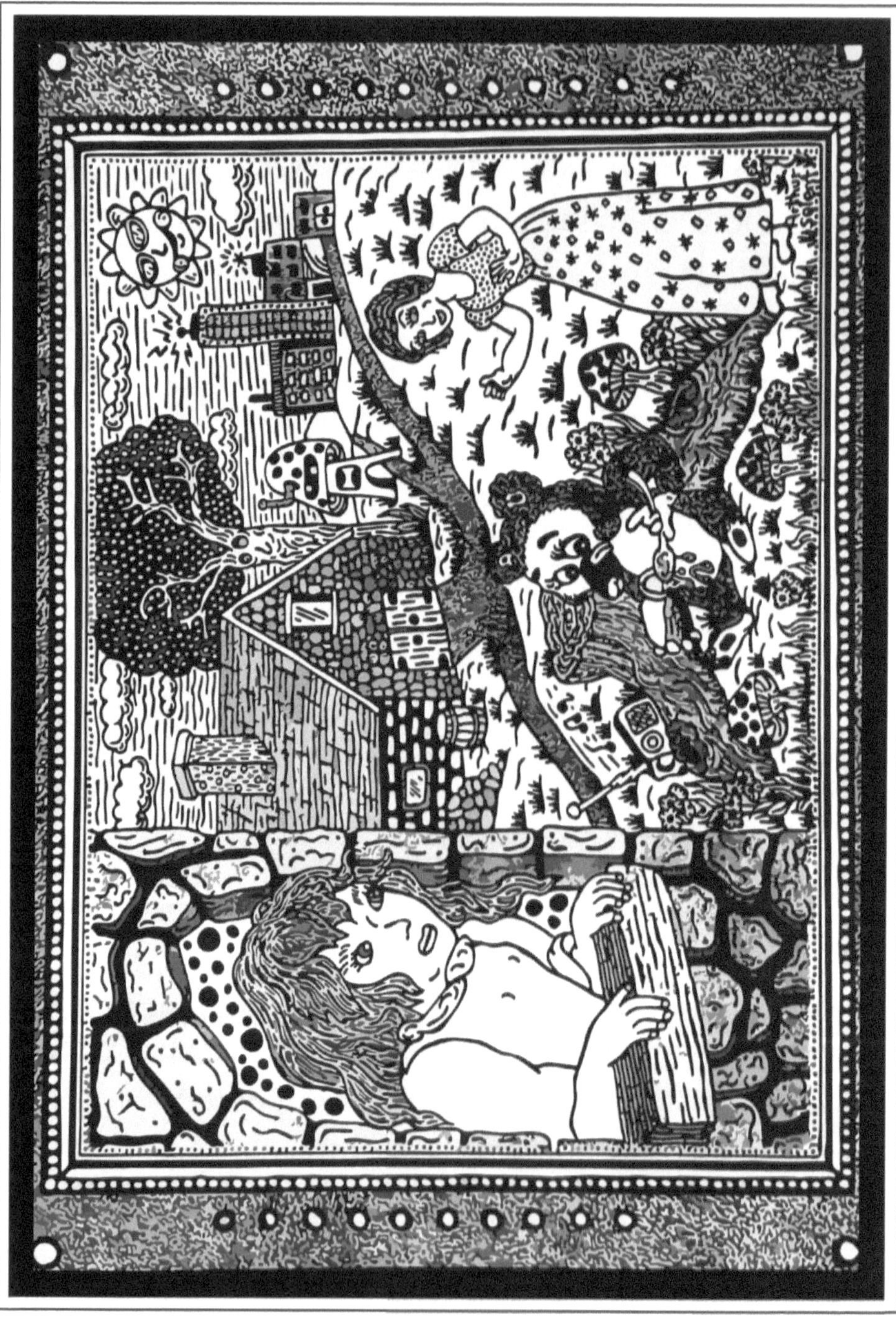

******

4588 ==> The homeless tramp living in a small tarp tent shelter is often happier and at peace than a rich man living in a mansion with armed security patrolling circles around his home.

******

4589 ==> How will you ever be happy if the mean eater eats the meanness out of your soul?

******

4590 ==> Is your life a TV movie? Everywhere you go, the cameras roll: the bank, the job, the store, the streets. Are you getting a union wage for all those TV appearances?

******

4591 ==> The little kids, for a school project, were asked to write Santa Claus a letter. One kid whose dad had not been home for a year because he was working overseas on some big engineering project wrote, "Please Santa, bring me a little baby brother so we can have a surprise for dad when he comes home."

******

4592 ==> The little kid put eight large bowls filled with oatmeal under the X-mas tree. Mother asks who the oatmeal is for.

Kid, "They are for Santa's reindeer."

******

4593 ==> The kindergarten class was talking about Santa Claus. One kid says, "It is really the parents who bring the gifts."

Another kid says, "I don't believe that because I know our parents don't know how to drive reindeer."

******

4594 (1/2) ==> The line-up at the lunch counter of the fast-food place was long and busy. It was the Christmas shopping insanity at the mall. One little boy was wailing and making all kinds of trouble, kicking and pulling at his mother.

I was a few steps behind them in the line. I looked at my cellphone and phoned a friend to see if we could have dinner together.

The mother pointed to me and said to the disturbing kid, "Look at that man. He is most likely reporting you to Santa Claus."

The kid looks at me and instantly becomes a sweet angel, making no more trouble. From time to time, he'd turn and give me a very suspicious stare.

Then, just when they were next to be served, I pulled out my camera to check how much battery power there was left. The kids' eyes lit up with fear. With one big pull, he freed himself from his mother and ran into the crowd. Mother took off after him.

4594 (2/2) ==> Reporting him to Santa Claus is one thing, but giving Santa a photo for positive identification, well, that is somewhat more serious.

* * * * * *

4595 ==> It is a nice feeling to go after work and cash your paycheck at the bank. Smug though you may be, you should feel great pity for the super-rich. The rich no longer think like humans; they think like mini-Gods. Every day is a casino reality. The money moves about, and there the rich steal a bit here and there. Armed with a smile and a handshake.

At least you, with your weekly paycheck, need not face the demonic frustration and fear of falling down to join the commoners.

You can walk down the street without bodyguards. You can stop and talk on equal terms. You are a human and most likely act like a human.

Some of us look to the future with mixed feelings because we may become one of the rich. Now let's check that lottery ticket.

* * * * * *

4596 ==> Her birthday was so slow to arrive that she feared she'd become a teenager before she turned seven.

* * * * * *

4597 ==> The family with the howling shit smelling kids went to the store to buy one of those plastic blow-up swimming pools for the kids.

Because this was a bigger item, the store did not put it on display but rather just stacked the boxes in a corner. The family wanted to inspect the pool to make sure there were no leaks. With hidden and subdued annoyance, the store clerk opened the box. He spread everything on the floor and blew the pool sides full of air. The parents inspected it, and the kids jumped in, wrecking the floor.

The father grabs a box and walks to the cashier. The mother tells the clerk, "We want a fresh one that has not been used as a demonstration model."

The store clerk, much frustrated, let the air out and neatly stuffed everything back in the box. As he taped the box shut, he looked at the family walk out. He thought, "I hope it leaks."

******

4598 ==> So, what happens if one day you wake and find you have outgrown your lover the way you outgrew your clothes when you were a kid.

******

4599 ==> Men seem to want women with touch control. Just push the button to turn her on and off.

******

4600 ==> You are working too hard. Give yourself a reward. Give yourself a raise – buy a ladder and start moving into those high positions.

******

4601 ==> There are some people stupid enough to listen to reason.

******

4602 ==> The determination of life insurance salespeople to succeed has made quite a few widows somewhat rich.

******

4603 (1/2) ==> A man walking down the busy street sees a little boy on the sidewalk playing in the sunshine with some toys. The people just walk around him. The kid is having such an intense passion of concentration with his playing. One would think it was his job.

The man asks where he got the toys. The kid points to the store he is sitting in front of. The man remembers his nephew will have a birthday soon, and some toys might be a good present.

4603 (2/2) ==> Inside the store, there seem to be many people buying toys. As he pays the cashier, the clerks say, "I don't know how the owner got the idea to place the little kid out front, but business has suddenly picked up."

******

4604 ==> Usually, those who have nothing to share are those who are the most eager to share.

******

4605 ==> Every doctor has his favorite sickness, which he convinces his patients to have.

******

4606 ==> The honest poor are always willing to lend some effort to help those above flush the toilet waste upon their heads. Compost oozed out of those above to help the honest poor below to fertilize and grow themselves deeper into poverty.

******

4607 ==> Money will get a man laid by many more women than real feelings of love ever could.

******

4608 ==> Why is Christmas like a factory job? You do all the work, and some fat guy in a funny red suit gets all the credit.

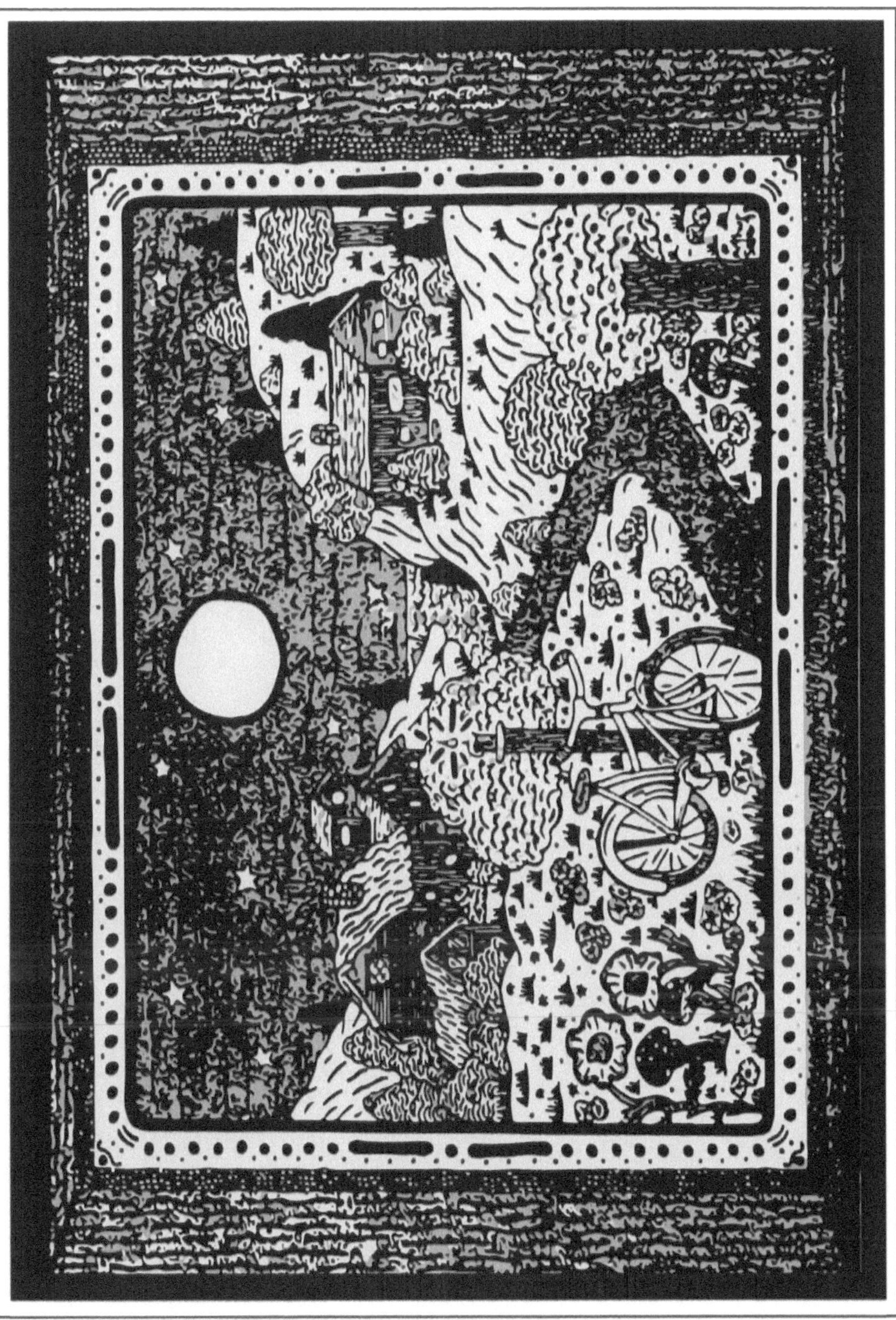

******

4609 ==> How will you ever be happy if the mean eater eats the meanness out of your soul?

******

4610 ==> To find the ultimate state of cleanliness, one needs but only to look into the homes of spiteful, lonely old widows who continuously fuss about.

******

4611 ==> The babysitter canceled at the last minute, and the mother was frantic. She had an appointment to see her secret boyfriend. In despair, she took the children, a girl of five and a boy of three, along with her.

Close to the boyfriend's apartment was a park with a children's playground. She left the kids there, telling the five-year-old to look after her little brother because the mother would be gone for an hour or two.

When her mother came back, she saw the little girl talking to some people. The people walked away, and the mother asked what they wanted. The little girl replies, "We were playing Santa Claus. I am Santa, and I am giving little brother away."

******

4612 ==> What do you call a big, ugly, mean goof goon listening to loud music on headphones? Anything you like, he can't hear you.

******

4613 ==> The mother was bleary-eyed, dim of vision. When the son brought his girlfriend home, the mothers said, "Well, you are certainly an improvement. You should have seen the blonde, brainless floozy he had last week. I knew she would not last long."

The girlfriend replies, "I dyed my hair."

******

4614 ==> Halloween is here.

Did you notice that travel agencies, train stations, and airports are filled with pumpkin heads trying to escape Halloween?

******

4615 ==> Meanness is a skill for too many have learned and perfected.

******

4616 (1/2) ==> The wife had forgotten to get her husband a birthday gift.

He tells her, "It is all right. The only thing I need from you is your love."

4616 (2/2) ==> She says, "I'd rather buy you a gift."

******

4617 ==> Often our greatest talent is the ability to deceive ourselves.

******

4618 ==> To have a vast education of misunderstanding is somewhat inferior to understanding only a little.

******

4619 (1/2) ==> Have you noticed that when one goes into a professional office, there is usually an impressive bookshelf filled with richly bound book covers. Books chosen for their rich covers rather than for content.

4619 (2/2) ==> Books no one ever opens.

******

4620 ==> The law being equal to both rich and poor forbids the rich as well as the poor to sleep under bridges, beg in the streets, and steal bread. The rich side-step this law with smiles and handshakes, covering up the stealing and begging. As for sleeping under bridges, well, someone has to occupy the big mansions. It is the civic duty of the rich to do so.

******

4621 ==> Is it better to be as stupid as those around us, or is it better to be intelligent, all alone and outcast from the idiot herd?

******

4622 ==> Too many good people have unknowingly become criminals by defrauding the government, but why does the government not become criminals when it defrauds the people?

******

4623 ==> He was from some remote mountain village hidden in the back woods, wild lands where there was no digital internet or phone service. His parents made some arrangements with a distant relative in a faraway big city so he might get a better book education.

On his first day at his new school, surrounded by more kids than he'd ever seen before, a teacher saw him talking into an envelope. The teacher asked, "What are you doing?"

He replies, "I am sending a voice mail."

******

4624 (1/2) ==> It is a curse at times to be psychic. To know, see, and feel life and things that are close to those around us, while the words to tell just seem to be blocked.

4624 (2/2) ==> No doubt, saving us from being erased from the picture by corruption.

Why must the honest mind-reading psychic carry everyone's secret?

******

4625 ==> When the Moon has risen to the center of the sky, we will meet in the eerie pale night. On our magic carpet under the big tree, we will share our secrets.

******

4626 ==> When you bet on the sports games, go to the Casino or buy a lottery ticket, do you rub your lucky rabbit's foot on your key chain?

You might consider, it was not lucky for the rabbit.

******

4627 ==> Who is in command of your spirit soul?

******

4628(1/2) ==> I was working for someone not inclined to be honest. The job was to collect charity to send mentally disturbed people on camping vacations. We did this sitting in a big office phone room high up in the clouds of an office tower.

I had worked with good faith because I thought I was doing a good job. Slowly, I found out that the only people with mental troubles who ever went camping with the money collected were my boss and his dumb, sleazy secretary. I did not like her, but she had a firm shape that was slightly arousing when she'd sit facing me and her legs spread slightly open to show she was wearing no underwear.

So, the boss and her did their mental disturbance camping in front of the living room sofa a few floors up in an apartment building.

It was a job situation that was not like a regular job as we know it. The secretary was playing with my mind too much. She had chosen me for a secret job.

We worked the telephones about four hours in the evenings. The boos usually just came in during the last hour or two. He had some other business to deal with. The secretary just about ran the scam during the first three hours of our work shift.

******

4629 (1/2) ==> The secretary was a strange animal. She asked me one night if I could come with her while she went to her car for some papers. She did not like being alone in the underground parking lot.

4629 (2/2) ==> What really played with my mind was when shortly after we returned from the underground parking and back in the office the boss would arrive.

I always got very nervous. The secretary just glowed a secret kind of pleasure all her own in her mind as she and the boss did the nightly book keeping. She lavishing the boss with sweet attention while my baby seeds deep inside waited for her to go for a pee.

Slowly as the weeks flew by, the boss started heckling me more and more. He had a strong dislike for me.

I became very mentally disturbed, being caught between her and him. I went camping for the summer.

******

4630 ==> The Christmas holiday season, where deeply religious folks celebrate the birth, life torture and murder of a brown skinned eccentric homeless man who did not carry or use money. These deeply religious folk celebrate by going to shopping malls to buy lavish gifts to give to each other. It makes them very happy to celebrate the misfortunes of a homeless man.

Religion is jealously trying to take the place of the winter solstice event.

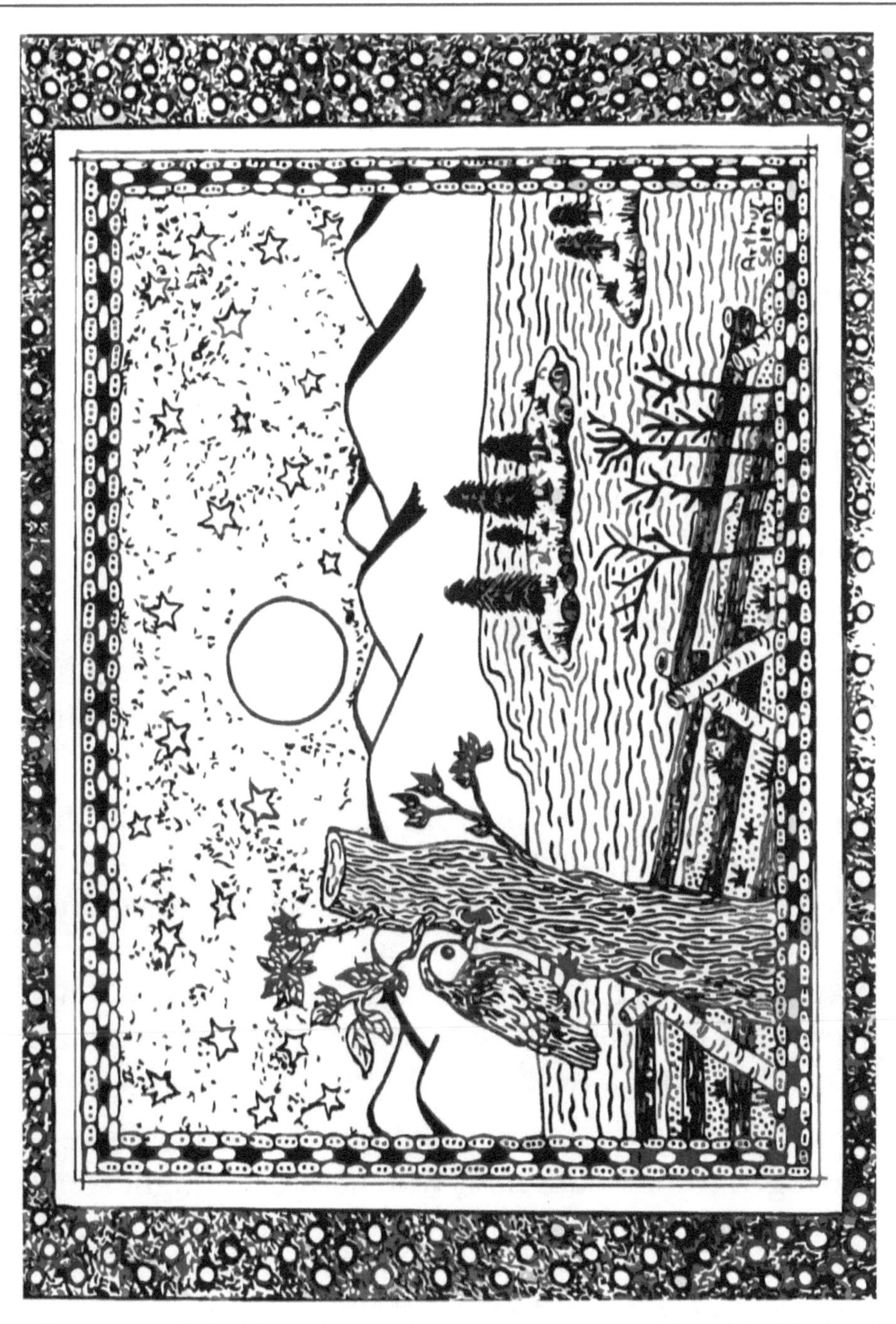

******

4631 ==> You notice that when you buy a new small electric item, the package always says, "batteries not included." Due to the frustrations caused by this, the marketing has started selling batteries with package labels saying, "toys not included."

******

4632 ==> The standard New Year's Company party. It is where old friends are forgotten. As are also a few various item of clothing left behind while frolicking with someone's wife.

******

4633 (1/2) ==> The elderly woman worked in a laundry, folding, washing clothes, and handling money transactions, providing coins for the machines.

A fellow parks in front and comes in with his rags to wash. She notices that he drove up in an old, decrepit rustic pick-up truck with a for sale sign on it. She asked how much he wanted for it. He mentioned quite a low price. He said the only thing wrong with it was that the radiator had a very small, slow leak, which he'd not had time to repair.

The elderly woman thought it would make a great gift for her daughter, who had just bought some land in the country. The fellow explained that he kept a dozen gallon wine jugs filled with water in the back and used these to top off the radiator.

4633 (2/2) ==> The woman paid cash for the truck. Put a "closed" sign on the laundry door and drove off to her daughter's land. Halfway way she stopped at a roadside rest area to check the water level in the radiator. It was low, so she got one of the wine jugs and proceeded to pour water into the radiator.

A family with a motorhome was having a snack at a nearby picnic table. The mother looks and says to her little children. Look at that silly floosie. As if getting drunk was not bad enough, she wastes all that good wine to get her truck drunk also.

******

4634 ==> The rich people never had time for their little kid. They were always away chasing money or being popular at corporate parties. The little boy's birthday was coming, and his parents asked him what he'd want for a present.

He replied, "I would like some warmth and time from you."

Dad gave him a portable room heater, and Mother gave him a wall clock.

******

4635 (1/2) ==> The parents had won a trip to some exotic tourist place. They brought the kids, four and five years old, to their grandparents for two weeks.

4635 (2/2) ==> The grandparents were very showy about their religion and took the kids to church with them.

The next day, when the kids were outside playing, one asked the other, "What do you make of this Satan fellow?"

The other kid replies, "Remember when we found out Santa Claus was really Dad. Most likely, Satan is really Dad."

******

4636 ==> Do you have any idea how fast you are going? Even as you sit on the sofa in front of the TV, the planet Earth is spinning you around at thousands of miles per hour.

And while spinning you around in big circles, the Earth is rolling around the Sun at still faster millions of length units.

******

4637 ==> There is nothing so ugly as a beautiful woman thinking bad thoughts.

******

4638 (1/2) ==> It was mid-winter in the Northlands. It snowed heavily, then the temperature warmed, and it rained. Then the temp dropped suddenly, and all that wet snow slush turned to ice.

4638 (2/2) ==> In the morning, the father tried to clear the driveway way but his cheap plastic snow shovel was useless against the ice. He got his kid's baseball bat and used that to smash the ice, which he then scooped up with the shovel. It was hard work. Soon he was tired and come inside for a rest.

After a coffee, he was just getting ready to go out again when his four-year-old kid came in carrying the baseball bat. He says, "I got the ice off the car."

Dad asks, "How did you do that?

Kid, "Same way you got the ice off the driveway, with the baseball bat."

******

4639 ==> Often after we have got half our wishes, we find we have doubled our troubles.

******

4640 ==> The little kid got dressed really warm and shoveled a pile of snow close to the street. He put up a sign, "Snow Man for Sale."

A car stops, and the driver asks, "Where is the snowman?"

The kid points to the fine print at the bottom of the sign, "Some assembly required."

******

4641 ==> So here we have Halloween. I would like to ask the witches out there if they have a broom to sell. I want the fast sport model, something capable of following my rich girlfriend's private jet.

I think she is keeping secrets from me. Why does she leave me at home when she flies about the planet?

******

4642 ==> You notice that these modern floosies are wearing dresses cut so low that a real man has to peek under the table to see what they are wearing.

******

4643 (1/2) ==> Two drivers had a smash-up with their cars. They got out and started yelling at each other. Finally, one driver says, "We should not fight like this. Let us be friends, set aside our differences, and reason this out."

The other driver pauses, then says, "I suppose you are right. Now, just what happened that your car hit mine?"

"I don't know, but let's toast to our new friendship first. We both need something to relax our nerves and get over this shock." He pulls a bottle of fine wine from his car and offers it to the other driver, who takes a big swallow, mumbles how fine the wine is, and takes a couple more big gulps. Then he hands the bottle back. He is clearly suffering from emotional shock.

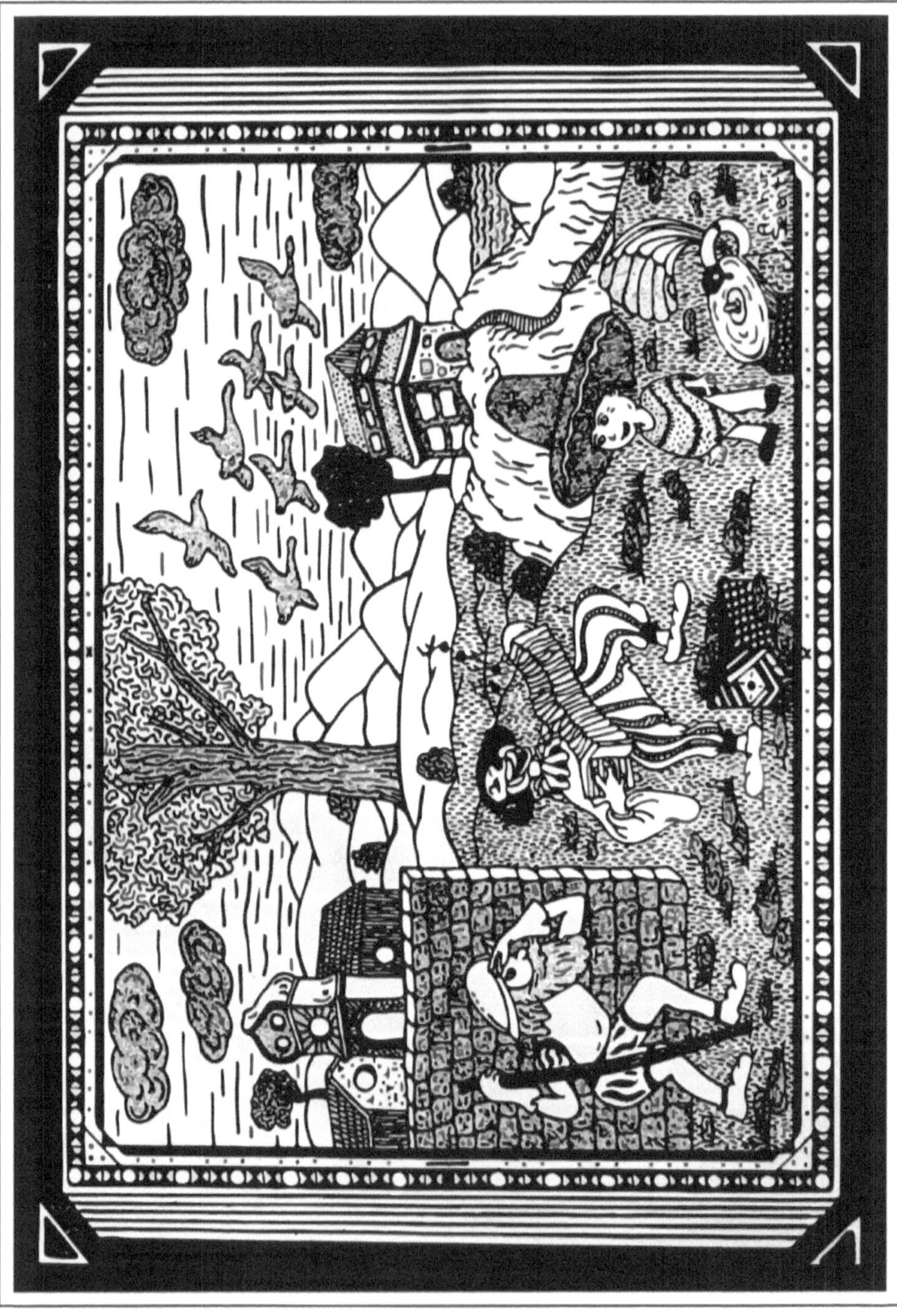

4643 (2/2) ==> The other driver caps the bottle and sets it down close to the other car. "Sorry, I cannot toast our friendship. The police have just arrived. You can keep the wine. It is leftovers from a party."

******

4644 ==> We could look at the mental condition of humans and their fashions. Various parts of the body must always be covered up, even when swimming. Yet all around us, we can view these private parts on animals, or we can go on the internet and see thousands of nude humans.

This social fashion was invented by people who have ugly, stinky private parts.

Maybe this is for the general good. I can only imagine the situation if reality were otherwise. Me with such beautiful private parts would just get grabbed and ravaged with each step walking down the beach.

******

4645 ==> He wishes to explore the industry of broken hearts. He needs a massive number of applications to help him forget those that expired past romances.

******

4646 ==> The fellow was a bomb disposal expert. On his business card, at the bottom in fine print. "If you see me running, then you'd better catch up to me and pass."

******

4647 (1/2) ==> The wife and husband decided they'd save some money by stealing a Christmas tree from the National Forest. The deal was that hubby would do the chopping and wife would pull the sled. They found a shoulder-high tree.

As he was chopping down the tree, the wife let out a shriek and ran away as fast as she could run. He looked up and yelled, "That's it, run away just when there is work to be done." "He went back to chopping."

It was evening when the heavily armed rescue crew arrived, and they found the three securely tied to the sled. His clothes were neatly folded and placed on top of the tree. Going off into the dense shrubs, the tracks of a big bear dragging the husband dripping blood for some distance.

It was getting too dark to follow. Overnight, the snow fell waist-high, covering all tracks.

The wife was in a complete breakdown. She phoned her daughter, "Honey, remember last month you advised me to triple daddy's life insurance? Yesterday, a bear ate Daddy, and now we are rich."

******

4648 ==> When you buy a lottery ticket or go to a casino, do you rub your lucky rabbit's foot on your key ring?

You might consider, it was not lucky for the rabbit.

******

4649 ==> The want of drink and the want of women have driven many a man insane.

******

4650 ==> It is always exciting the first time. Afterward, it just becomes a routine habit.

******

4651 ==> There would be no wars if the truth were told to the people.

******

4652 ==> He had the keys to the top-secret place. He kept all the doors locked tight, but his lips flapped as the words floated from his tongue, vibrating like a musical reed.

Now everyone knows.

******

4653 ==> They have two faces, one sneaky and the other tricky.

******

4654 (1/2) ==> The rank political cheese stinking of corruption gets out of his big luxury Limousine and, surrounded by his heavily armed henchmen, walks up to the stage at the farmer's exhibition fair. This was an area where mostly poor immigrants had settled, and many still spoke their old homeland language.

He starts his speech. "I come with the warmest greetings and feelings of friendship."

The crowd claps their hands and shouts, "Poopsy."

"Great prosperity is on its way."

"Poopsy"

"Economic benefit and jobs."

"Paradise and streets of gold."

"Poopsy." The crowd is worked up, hooting and yelling.

The speech over the Political cheese says to one of his armed henchmen as he walks back to his shiny new Limousine, "What a nice crowd. They have nicknamed me, Poopsy, which sounds sort of cute, like someone fondly calling a child."

Just then, a farmer leading a bull crosses their path. The bull stops and has a big shit before moving on.

4654 (2/2) ==> As the political cheese gets close to the steaming pile, one of the henchmen says, "Better walk a little to the right. There is a big pile of poopsy on the path."

******

4655 ==> There would be no war if the truth were told to the people.

******

4656 ==> Who is in command of your spirit soul?

******

4657 ==> Are we born with blank paper waiting to be imprinted with love?

******

4658 ==> At the party, she is like a queen wasp surrounded by adoring drones.

******

4659 ==> A crowd has many heads but few brains.

******

4660 (1/2) ==> She sleeps at the back of the garbage dump. She carries the stench like designer perfume. Gapped front tooth surrounded by multiple tawny layers of lipstick. A face that once was pretty is now hiding behind a painted Halloween mask.

4660 (2/2) ==> She really was ugly enough to scare the night goblin. The garbage smell mingled with the rankness of her unwashed vagina.

This late at night, she semi-staggered under the street lights, pretending to be slightly drunk, waving to the men driving back and forth, hunting for a rental girlfriend. Of course, there was no romance. One car, one truck, all the same. Jump in and get ravaged by some sex starved man. Afterward dumped like garbage onto the streets.

At the end of the night, the garbage walks back to the garbage dump and her cardboard shelter covered with a tarp. No rent, no car, no electricity bills, she had made enough money to live another day or two plus buy some drugs.

******

4661 ==> The warm intimacy of the marriage bed produces a kind of bonding, a mysterious partnership between two persons, even after they have ceased to love each other, but still go through with the honeymoon pretense each time they practice breeding. Two so tight they will not let anyone else into their secret.

******

4662 ==> House guests are like fish; they go bad after three days.

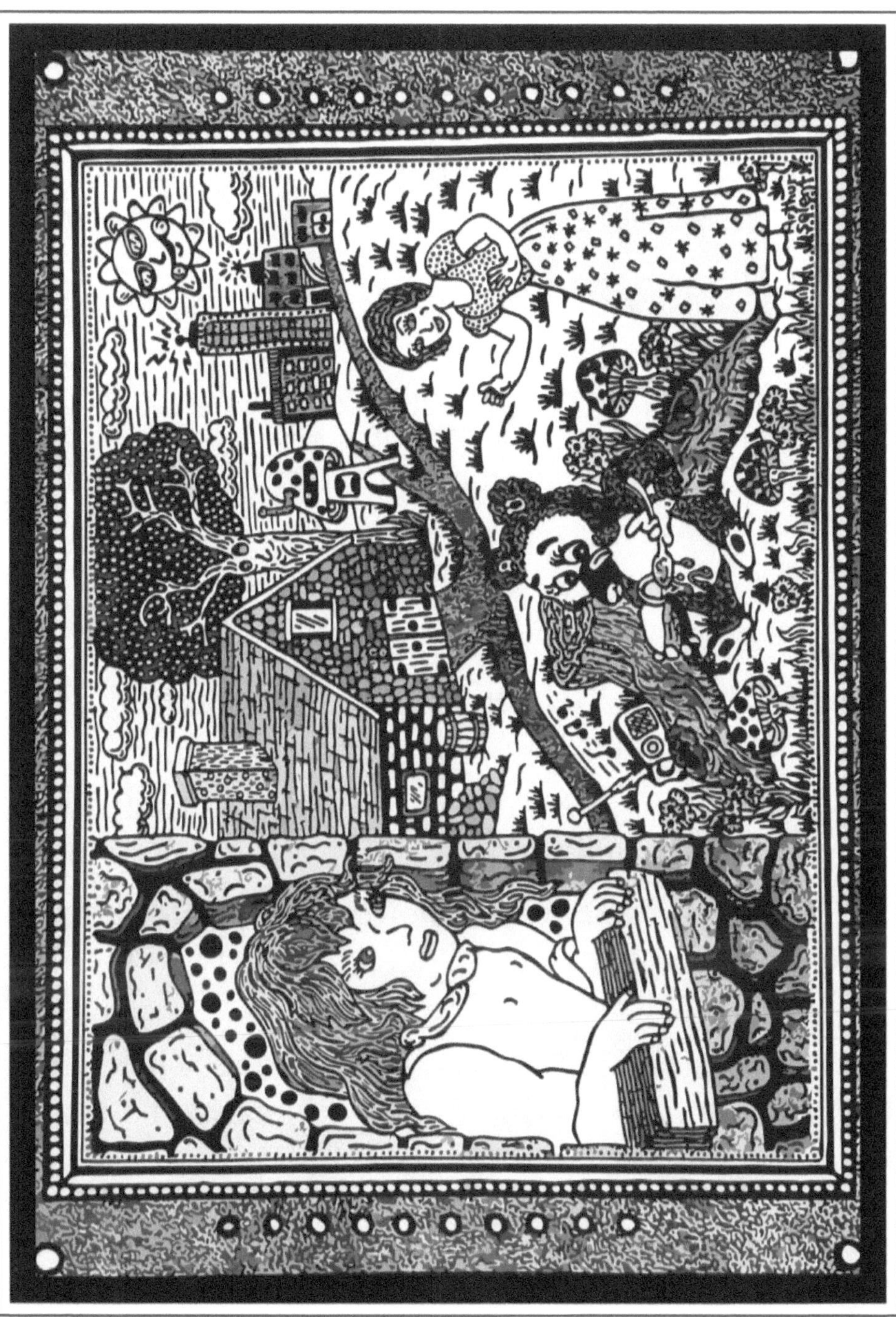

******

4663 ==> A mother takes many years to make a man out of her baby boy, but another woman comes along and makes a fool out of him in minutes.

******

4664 ==> He is a friend of the mother, but he only thinks of the daughter.

******

4665 ==> I really do think about things that would astonish you.

******

4666 ==> The virus people killing the bio industry are coming into direct conflict with the military people killing the industry.

Do we have enough population to tolerate two people killing industries?

How much more money are the political cheese going to pump into these two insane delusions?

We are creating a very bad future where the biggest profits are made from us killing each other.

******

4667 ==> Love your neighbor, but keep your fence strong.

******

4668 ==> Since religion has often created so much evil, what would humans do without religion?

******

4669 ==> It is not easy to get out of ruts carved deep into a muddy road. So likewise does the mind roll along in the ruts made by others.

******

4670 (1/2) ==> The middle-aged man and woman went to a rock concert. The crowd was packed in, standing shoulder to shoulder. It was dark with Laser lights flashing on the ceiling.

Directly in front of the husband stood a young woman, the usual sleaze one sees at these events, dirty, drugged, and barely dressed. Her thigh pushed into his crotch ever so slightly, then moved firmly. His erection suddenly woke up. Surely, she must feel the hardness, but she did not move away. Exited, he wondered, could he get away with it in this crowd? It was dark, and no one seemed to notice. His wife, beside him, was looking trance-like towards the stage.

He made his move, lifted her mini skirt, and took his manly thing out of his pants. He slid it between her thighs into the warm, wet, slippery.

4670 (2/2) ==> Just then, she moaned, shivered, and trembled. She turned and said, "Oh, daddy, you really know how to do it." She slipped away into the crowd.

He noticed his wife looking at him. He felt guilty and caught. He says, "I don't know what that was all about."

Wife, "Oh, but I do. It was my hand under her dress. You seemed to be enjoying yourself so much that I decided to help." She held her fingers under his nose.

******

4671 ==> Do you think we could tolerate each other if we went on a date?

******

4672 ==> I just want to be the real me when I am around you.

******

4673 ==> Most of the people have something to say, but cannot say it.

The remaining people have nothing to say but cannot shut up.

******

4674 ==> How often have great talkers been found to be little doers?

******

4675 (1/2) ==> She was a mysterious beauty. Almost every guy at school had a secret fantasy desire to be alone with her on a romantic to be alone with her on a romantic date.

Her mother was also good-looking and not aged at all. Her mother was single; she was too much of a slut to marry. She liked a variety of men too much. She was a hunter of men.

She could walk into a crowd or busy place and within an hour emerge with the captured trophy, a hypnotized, entranced man at her side. She could read a man like an X-ray reads a hard bone. The man easy to captured and led on by soft suggestions into his mind, driving his emotions with the excitement of some fast, fresh new girlfriend experience.

The young schoolgirl was blooming with the springtime flowers, just opening petals for the first ray of light to let the bee in for a taste of nectar. She found herself becoming very interested in men. What would it feel like?

She began to look closer at her mother's boyfriends. She looked for chances to get close and brush against the lover when her mother was busy cooking or making tea. She could feel awake, a sort of tense emotion when she slyly made contact with the lover. For sure, he became aroused. She was young and blooming with curiosity.

4675 (2/2) ==> She chose one of these experienced lovers for her need of secret education. She will borrow one of her mother's lovers. Why this one? Because he had a small, soft manly thing. She had seen it when he'd gone to the washroom late at night, walking nude. Best to start with a small toy.

She wondered what it would feel like. It must be wonderful because mother never seems to get enough.

Mother was making dinner in the kitchen. She sat close beside him on the sofa. She reached over and put her hand on the little manly thing hidden in his pants. It got big and hard, what a surprise. He put his hand on hers and held it loosely. He did not say anything. Her other hand gently caressed his thigh. She felt him get so aroused. She said, "Come to me tomorrow at noon. I am alone then. Don't tell Mother. This is our secret." The guy was all confused and so aroused. She pulled away, got up, and went to help her mother in the kitchen.

The guy had a fitful night, the thought of her cooking his mind with lust and fantasy urges. The desire of having such a fresh-faced, eager thing in his arms excited a secret romance with the nervous fear of getting caught, only adding color to the dream.

Even though he knew it was some what wrong as society would judge, he slowly made his feet walk to her place at noon.

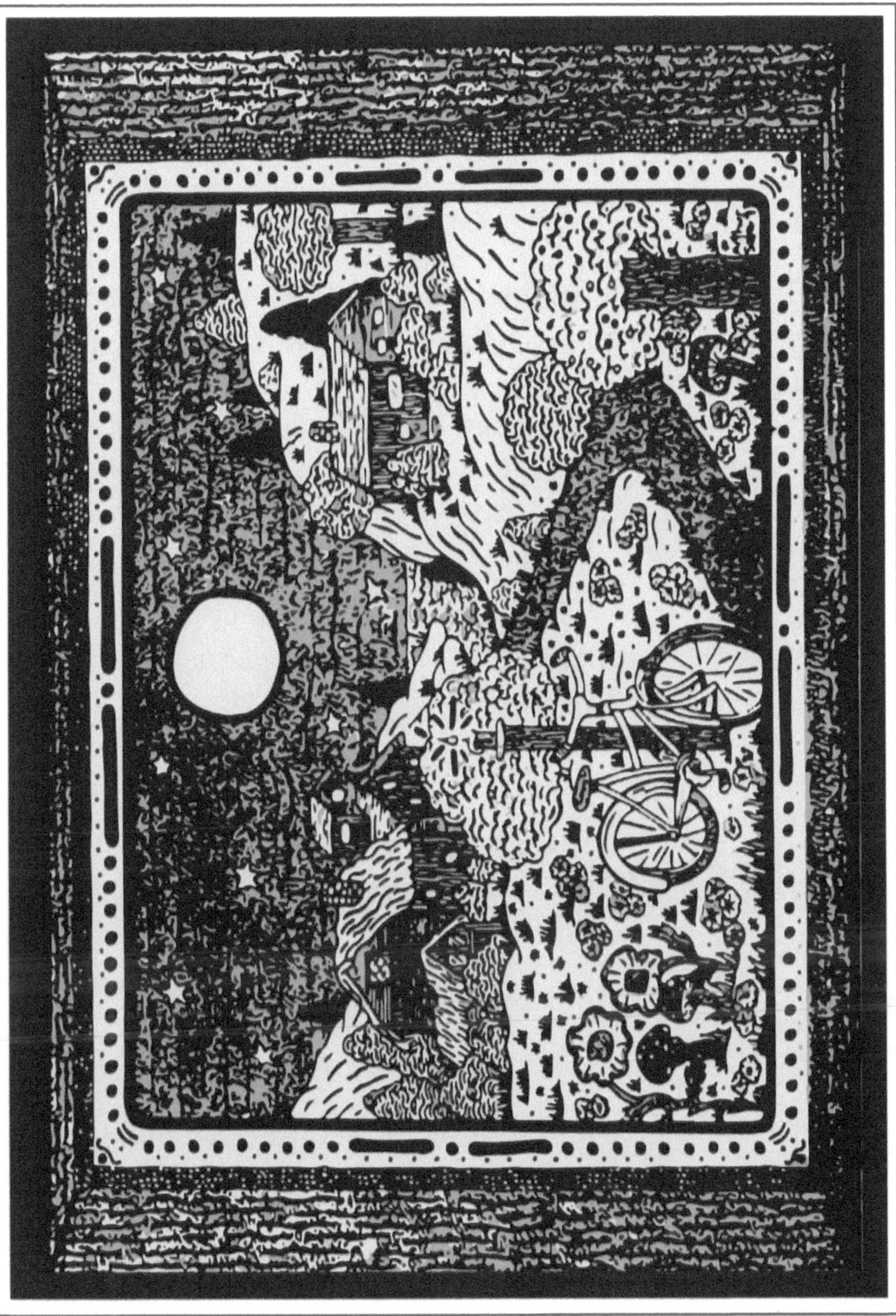

******

4676 ==> He is in the fortunate position of being an irresponsible money sack who can say and do what he wants.

******

4677 ==> If then people have to keep a big secret, it is possible that one will make the other nine dead.

******

4678 ==> Tax time is when the use of powers of deduction is most useful.

******

4679 ==> We must not fall for the nonsense of those who think they talk sense.

******

4680 ==> It was never intended that the leaders of the flags should become a ventriloquist's dummy sitting on the lap of the puppet master.

But sadly, that is all we get.

******

4681 ==> Better is it to have a firm grip on nonsense than it is to drift on the troubled seas of thought.

******

4682 ==> When you lock your door, you contribute towards keeping your neighbor honest.

******

4683 ==> Much-washed and well-groomed people grow dull; they miss the stimulation of fleas.

******

4684 ==> A tourist is someone who drives day and night just so he can take a photo of himself standing beside his motor home.

******

4685 ==> Some people cook, others just open tins and heat the contents.

******

4686 ==> You have to brag about yourself. You will never get anywhere unless you advertise.

******

4687 ==> Nature is waiting for you. She will make your days interesting and keep your mind content.

******

4688 ==> If you can count your money, then you obviously do not have enough.

******

4689 ==> Who has more purpose or meaning? Him that is on the table or those that is in chairs around the table?

* * * * * *

4690 ==> Where they go, they go with their Bibles. When they arrive, they soon have all the land, and homeless natives now have the Bibles.

* * * * * *

4691 ==> The boat sank after the explosion, and he was the only one to float to a nearby island. He blessed his spirit helpers for saving his life. He walked and wandered the coastline beach.

At one place, he saw piles of ashes and evidence of some active human presence. Some of the ash piles were weather-washed, but a few looked as if the fires had been only a day or two in the past. Beside one ash pile lay a partially burnt cross with a half-burnt human body tied to it with wire.

He thanked his God that he'd found signs of civilization. Certainly, he would be warmly welcomed by a society that tortured and burned people on crosses. After all, they shared the same God.

He wandered about some more, going in all directions, but no humans. Then it dawned on him, God's people had come by boat. He was alone; God's people had gone away.

******

4692 ==> We have found a real human. He is ours now.

******

4693 ==> His trouble seems to come from him, trying to fool himself. His eagerness to fool us for so long led himself lost in the mental forest.

******

4694 ==> She knows what she wants and has the brains to get it. So don't even think she is headed for hell. The devil would not let such a cold heart into his furnace.

******

4695 ==> The Political cheese authorities are worn smooth by long obedience with regulated coming and goings. Their heads never filled with new things, they shuffle about on the paths of yesterday.

******

4696 ==> Corruption is like fruit. It always looks good on the outside, but the worms are inside.

******

4697 ==> Do not borrow trouble. Instead, save up all you own troubles until you have enough.

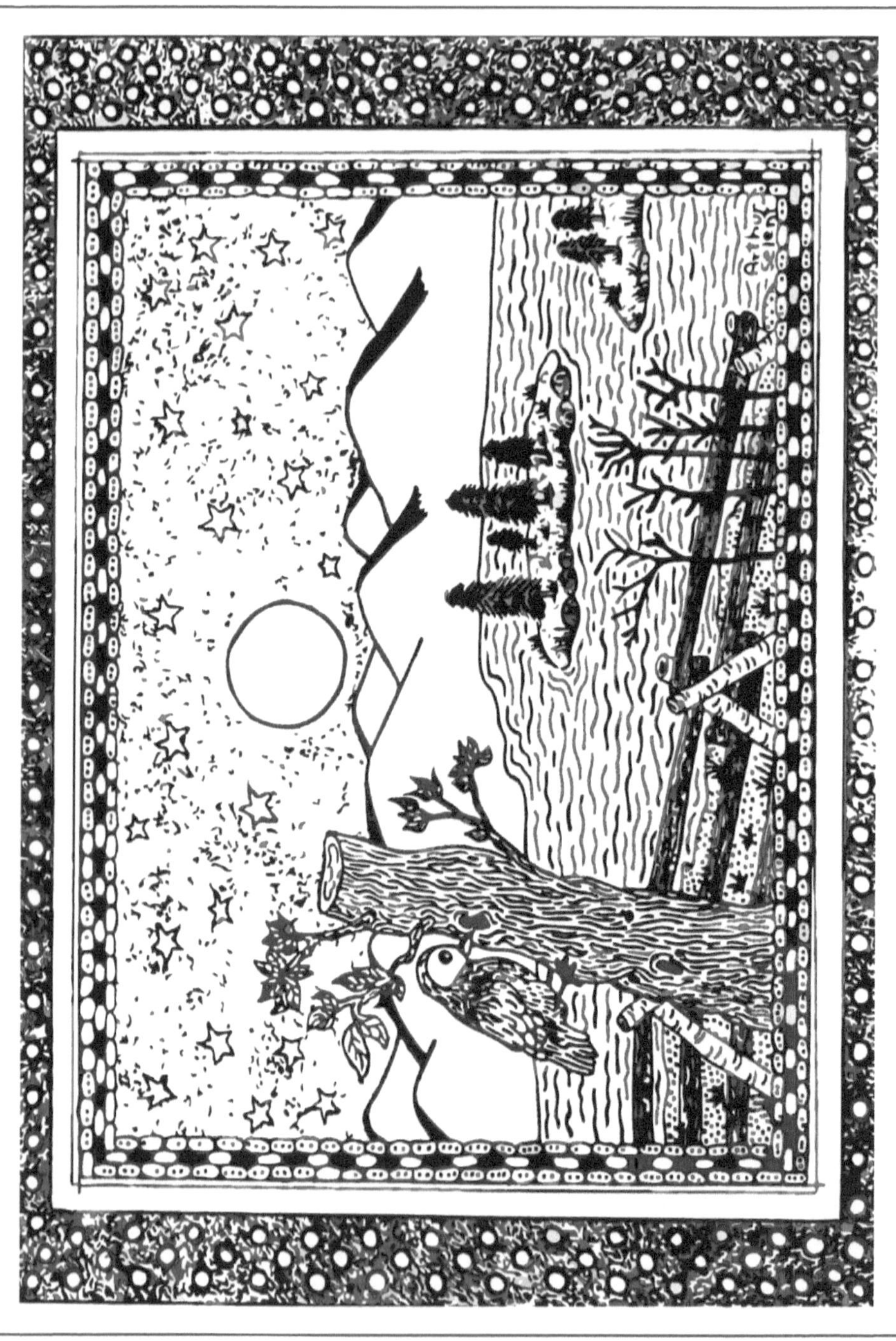

******

4698 ==> His trouble seems to come from him trying to fool himself. His eagerness to fool us for so long led himself lost in the mental forest.

******

4699 ==> She knows what she wants and has the brains to get it. So don't even think she is headed for hell. The devil would not let such a cold heart into his hot surface.

******

4700 ==> The Political cheese authorities are worn smooth by long obedience with regulated coming and goings. Their heads never filled with new things, they shuffle about on the paths of yesterday.

******

4701 ==> Corruption is like fruit. It always looks good on the outside, but the worms are inside.

******

4702 ==> Do not borrow trouble. Instead, save up all you own troubles until you have enough.

******

4703 (1/2) ==> In the old days, when a man or woman wanted to meet a new lover, they would attend dances. It was a fast start to romance, holding the other close on the dance floor.

4703 (2/2) ==> Today, when someone wants romance, they search on the internet and choose a lover from among photos of penis, vagina, and face. An appointment is made, and instant romance behind closed curtains.

******

4704 ==> The homeless, hungry man shuffled down the crowded sidewalk. He carried a large sign, "I surrender. Whatever crime is unsolved, I did it. Tell me the crime and I will confess. Now arrest me, give me a free warm room, and free meals in a safe security security-patrolled gated community."

******

4705 ==> The success of political lip-flapping is to say something which in fact is nothing but looks as if it were really something.

******

4706 ==> All in the village knew that old man, knew him so well that they could imagine what he was thinking. He comes, takes the wages, earning good money because he was skillful with his hands and mind. He comes in response to the job, giving his labor in trade. The village repairman, the children's grandfather.

******

4707 ==> I did not realize they were talking about me because they were saying so many nice things. How could anyone be so nice?

******

4708 ==> No one can take it with them. If it were not so, then we'd see moving trucks follow the coffin.

******

4709 ==> It is the half-fool and half-smart that makes all the trouble. The fools by themselves do not know enough, and the smarts by themselves know too much.

******

4710 ==> The haggard housewife went to see Doctor kill Em. She says, "What is wrong with me?" Everything sags and flaps, my face is all wrinkled, my teeth are falling out, my hair is falling out, and my husband no longer sleeps with me.

Doc kill Em replies, "Your eyesight seems to be working fine, but other than that, you have old age."

******

4711 (1/2) ==> The young university fellow was on summer vacation at some resort heaven beach. A fortune teller had set up a simple booth near the food sales area. He sat down and paid her fee.

4711 (2/2) ==> Psychic says, "You will meet a very attractive young woman. She will want to examine every part of you."

The young fellow had been hoping for romance for many months past and was aroused to interest. "Where will I meet her?"

"In her biology class."

******

4712 ==> If lemons come into your life, then making lemonade might be a good idea.

******

4713(1/2) ==> There were two of them, all rugged, experienced mountain wilderness guides. They were hired by a rich investor who sent them to get the gold at the end of the rainbow. Off they set, in high spirits. They camped here and there, watching the weather and chasing rainbows. They always got to the end of the rainbow too late.

Months went by, and still they could not catch the end of the rainbow, but the rich investor kept paying their wage, so they persisted.

Then one morning, as the deep fog lifted, there was the most brilliant rainbow. The end of the rainbow shone right into their camp. There sat three big clay pots filled with gold. The pots were too full and heavy to be easily picked up and moved.

4713 (2/2) ==> There, beside the shores of a lake where they camped, they had a serious meeting. Do they keep the gold and retire it in luxury, or do they bring the gold to the rich investor?

Another problem came to light.

The gold was too heavy and too much to carry back to civilization. It would require a half dozen trips of many days walking.

Now, suddenly, each did not trust the other anymore. Each took half and moved the gold inside their tents. It was decided that they'd work on a solution to get the gold transport worked out after breakfast tomorrow. Each crawled into their tent for the night.

Each silently sharpened their knife while waiting for the other to go to sleep.

******

4714 ==> If you light a fire for a stupid man, he will be warm for the time the fire burns. If you light him on fire, he will be warm for the rest of his remaining life.

******

4715 ==> Every insanity has a hero to defend itself.

******

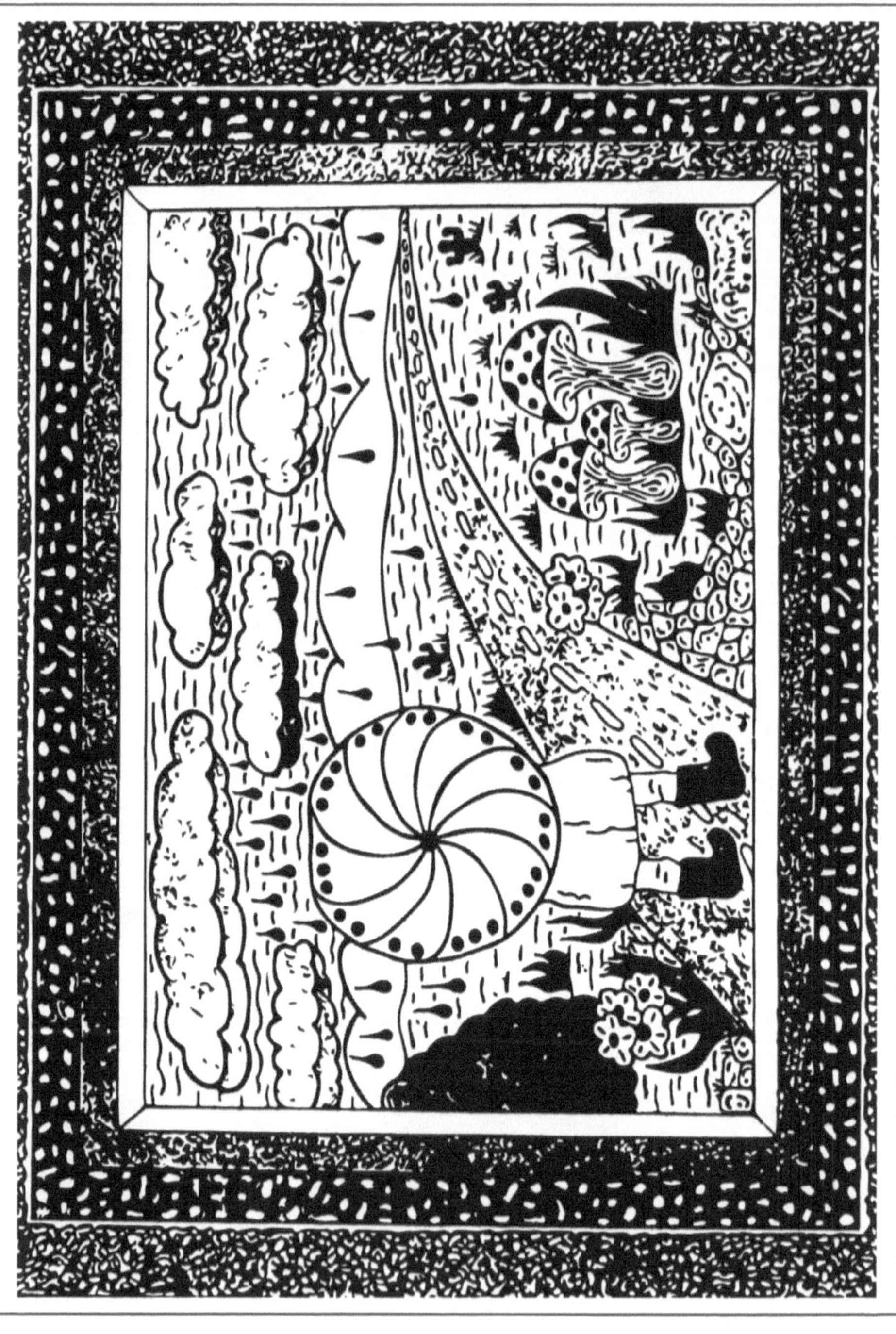

4716 ==> We only hate wealth if we cannot get it.

******

4717 ==> What would life be without a few social media girlfriends? At least we don't have to smell each other and can turn off when in ugly moods.

******

4718 ==> Year after year, the grand graduates hear the same brain delusions thumped into their minds. The teachers mean well, but they are only playback machines of recordings long ago made by others.

The graduate, inflated with urges to become important, rich, and successful, marches forth mixing logic and reality into a confusion of delusions and self-belief, but no experience or observation. In venting great fantasy of slaying the corruption of the old, sinful world. Yes, this corruption has managed to stay alive no matter how many times it has been beaten down and replaced by new corruption games.

It may well be that the last living thing left on the planet in the end might be corruption.

******

4719 ==> When we are right and truthful, we can only hope others will tolerate us enough to let us live among them.

******

4720 ==> Two weeks ago, he was at the Casino playing blackjack. The cards were lucky. He was betting big and winning a few thousand.

The other players at the table noticed his winning run and closely watched and copied his methods. They were jealous. He sensed this and decided he'd won enough.

He went over to the eating area by the food sales and sat at a table, ordering a meal. The waitress said there would be no charge. It was a gift from her. She also said she gets off work in ten minutes and to meet her in the parking lot.

He waited outside. It was a warm summer night. She found him, and he led her to his car. She directed him to her place.

Later, when the wine bottle was almost finished and his baby seeds were rushing into her warmth, she says, "Tell me what methods you use to win."

He almost told her the secret, but as his romantic passion had just climaxed, his mind woke up. He told her that he had to return home to his wife and four kids.

How could someone so attractive turn ugly so fast?

******

4721 ==> They came from far away over the ocean. Arriving with their Bibles, saved from shipwreck over the raging seas, they fell to their knees and gave thanks to their God.

Then they slaughtered the natives, taking and robbing all that could be owned. Then again, they fell to their knees and thanked their God.

******

4722 ==> You can see the insanity, mental delusions of Godly worshipping flags when they go to war because God commands them to slaughter in the pretense that their flag must be defended against imagined enemies that take considerable effort to create.

******

4723 ==> They know a lot of things that are not so. But it is so top secret that they must invent a story to cover up what was not so.

******

4724 ==> It is natural to ask a stranger where they come from, even though we know they crawled out of their mother's piss hole.

******

4725 ==> Humans are like ripening corn. The older they become, the more lowly they bend their heads.

******

4726 ==> The best start to a nice day is a leisurely breakfast.

******

4727 ==> When we start to argue, the one who is right may not so easily win.

******

4728 ==> The vanity of education often tempts one to forget just how stupid they really are

******

4729 ==> It is implied that the average person may quietly, secretly step away from being honest if something that pleases their desire can be obtained secretly.

******

4730 ==> Reason and common sense look very ugly when they do not merge into our delusion-induced desires.

******

4731 ==> To be a skillful hypocrite does require some intelligence.

******

4732 ==> The best we can do is work with what we have. We cannot work with what we do not have.

******

4733 ==> His brain is so full of education that all the halls, rooms, stairs, and exits are sealed shut by sheer abundance of education. The lips flap, the tongue wags, and all that comes out is a recording of entrenched brainwashing placed there by others, lacking any thought.

******

4734 ==> The small-time criminal had some luck, and he completed the job the crime boss wanted done. The boss decided to reward him. He asked what the crook wished for.

The crook replied, "I'd like to see some big-time action."

So the crime boss bought him a giant wall clock.

******

4735 ==> As we see the change in the world, so also see the change in ourselves.

******

4736 ==> Happy are those who have something to do, something to hope for, and someone to love.

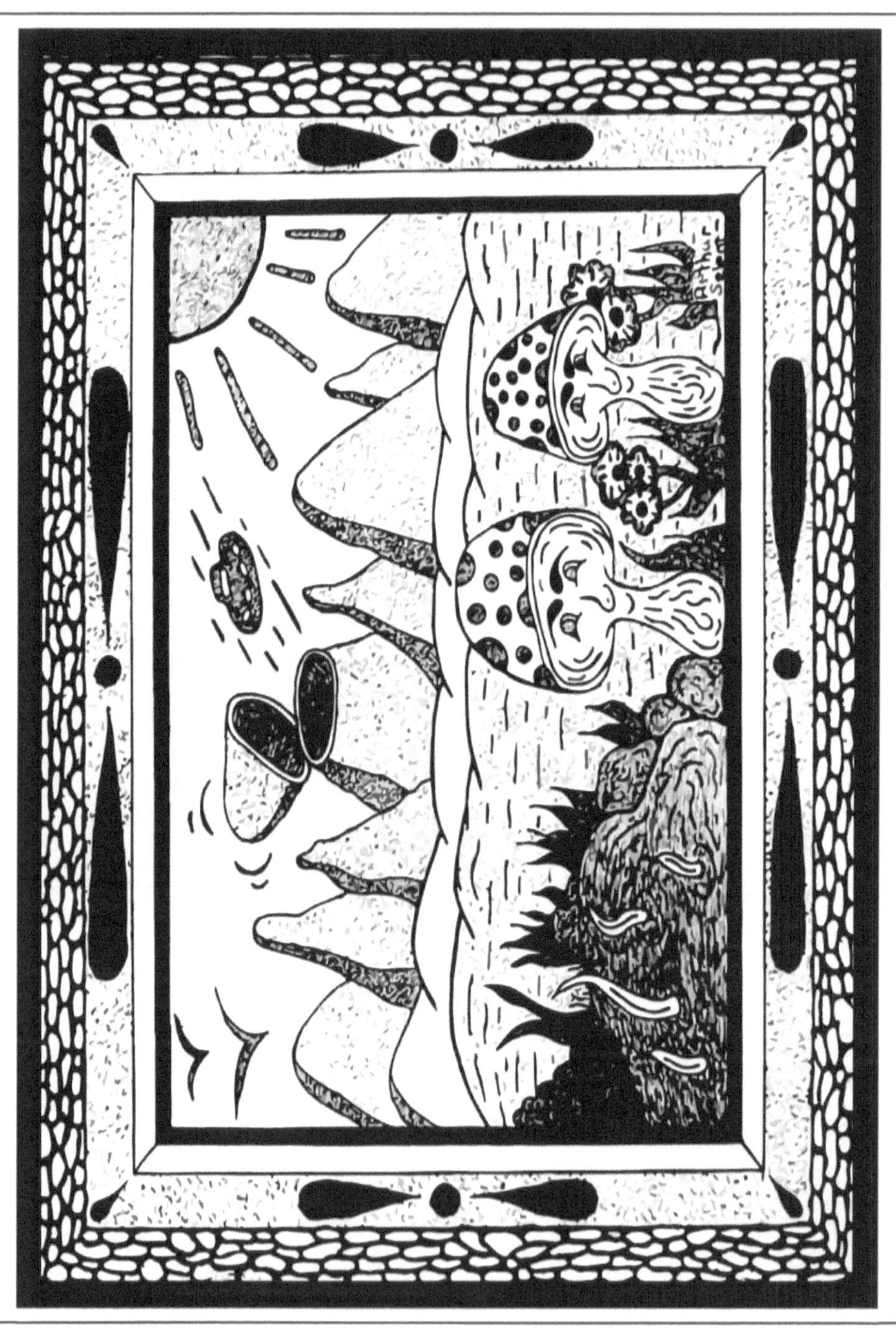

******

4737 ==> I am your radio. Turn me on.

******

4738 ==> The preacher noticed a very attractive young lady in the congregation. Week after week, he noticed her. He began to think of her ever more. He formed the impression that she might be of loose morals and in need of salvation.

One Sunday after the service, the church had a backyard feast for the folks to mingle, dingle, and get to know each other.

She was there. The preacher came close and started small talk. He says, "I prayed for two hours last night asking that you be guided into the loving embrace of God."

She says, "All you have to do is phone and I'll be there in ten minutes. You can embrace as much as you want. I know what it is like to be all alone night after night."

The preacher, suddenly excited, looks around to see if anyone is listening, then he nervously and softly mumbles close to her ear, "Could you come tonight after the dinner hour?"

******

4739 ==> You notice how we are directed in our thinking by the entertainment business. In one minute of channel surfing on TV, we see eight guns, three shootouts, and three acts of violence. This is the fun fantasy of the industry, pumping the little children's minds full of visions to create in real life.

******

4740 ==> For both the mind and the imagination, reading guides the great thinker.

******

4741 ==> The joy of shopping. Buying things because of advertising package lures. We never see what we want to buy until we take it home and open the package.

So today we have forty-seven different package designs on the store shelf selling the same tea at forty-seven different prices.

******

4742 ==> A focused mind with a determined spirit can have tremendous influence on the future.

******

4743 ==> But even those who see the distant light will lose sight of it when the road rolls down into valleys and around the mountains.

******

4744 ==> Our own will will make us great or small. Sounds very educated. But what of our path? Does it also make us great or small?

******

4745 ==> What we can do very well and what interests us the most puts us on the road to happiness if we direct every bit of energy, ambition, and natural ability of our soul into these two above-mentioned things.

******

4746 ==> We must open the windows of our soul to learn. We must open the window and let the light shine in. Let us hope it is not a windy day.

******

4747 ==> Our choice of attitude decides which path we will travel.

******

4748 ==> The human two-legged mobile compost shit making bio machine has some brains, let us hope this is true. As well the human has mobile feet and can, by turning around, see in any direction. Then why does the human so often steer itself in the wrong direction?

******

4749 ==> The business deal, hold fast to your offer and compromise only if the deal might be lost.

******

4750 ==> We are as creation made us, and since creation is satisfied with its work, then we should also be satisfied with ourselves.

******

4751 ==> Good health and a good conscience are something not easily bought with money.

******

4752 ==> When we get to the end of our rope, we can only hope the rope is not too short.

******

4753 (1/2) ==> The young widow was no longer young. Her freshness had undergone some heavy wear and tear. She had considerable income and never worked. But she had an air of authority and assurance that made it impossible for him to refuse her.

Day and night, she commanded him. Now we must go to bed. Now we must eat. Now we will go out shopping. She had her way, and there was no resisting for him. He was her pet and needed her for food and shelter.

4753 (2/2) ==> He was her dildo. Her sex toy. But the wage consisted of only basic needs, food, and shelter. There was no saving up for a future escape.

******

4754 ==> These girl mothers and public girls with all the shame and misery of women. The poor women who become the ravaged prey of the wandering male with money in his pocket. The flower of innocence slowly debauched and wilted to fading away.

******

4755 ==> They were having a backyard party. A variety of people from the guests were feasting, drinking, and talking. The couple's five-year-old son was talking to a visiting investor. "Dad says you are a self-made man."

The investor replies, "That is somewhat true. I am a self-made man."

Kid, "Then why did you make yourself look so ugly?"

******

4756 (1/2) ==> The ugly man thought it would be a great prank to send a job application to the "Lonely Ladies Society." He applied to be a comforter.

4756 (2/2) ==> Three weeks later, his photo and application were returned with a note.

"We are not that lonely right now. If you wish to appeal our decision, then feel free to contact us. Your appeal will only be considered if detailed nude photos are presented."

******

4757 ==> Egotists do not talk about other people; they are too busy talking about themselves.

******

4758 ==> Strong drink talks mighty loud and brave when it runs out of the jug and down the tube into the two-legged mobile compost-making bio entity.

******

4759 ==> The rooster makes all the noise, but the hen is the one who lays the egg.

******

4760 ==> Careful of those who know the answer before they know the question.

******

4761 ==> Some never seem to tire of turning others into ridicule and gloating on their defects.

******

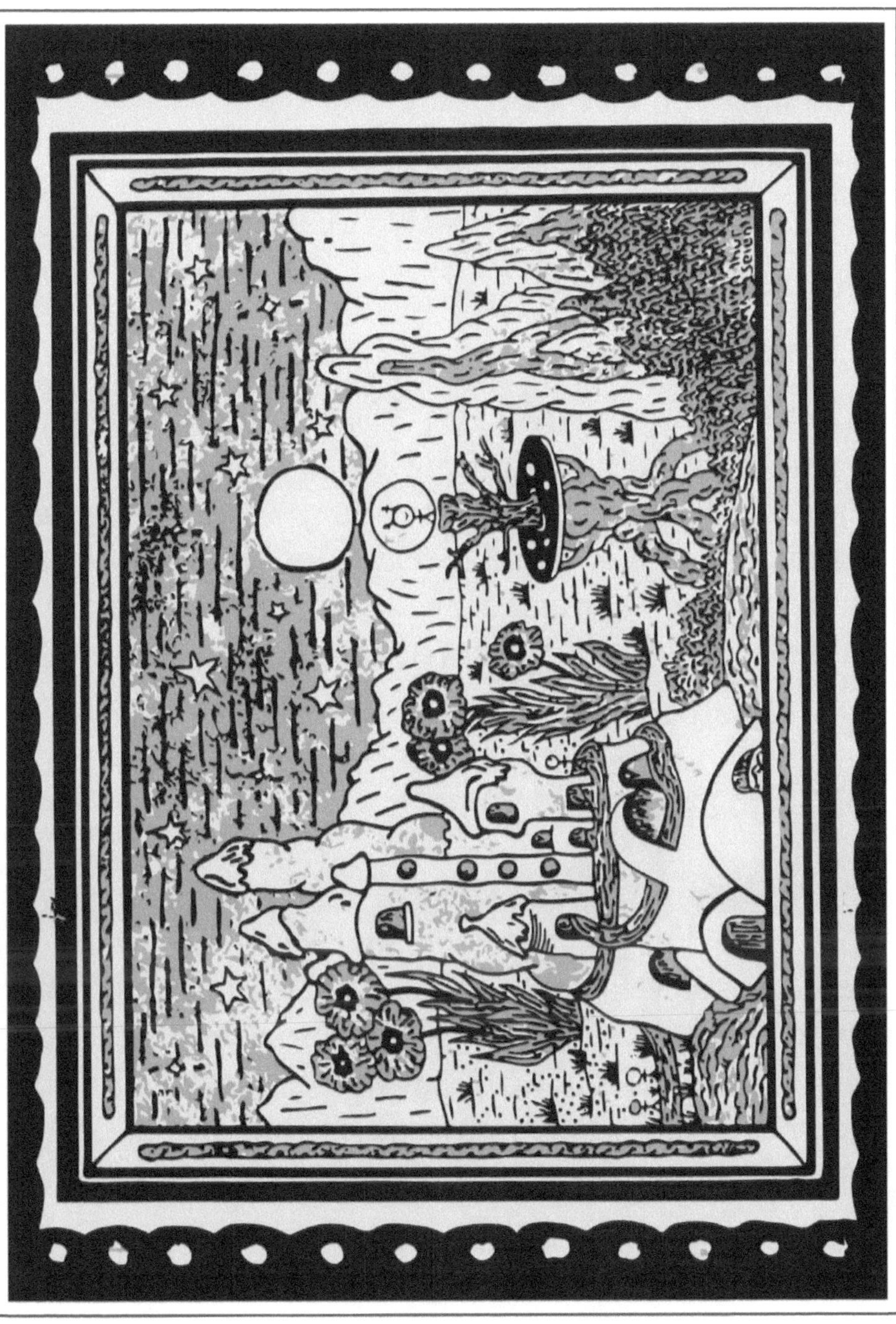

4762 ==> There is nothing more frustrating than being all rested up and ready for action but having nothing to do.

******

4763 ==> It is easy to admire hard work if we are not the ones doing it.

******

4764 ==> He had a vast passion to follow the vocation of doing nothing. He had an unbelievable aptitude leaning towards the lazy side. Anything serious, and his mind became confused with a sudden need to wander away on the pretense that something more important needed doing elsewhere.

The company paid top union wages. He was their top Union employee, passing his work onto others to keep them looking busy.

******

4765 ==> The two married couples went to a school reunion party to meet old classmates not seen for many years. As they were getting drunk and meeting old friends, he suddenly says to his wife, "Would you have married me if my dad had not died and left me his fortune?"

She replies, "Honey, I would have married you, no matter who died and left you a fortune."

******

4766 ==> To show your woman that you are very serious, it is a good idea to firmly place your foot down after she has finished vacuuming around your chair.

******

4767 ==> The rich man was in a mad rage at the dinner table. He ranted and raved to his wife, "I am going to get rid of our driver. Today, he almost killed me three times."

The wife replies, "Honey, be a sport. Give him one more chance. Don't worry, we have the highest insurance coverage on the car."

******

4768 ==> The little four-year-old girl asks her mother, "Did God make you?"

Mom replies, "Yes, he did."

"Did God make me?"

"Yes, he did."

A pause of a minute then the little girl replies, "He's like those TV ads making the new and improved product. His work has improved since he made you and daddy."

******

4769 (1/2) ==> The man and wife rode down a very crowded elevator from their new high-rise apartment above the clouds. The husband was enjoying the ride; he was at the back of the elevator, and a fresh, firm, beautiful young woman was pressed against him. She had a very short mini skirt on. He positioned himself so that his crotch rubbed against her. He got a hard erection.

He reached his hand down and timidly touched her thigh. He slid her dress up just a little. She seemed not to notice. She wore no underwear. His wife had her back to him and was facing the door, as was everyone else.

Not having any reaction, he slid her dress higher and unzipped his pants. His mind was fever hot. Could he do it that fast? He slid inside her. She did not resist. He felt relieved. She had not screamed. He was almost finished when the elevator stopped on the ground floor. The door opened and everyone began to leave. She pulled away, turned, and laughed, saying, "You silly man." Then she lightly slapped him.

His wife pulled him along and asked what that was all about.

He replied, "I think I stepped on her foot." Inwardly, he was on fire. So close to finishing, and fate stepped in. He was also in shock.

4769 (2/2) ==> How could he have dared to do such a thing? He looked at his watch. Maybe she lived in the building and rode the elevator at the same time each day. He just had to meet her again; the job was not finished.

He stumbled after his wife in a hypnotic trance. All his mind saw was her smiling face and feeling the sensation of her female warmth. The great catch that got away, fumbled from his grasp when the door opened. His hand rubbed his nose as he smelled his fingers.

******

4770 ==> The floosey flirt was toying with the uncultured farm land at a convention. She was working his erotic passions to a boiling fever. He overcame his shyness and asked, "Could I have your phone number and email?"

She, "It's in the phonebook."

He, "What is your name?"

She, "It is also in the phone book"

The realization dawned on him. He was not going to get any action with her.

******

4771 (1/2) ==> The speaker at the school was explaining to the engineering students the difference between "substitute" and "replacement."

4771 (2/2) ==> He says, "If you have a broken window, a substitute would be plastic or plywood. A replacement would be a glass window pane."

The speech finished, he shuffled off stage while another speaker presented their lecture. He noticed a scuffy, attractive young woman scantily dressed sitting on a stair step, painting her toenails. She looked like she lacked morals. She was not so clean. He could smell smells that awoke a dirty urge of arousal. He comes close, ready to proposition some romantic action.

She turned to face him and said, "You certainly are no substitute. You are the real pain."

******

4772 ==> Be careful of swallowing your ego, for you will gain some weight.

******

4773 ==> The man wanted a divorce on the grounds that his wife was a hystorical. The Judge asks, "You mean hystorical?

The man says, "No historical. Every time fights, she mentions things I did wrong years ago."

******

4774 ==> Have you noticed how little boys, as they grow up they join Boy Scout groups. They go camping and explore wilderness cooking and learning how to track nature. They learn all kinds of neat things.

Then, when they get to be about fifteen, they suddenly put their educations to use by tracking females.

******

4775 ==> The woman inherited some land and decided she'd try home steading. She got a cow and asked her neighbor how long cows should be milked.

Neighbor replies, "Same as short cows."

******

4776 ==> The circus hired a new driver for one of their trucks. He got lost, and the circus management all piled into a large, decrepit car to go look for the truck.

They saw, as they drove about, an old fossil repairing his roadside fence. They stopped to ask, "Did you see a truckload of apes driving by?"

Fossil replies, "No, did you fall off?"

******

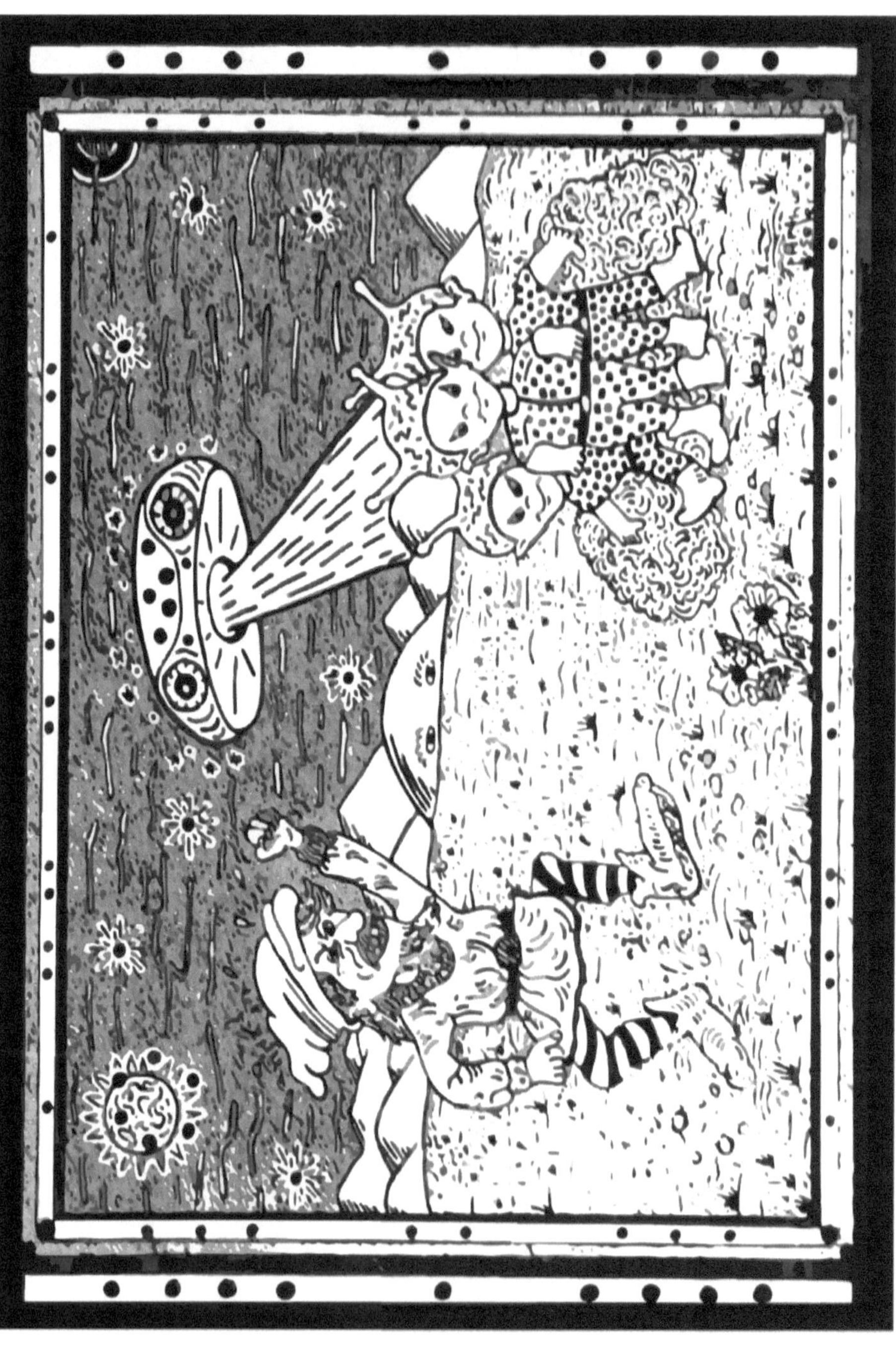

4777 ==. Did you know that some music players keep their instruments in the fridge so they can play them cool for their friends.

******

4778 ==> By the time we have money to burn, the fire has already gone out.

******

4779 ==> Those of us who have no one to blame but ourselves are in serious need of a companion to shoulder the blame.

******

4780 (1/2) ==> One can see how the mind can be led down the wrong road if all the facts are not known. The interior design agency sent two employees to look over a mansion: a young, attractive trainee woman and an elderly, experienced senior employee.

They walked into every room, looked out every window, peeked into every closet, paced every hallway, and climbed every stair. They then went to a park that had some picnic tables and fast-food sales.

As they sat at one of the crowded tables eating their meal, some old prune church ladies (hags) came and also sat at their table.

4780 (2/2) ==> The designers finished their food, and he says, "What are your thoughts? How should we start?"

She says, "This is all so new to me. I've never done something like this before. I am eagerly excited. Maybe we could start in the bedroom and get it over with first. It is uncluttered and ready for some fast action.

He said, "It will be a fun job." They get up and ample away. The two old church spinsters watch them as the one says. "You'd never have seen sin when we were young. She wants to start in the bedroom, and she is so young with no brains and so eager to turn a soft noodle into a hard seed planter. That man, three times her age. She's likely digging a gold mine."

******

4781 ==> Divorce is always directly caused by marriage.

******

4782 ==. The bad part of doing nothing is that there are no days off.

******

4783 ==> A career girl uses her brain to get ahead. A floosie girl uses her brain to wiggle her rear compost outlet.

******

4784 ==> A clever move gets most of the blanket.

******

4785 ==> The police had a roadblock and were checking cars for a bank robber that gotten away. The car stopped, the officer looked casually, and said, "For being the 100th car, we are giving free coffee vouchers. Here are your free coffee tickets."

The driver says, "Thanks, I'm going to need a coffee to settle my nerves. This driving without a license is scary stuff."

The floosie woman sitting beside him says, "Just ignore him, officer. He has an overabundant imagination when he's had too much to drink."

The little kid in the back seat says, "I told daddy he'd not go far in this stolen car, but dad said it was the best choice because it had a full tank and the keys were in the ignition."

The officer was shocked but then started laughing, "You folks are funny, but you have to move along. You are blocking traffic.

As they drove away, the wife says, "It's a good thing we told the truth; who knows what would have happened if we lied?"

******

4786 ==> How romance creates its own fairy tale. The night, warm and mild, the full moon. The tall mountains with their snowy wigs, silver crested ripples glittering on the lake. Romance-induced moods swoon without any cause.

The lonely evening walk along the beach. How quickly the strangers meet, both possessed with a fantasy urge to embrace and love, gambling against the dullness of life. The beach quickie.

Later, both tourists, complete strangers, go their separate ways to their hotel rooms. The dream vacation has found a dream. No one back home will ever know.

******

4787 ==> Did you know that there is a mile between the first and last letters of "smiles"

******

4788 ==> Romance is always so eager, hot, and exciting in the beginning, before we know too much about each other.

******

4789 ==> Many of us are not failures; we just started at the bottom and like it there.

******

4790 ==> The missionaries with their arrogant self-righteous attitude arrived at a jungle village and set up their concept of reality. As they brainwashed the savages and infused their religious delusion, the savages would fake great attention as they touched the arms, shoulders, and thighs of the missionaries, muttering, "So tasty." The mission folk thought this was some sort of social affection routine.

They had hardly been there two weeks when one night, silently, they were captured, tied, and placed in bamboo cages.

The savages removed from hiding a large metal tank, moved it with considerable effort, and placed it in the center of the village park. Some carried firewood to place under the tank, others carried water in animal skin pails and filled the tank.

The three missionaries were brought, undressed, and flung into the tank of water. A fire was lit underneath. The missionaries waited for the bath to warm up. Young savages with long sticks beat and pushed anyone back into the soup.

One missionary says, "At least they will get a taste of God and religion."

******

4791 ==> The best way to stop old fish from smelling is to cut off their noses.

******

4792 ==> Political cheese is like headless nails. Once in, there is no way to pull them out.

******

4793 ==> The history of stupid people goes a long way back, so don't think that you are a new invention.

******

4794 ==> Alcohol acupuncture – having to pay for the drinks.

******

4795 ==> A bachelor is a man who believes in women, wine, and goodbye.

******

4796 ==> The minute after you throw something out, you are bound to find that you need it.

******

4797 ==> The one who thinks he is still popular, as he never was at all, is commonly referred to as an egotist.

******

4798 ==> The teacher was explaining the evils of strong drink to his class. He got permission to use school money for the lesson. He bought the largest bottle of strong drink the store had.

He put a very little in a small glass. He dropped a few worms in the glass as the class watched. The worms died quickly. Then he said, "You can see what effect strong drink has on the worms. How does this relate to humans?"

One student answers. "People who drink don't get worms."

The teacher who had not been listening too closely said, "Right you are." He placed the almost full bottle in his lower desk drawer to take home after school hours.

******

4799 ==> The old man asked the doctor about his wife's condition. Doc says, "Her mind is completely gone."

Old man thinks a while, then she says, "Should have expected this. She has been giving me a piece of her mind for forty years, and now there is nothing left."

******

4800 ==> All his life, the fellow made it a point to go to church once a month. As he says, "When at last I go to the golden gates of heaven, the Lord won't say, 'Who is that?'"

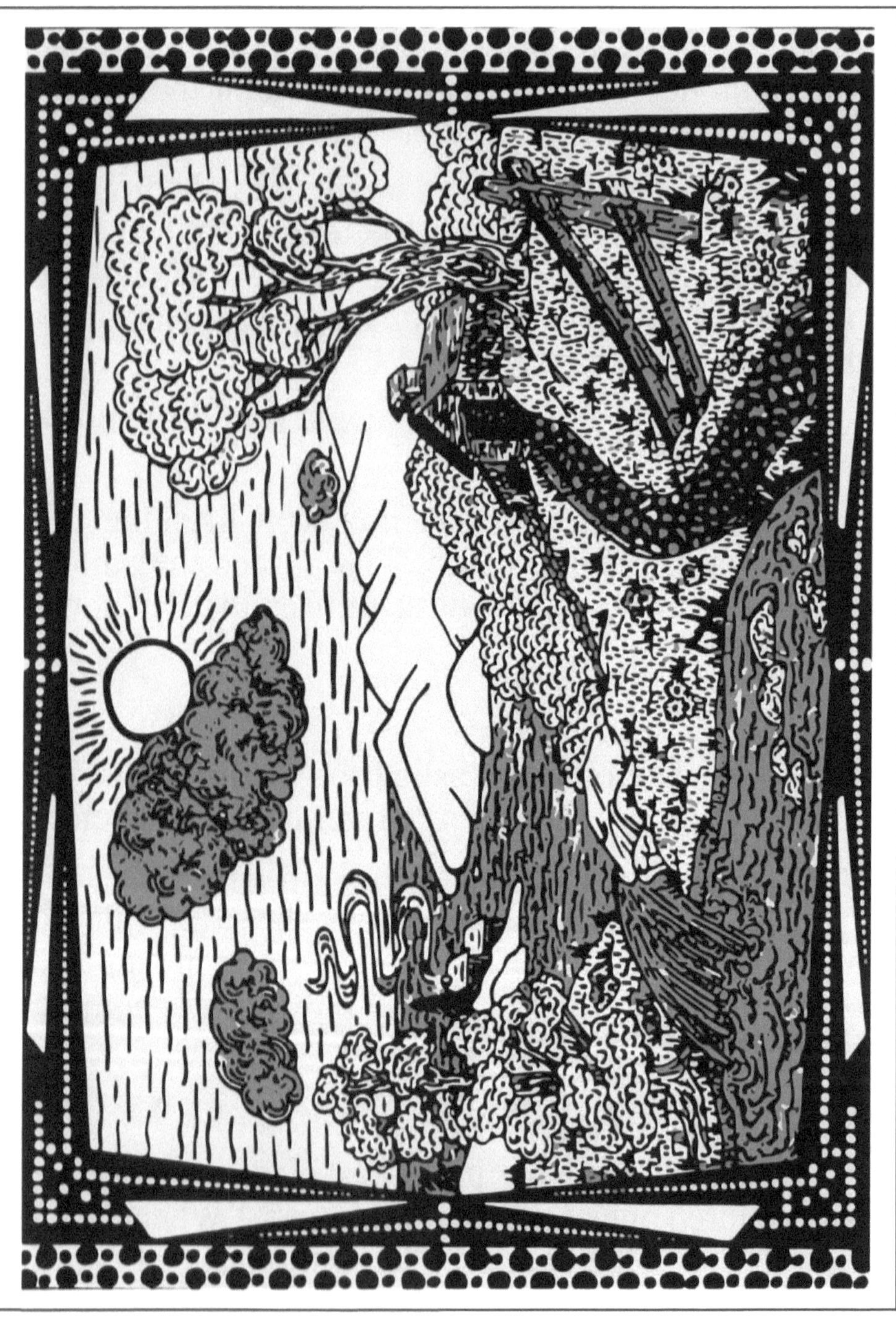

******

4801 ==> The attractive woman went to a prominent psychiatrist and complained about her love life failures.

The quack head shrinker replies, "This is common among some women. I have cured this a few times. It will require two years of appointment treatments. We will play out the romantic seductions and look at what keeps going wrong.

The woman says, "That will take care of your sexual needs and most likely mine also, but how will that solve my love life failures?"

******

4802 ==> Strip Poker: a card game where the more you lose, the more you have to show for it.

******

4803 (1/2) ==> The religious cult made him the supreme commander, the power of civilization. What he willed was made to happen. What he wanted, he got. He could go to any woman, office girl, store clerk, housewife, or daughter to satisfy his needs. None refused him. He could go to any bank and walk out with pockets of money.

4803 (2/2) ==> Gold-digging sneaks made attempts to get close to those pockets dripping with loot. But as they got closer, they were used more and more as slaves to make his desires a reality. All work and no sharing of the gold, they soon drifted away.

Then the year was over. He was burned alive by the religious cult that sold seats to the event. The super-rich paid more so their children could sit close to the smell and sizzle of flesh. It was a grand yearly event.

The religious cult then elected a new supreme commander, and everyone lined up to pay for the honor of kissing his ass.

The profits were counted, and the cult went back to making wine and selling black market happy drugs using secret undercover middlemen agents.

******

4804 ==> My hair is getting more grey. You are getting more soft and flappy. Should we perhaps consider divorce before we talk about marriage?

******

4805 (1/2) ==> The young man was recovering in the hospital from a small car accident. It was minor and he would recover by the end of the week. He fell in love with a young trainee nurse who washed him every day.

4805 (2/2) ==> Yesterday, he'd been so aroused when she washed his penis that he'd ejaculated. The nurse laughed and said, "You silly fellow." She tickled him briefly.

The man said, "I am falling in love with you. I want to be sick a long time so you can care for me."

The nurse says, "The Doctor also loves me. He wants the money, so you will be sick as long as he can arrange it. You will be mine only until he finds out we are copulating. Think of how sick you will become then."

******

4806 ==> The soft can overcome the hard. The gentle can overcome the powerful. Many think this, but very few, if any know how to leverage this.

******

4807 (1/2) ==> The girl had a school friend lover. The two of them were always in each other's arms whenever they got a chance to be alone.

When the girl got into her late teens, she decided to get a rich husband. She asks her boyfriend how much money he has.

He replied, "One thousand, but it's in the bank."

4807 (2/2) ==> She replied, "I cannot marry a man unless he has at least a million. Go get a million."

He left heartbroken, and was gone for forty years. When he came back, he found his old girlfriend. She asks how much money he has. He replies, "Only one hundred and it is in the bank."

She, "Well, it is enough for these times. When do you want to marry?"

He, "Oh, I cannot do that. I am married now. My wife is rich and just bought a mansion on the edge of town. We thought is best for our children to have a nature experience growing up.

******

4808 ==> The city folks went to a riding stable and asked about renting some horses to go riding.

The stable worker asks, "How long?"

The city folks reply, "The longest horse you have, there are five of us going riding."

******

4809 ==> A wife's marriage that has suddenly improved should note that the husband has found the secret path to the maid's room.

******

4810 ==> At the wedding party, the guest remarked that it must have been love at first sight.

The new husband replies, "Actually, it was love at 2nd sight. At first sight, I did not see she had money and a lot of it."

******

4811 ==> The little village now has a new towering 10,000-story building. It is called a "Library"

******

4812 ==> How many nervous carpenters bite their own nails?

******

4813 (1/2) ==> She was twenty-four years old, firm, trim, and considered to be good-looking. She was in love with the doctor at the sanatorium asylum. He was the only male she was allowed to be alone with. He made all the rules. He was married with children. He returned her love with considerable lust and passion. He would come into her room, lock the door, and ravage her to his satisfaction. Her bored existence had no other sensations.

Slowly, as he copulated, she played with his mind. She wanted to be released from the asylum. She had no outside connections to swing the deal.

4813 (2/2) ==> Bit by bit, she got his mind twisted that he signed her release papers.

He walked her to the front gates and said, "I got you a little apartment. I'll be there later." He held out to her some keys and the address of the apartment.

She says, "Sorry daddy, the party is over." She walks away, leaving him dangling the keys and a piece of paper.

******

4814 (1/2) ==> Louise was tall and attractive. She was nineteen. Her and Jacky Boy were secret lovers, copulating whenever they had a chance to be alone. He said that because he was going into the army it would be better if they kept their love secret until he returned.

The war started and he got sent overseas to do the dirty work. He wrote her once a month.

The local Political cheese had a big fund-raising dinner party. Louise offered to help and was put to work in the kitchen along with two other girls, Jenny 18 and Beth 22. The women were cheerful and got along ever so well.

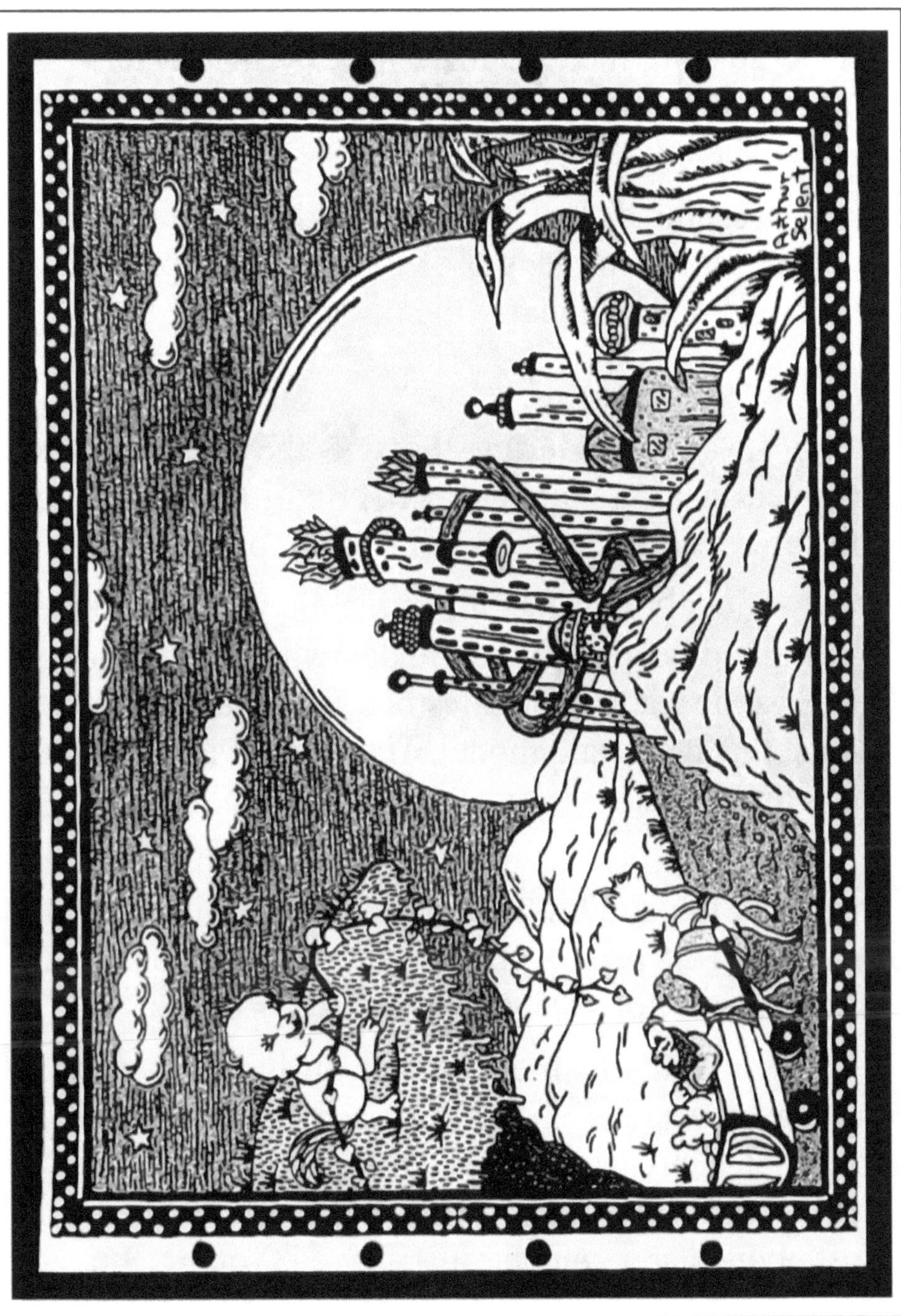

4814 (2/2) ==> Louise started singing and in her made-up song mentioned Jacky Boy. The other two stopped their work, shocked. The good cheer faded away. The questions started and the talk flew fast.

It seems Jacky Boy had secretly copulated with all three for some length of time. He had promised all three he would marry them.

******

4815 (1/2) ==> During the war the car factories stopped making cars and converted to making war machines. New cars were almost impossible to get.

The fellow walks into a big city car dealership selling old decrepit junk. He describes what kind of used car he wants. The salesman says it is impossible to get that make and model. There are twenty people already waiting.

The fellow says, "That is too bad. I am prepared to pay double in cash, no questions asked. You make the paperwork out to a small sum, and you keep the rest for yourself."

He walks to the exit and on his way, as the salesman watches, he throws a hefty brick of big banknotes into a waste basket. He had just taken two steps when the salesman yelled, "Hey fella, the yard just phoned and your car just arrived. You must have some luck on your side."

4815 (2/2) ==> He turned back, and the salesman had the papers already on his desk. He made the sales price out to be some very small amount. The fella signed, got the keys, and drove away.

Two days later, the salesman phoned, "That money was counterfeit."

He replies, "That is why I threw it in the waste basket. Thanks for the car, it seems to be working fine."

******

4816 (1/2) ==> The corporation management was in a frenzy of frustration; there was no money in the corporation's bank account. Employees had not been paid for weeks. Sales were down, production was down. They even hired an expert, but he left when they did not pay him. No money could be found anywhere.

Management then took out many different kinds of insurance on the business buildings. They planned to make a campfire.

Then along came a wimpy potbellied man carrying a briefcase that looked like it had been salvaged from a garbage dump. Within an hour, he'd found a few billion in cash just lying in the bottom drawer of the president's desk. No one had thought to look there. The drawer having been locked at, and the key has been lost.

4816 (2/2) ==> The corporation president asks the wimpy potbellied man. "How did you find the money so fast?"

He replies, "I am from the Income Tax Department. I know where to look.

******

4817 (1/2) ==> A very strong man at the summer farmers' drunk party bragged about his strength. A smaller, wimpy man, a newcomer, and somewhat an intellectual fellow laughs. He says to the brute, "I can wheel borrow a load to the barn which you cannot wheel back. Want to bet some money?"

Finally, something exciting was about to take place. Everyone made bets. Some farmers ran from the yard to the back gardens to get money from their wives for betting.

A big wheelbarrow was found. It was still damp from having quickly been hosed with the garden hose to wash the cow shit off from that morning's barn cleaning.

The wimpy fellow places the wheelbarrow close to the strong man and says, "Now get in the wheelbarrow. You are the load of shit, now wheel yourself back."

The strong man, slightly drunk, wanted to fight but then became friendly and laughed the joke off.

4817 (2/2) ==> A week later they found the wimpy man, dead floating on top of the sewage lagoon.

******

4818 ==> They are making a killing at the stock market. Brokers are being pushed out of tall commercial office buildings. They ask that the public not walk the streets. Two cars have already had their roofs caved in by brokers taking their gold with them on their rapid fall.

******

4819 ==> They called the wedding off at the last minute when it was found the bride was religious, she worshiped money and he didn't have any.

******

4820 ==> The God preacher put a sign along the walk to the church, "If you are tired of sin, when cum inside."

A few days later, someone had sneaky like written under the sign, "But if you are not, then call Susan XXX-1234."

******

4821 ==> The woman got rid of 300 pounds of ugly excess fat overnight. She threw him out of the apartment.

******

4822 ==> The doctor told the cannibal that he must not eat rich foods, so he went home and released the millionaire he'd been planning to have for supper. Instead, he ate the homeless man he'd been saving for a rainy day.

******

4823 ==> The owner of the village laundry put up a sign, "Ladies wishing to drop off of all their clothes, please report to the office for special attention."

******

4824 ==> To be a good plant manager, one must have a garden with plants.

******

4825 ==> A rich person acting meanly, acts poorly, and will not find joy with their wealth.

******

4826 ==> The public was upset about the number of young people drinking too much, so the store selling strong drinks put up a sign, "Alcohol is a slow killer."

The next morning was found written at the bottom of the sign: "So, who is in a hurry?"

******

4827 (1/2) ==> The town was having a lot of homes and businesses being broken into and a wealth stolen. The police were under pressure to find the thief.

At each break in the thief wrote, "Thank you" on the wall. Finally, the police grabbed someone. He went before the court, and after some questions, the case was delayed a week so the police could do more investigating. He was put in jail for a week.

The town being small, there was only one watchman on duty at the jail at night. And only one prisoner.

The crook says to the watchman, "If you go to the church and test the bricks on the north corner, you will find one loose. Remove this, and behind it is a hole where there is a stash of money. Put the brick in place. Use this money to buy us both a nice warm pizza. At the end of the week, whatever money is left is yours to keep."

The watchman went after work and found the money.

The next night, like the best of friends, they sat together eating pizza, the jail door open.

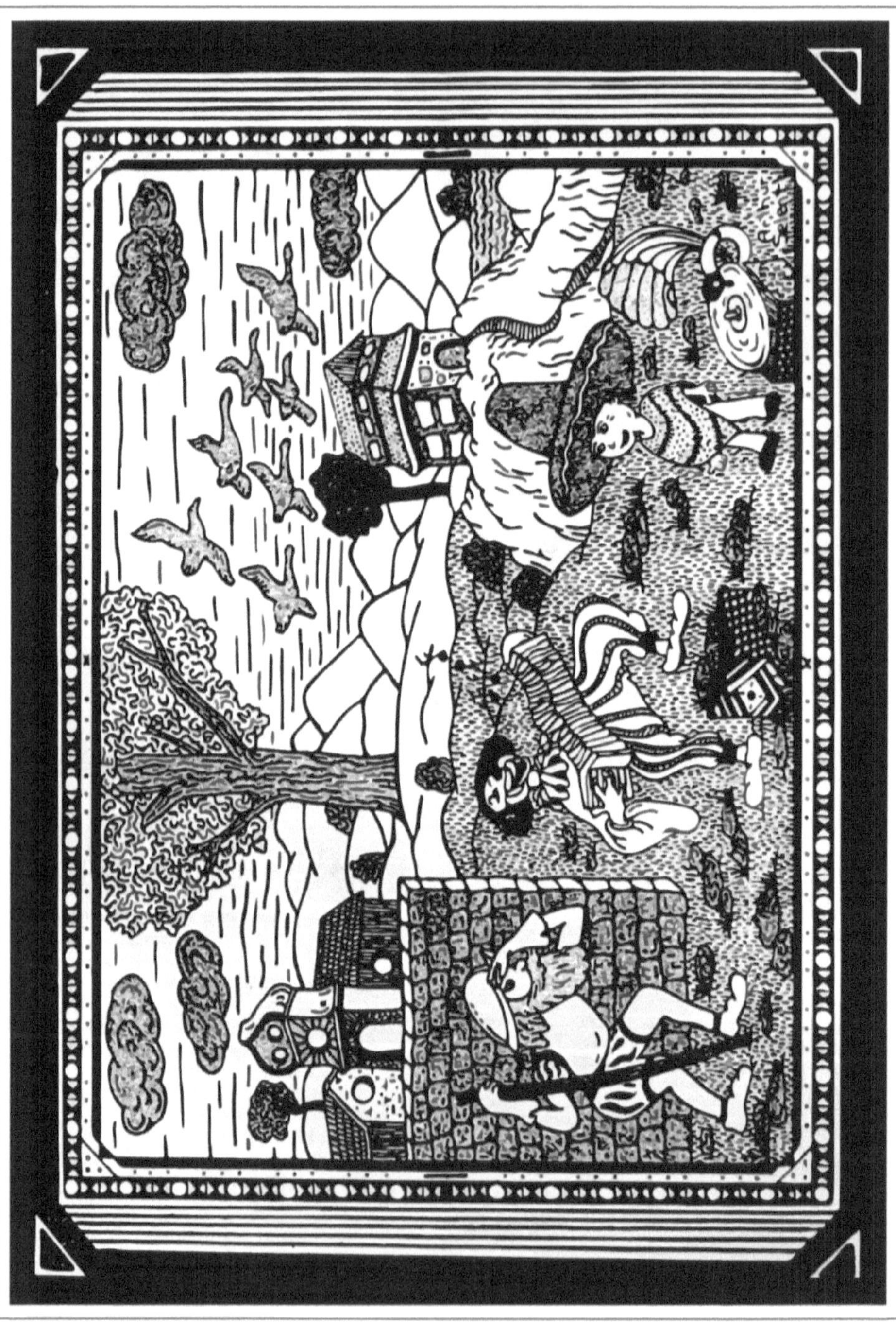

4827 (2/2) ==> The prisoner says, "Go to the bridge. Under the South Side are three large rocks, dig behind the middle rock, and find there a sealed jar with twenty thousand money units, a year's wage. That is yours to keep if you will let me out for six hours so I can visit my girlfriend."

The watchman was amazed at the money and the next night let the prisoner out, saying, "You can have an extra hour. Return before seven hours pass."

The watchman hid the money and began to think of stories to explain the jailbreak. Then to his surprise, the prisoner returned in the best of moods.

That night there had been four break-ins. Much wealth was stolen and, "Thank you", written on the walls.

The court released the prisoner. The night watchman dared not to say anything. He went into his office, and there on the wall was written, "Thank you". The money was gone.

******

4828 ==> Who do you belong to?

******

4829 ==> I am not the sweetest cookie in the box, so don't even think about romance. My secretary, lawyer, banker, and six wives would never allow such a thing to happen.

******

4830 ==> The big people are complaining that wages are not fair. They claim their pay is equal to small people's pay. But small people eat less, and their clothes also cost less.

******

4831 ==> Due to the high price of gas and diesel, people should prepare for the future by growing tall grass and clovers around their homes. With the future of horse and wagon coming, we must prepare food for the horse.

******

4832 ==> Do you know what happens to a liar when they die? They lie still.

******

4833 ==> Most Politicians would never get elected if they did not tell lies to cover up corruption.

******

4834 (1/2) ==> The new army grunt was sent overseas to fight a war against some people the homeland was trying to create into an enemy. He was in this foreign land of peace and was bored and homeless. He yearned for nights of sin.

4834 (2/2) ==> He went to his commanding officer, "Sir, I need a month off. My wife is dying in the hospital."

The commander replies, "I have some good news for you. We just received a memo saying your wife has just been released from the hospital and is expected to fully recover quickly."

The grunt replies, "You sure as big a liar as I am. I do not have a wife."

******

4835 ==> Because the majority of people tend to be truthful and honest, most of the time they think all they see and hear on TV or the internet is also truthful and honest.

******

4836 (1/2) ==> Hard time coming to rich lands, and a newly graduated lawyer was not doing so good at setting up his office and getting business to prosper. He saw an ad for entry-level employment at a big corporation. He applied for the job.

On his first day of work, he was given a broom and told to sweep the floors. He reacted with shock and said, "There must be some mistake. I am a newly graduated lawyer and was expecting my own office."

4836 (2/2) ==> The boss says, "Sorry to hear that. This is the best job in the company. You even have your own closet office where the brooms, mops, and washroom papers are stored. The fellow you are replacing had the job for sixteen years but he retired last week. I will show you how to use the broom and mops. The other workers will never guess your inexperience."

******

4837 ==> Most folks would rather not be mixed up with the naked truth.

They prefer the well-dressed company of lies.

******

4838 (1/2) ==> The smart ass just graduated sniggered with malicious joy as he phoned the businessman.

"Hello."

The lawyer starts talking, saying, "Your wife got her hands on some pictures worth millions."

Rich businessman, "Terrific. She always had a knack for finding bargains."

Lawyer, "Yes, that may be so. There are some legal details pertaining to the pictures. That is why I am calling you."

4838 (2/2) ==> Richy, "Spare no expense. Give her whatever she needs."

Lawyer, "She has a half dozen photos of you and your secretary copulating on a beach and some photos of you two sleeping naked, arms around each other in a motel room. She wants two million and a divorce.

******

4839 ==> They are trying to develop a new deodorant that makes people invisible. Then no one will know where the smell is coming from.

******

4840 ==> You notice there is nothing to these new swimsuits for the ladies. One wonders if it is one long string or two short strings tied together. It is certainly not three strings. Grandfather says that were three strings, then we would be able to see the swimsuit.

******

4841 (1/2) ==> The church service was over, and the mother was walking home. She says to her daughter, "The choir was singing off-key."

The daughter, "The preacher creature was flapping his lips a lot but didn't say anything useful."

4841 (2/2) ==> The Son says, "Well, I thought it a fine diversion when a slight technology mishap happened and the collection plate slipped and two hundred dollars fell into my pocket."

******

4842 ==> A machine is a wonderful servant, but all too often it makes a fool of the master.

******

4843 ==> A naive young missionary believing in the power of God upon himself went fearlessly to wander about jungle lands looking for savages to brainwash with religion.

As he trod along a path surrounded by dense vegetation, he heard soft foot steps behind him. Turning, he saw a big, muscled lion following him. He knew he could not outrun the lion, so he got on his knees and prayed to God for help. He prayed and prayed, then realized the lion had not attacked.

He looked around, and there was the lion beside him also praying. Says the missionary, "It is wonderful to find a fine fellow of the same faith."

Lion says, "Shut up. I am saying grace for the meal I am about to have."

******

4844 ==> The religious cult invaded a jungle village, bringing their Bibles and preaching hell fire, and brimstone sulfur pits.

Later in the week, when the cult had ravaged the village with sin and moved on, one savage elder says to his family. "So much wind, hot gas, thunder, and rumble but no rain."

******

4845 ==> The preacher minister creature was on vacation in a faraway land. He liked to wear his religious uniform in public. He imagined it gave him a distinguished, authoritative look.

He saw two boys pushing a firecracker up the ass of a cat, but the firecracker seemed too large. He asked directions to the bus station. Then being so far from home where no one knew him or was likely to remember him, his sinful thoughts liked the fine bodies of these two young demons. He said, "Could I invite you two fine fellows for lunch. I will show you the road to heaven."

One evil rascal laughs. "You can't even find the road to the bus station, so how are you going to show us the road to heaven?"

******

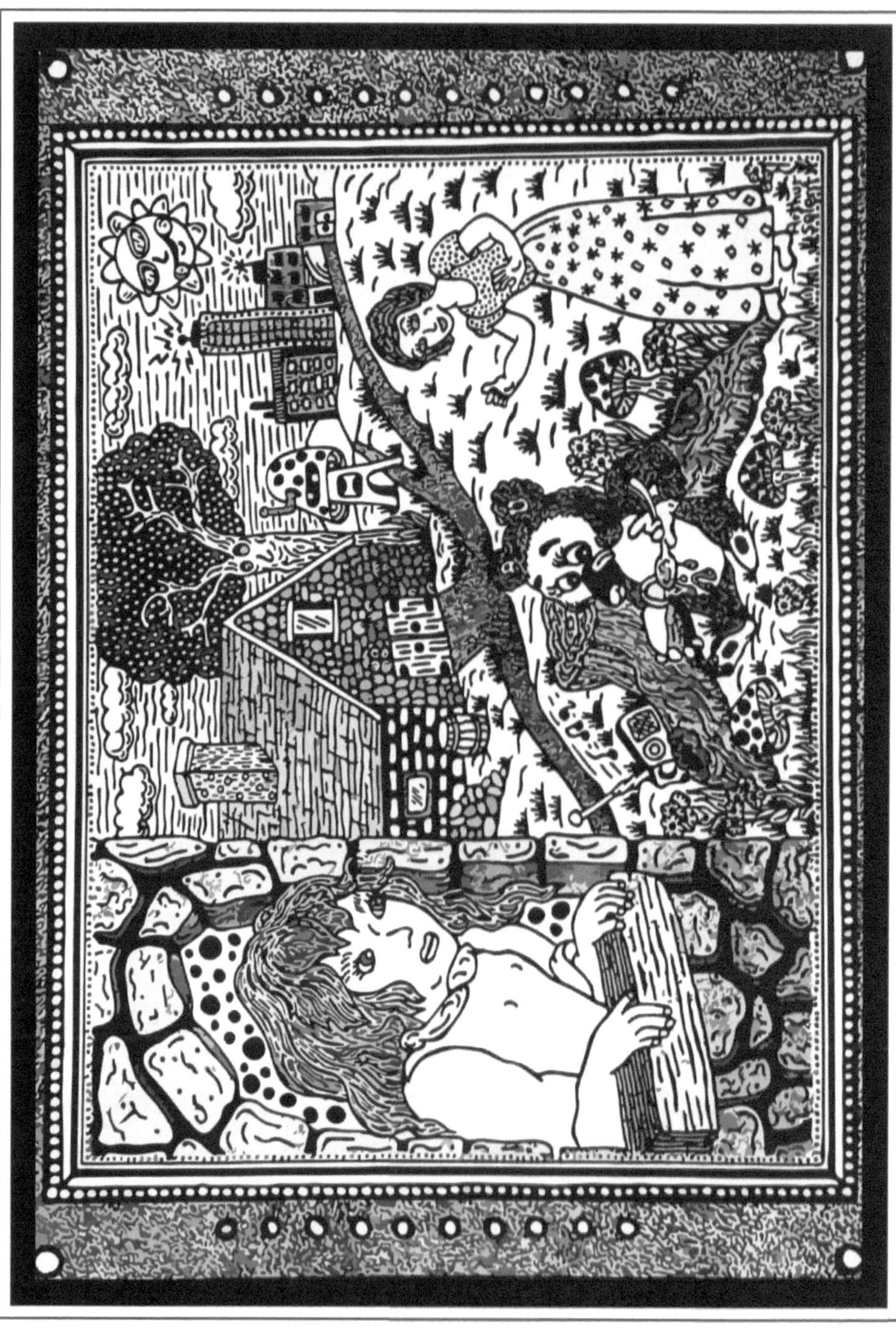

******

4846 ==> If you really want to be among friends who say nice things to you, then just say, "Give me the bill", whenever some service needs to be paid for.

******

4847 ==> Some folks you just cannot trust, no matter how long you have known them.

******

4848 (1/2) ==> The religious zealots marched day and night through hell itself, sun, heat, and cold snows. Finally, they come upon paradise, a fertile land of grass huts and gardens. Inside the grass huts, toothless, dirty farmers copulated day and night to increase the future work force.

The zealots in the fury of their mental delusions squatted their shit piles off to the edge of the cultivated areas. In one flat area they like demons on fire built a church. They began their Sunday morning mental delusion preachings.

None of the natives comes to the church. After a few months, the zealots started giving a feast after the Sunday preaching. Suddenly, the church was full, and others stood outside waiting. The natives, like jolly school kids, laughed, gossiped, and ate and ate.

4848 (2/2) ==> Each native had secret containers hidden under their large, loose clothes. Only for church did they bother to wear clothes. All week they ran about naked.

Then one day, the Zealots ran into trouble getting food for the feast due to some kind of small tribal war. Everyone was fighting, and no one was growing food. Suddenly, the church was empty again.

One Zealot asked a simple-headed native why they didn't come to church

Native replies, "No God feast, no need to come to church."

******

4849 (1/2) ==> The high command sent a ghost to keep an eye on the minister. It seems the high command thinks the minister is lacking in work activity.

Sunday morning dawned such a beautiful day. The minister looked out the window and phoned his trainee. "You will have to give the sermon. I am suddenly sick, must have eaten a sour cherry. Just pick one of the old sermons and read that to the faithful."

The minister kept copies of his sermons so he could sometimes repeat a forgotten sermon when not in the mood to invent a new one.

4849 (2/2) ==> It was still too early; no one was at the golf course. He teed off. The ghost laughed, grabbed the ball in flight, and dropped it into the hole. The minister went wild with joy. His first-ever hole-in-one.

This repeated over and over until he got to hole number thirteen. Here, the ghost threw the ball back at the minister. He was persistent and teed off over and over. The ghost responded by throwing the ball more forcefully, hitting the minister in areas that hurt.

Other goffers started arriving. The minister fearful of being recognized, quickly drove home. His nerves were shaken by the activities at hole thirteen.

The ghost laughed at his joke.

The golf clubs were set neatly away in the basement and forgotten. The minister went back to preaching a story invented thousands of years ago.

******

4850 ==> We can never push our commander leader too much in their corruption insanity, for at times, they do have honest moments when they are simply stupid.

******

4851 ==> The survivors thought themselves the lucky ones, escaping most of the ugliness that tore apart the cities and left piles of rotting dead in the street and rooms. The survivors had found land and tools enough to feed themselves but it was a life of battle. Vagabonds and robbers were constantly watchful for secret advantage when no one was around.

Many survivors became smug as they learned the old ways and fed their families. In their success, they then were struck down by one of the many new germ virus bio experiments released into the population. The virus that got out of the profit game escaped to rapidly mutate over and over.

Pity the humans that survive.

******

4852 ==> What you drive is what shapes your outlook upon reality.

A bicycle rider is quite different from a truck driver, and both are different than a mini-car driver or bus rider. One notices one's position to the obstacles along the road.

******

4853 (1/2) ==> The fellow went to the restaurant, a modest fashion place. The place was about half full. He took a seat at a window table.

4853 (2/2) ==> The people walking the sidewalk looked at him as he ate. The meal was big, and the manager would bring samples of this and that, placing them on the table. He ate so much.

The next day, he thought he'd go back. This time, he sat near the back out of sight. His meal arrived, and he noticed it was so small compared to his previous meal the day before. He called the manager for an explanation.

Manager, "Sir, yesterday you sat at the window and advertised my food. Today, you're back here, hidden away, not doing your job."

******

4854 ==> A walking travel person hiking the wilds of the planet cannot afford to get lonely. They feel like they just have to talk to someone face-to-face.

The wild one coming out of the wilderness only to find that dainty snobbish society does not want companions.

******

4855 (1/2) ==> There were at business school. Management put on a dinner for the students to practice speeches and business theories.

One simple fellow noticed that his seat was beside the school brain, who was the only one at school to have won a business start-up grant. He says to the brain, "How did you get to be so smart?"

4855 (2/2) ==> The brain says, "It is a long history. A secret no one outside the family has ever been told." He pauses, then, "You seem an honest fellow, I'll tell you. My family owns a fishing fleet and a fish shop at the market. Sometimes we catch a wiky fish. We never sell this fish because it makes us smart; we save it for our own dinners. If you go to the fish store, you just tell them I sent you to buy some Wiky fish for me,

The next day, the simple fellow goes to the fish store and is told that the Wiky fish is costing a thousand money units. He is shocked but has to have it. As he starts to leave with his smoked Wiky fish he sees a sign, "Smoked Salmon, one money unit." So he gets some as well.

Later at dinner hour he got the two fish mixed up but no matter, he ate both.

A few days later the brain happens to meet him. The fellow says, "I don't notice myself getting any smarter. The Wiky fish tasted just liked smoked Salmon."

The brain says, "See you are already a little smarter. Say, can I buy you a coffee. I've had a good week selling Wiky fish and my sales commission itches to be spent."

******

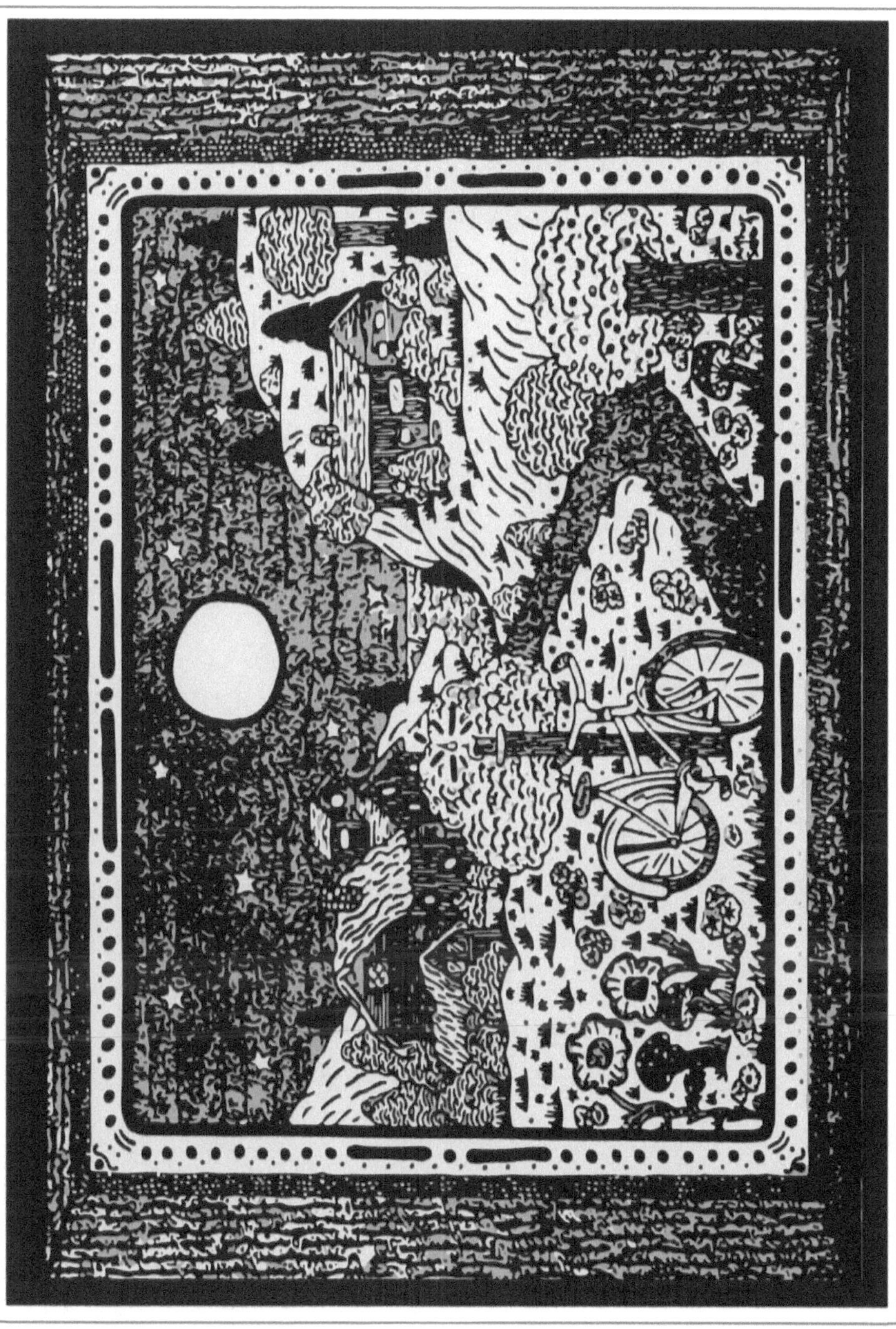

******

4856 ==> The election was just a week away. The Political cheese gave a big dinner speaking affair for fundraising. The rented hall was filled. One cheese was throwing his ideals out with clever words.

The village idiot approached, carrying an oversized screwdriver. Two big security goons grab him and ask what he is doing.

The idiot replies, "The cheese has a screw loose, and I am here to repair it. This could take some time. I'll have to check if any other screws are loose."

******

4857 (1/2) ==> The church beside the pond decided for the long weekend to have a family fishing contest. They bought fifty modest-sized fish from a faraway fish farm and released the fish into the pond. Each fish is just big enough for a one-person meal.

The weather was nice. Overnight tents were set around the pond, and the smell of campfires and roasting foods drifted about. The little children were all excited and each hoped to catch the really big fish.

The weekend days and nights were long. Many even fished at night, going without sleep. This was an ego event, and the winner would be an important person.

4857 (2/2) ==> As each fish was caught by a kid or parent, it was measured, weighed, and recorded.

The winner, with a massive fish the size of one's arm's span wide open accepted the prize. It had taken two strong men to lift the fish onto the scale. The winner told how his two-year-old son had fought the fish for an hour before finally getting the fish in the boat. The fish that was still slightly frozen from its sleep in the fish store freezer.

******

4858 ==> Could we all just talk a little faster? We must say everything before the future arrives.

I will go first, "Everything." There, I have said it. Now is your turn to say everything.

******

4859 ==> He is in the political game now, so he traded his brain for a suit jacket and everything free. Look how smartly the pup-pet strings make him dance.

******

4860 ==> There are many books out there that tell one how to "Know oneself." But these books set one up for a rude awakening by failing to notify one, "Not to tell anyone."

******

4861 ==> After all these thousands of years the planet realized with surprise that once there lived an honest person. When that person retired, there has never been an application made to fill the job vacated.

******

4862 ==> How many self-made people owe their success to nobody?

******

4863 ==> No matter how much he cheated, he could not win the game because his fellow players could cheat better. When he had five aces, the others had six aces.

******

4864 ==> The luxury of great riches is that it allows one to escape good advice.

******

4865 ==> War, no matter how necessary and no matter how justified, is always a crime.

They lock a person in jail for a single murder, but make mass murderers military people killing a great hero.

******

4866 ==> A rolling stone gathers no moss but develops a unique polish which the jealous moss farmers wish they had.

******

4867 (1/2) ==> A woman phoned the city bus works and complained that the roaring bus going past was shaking her house. She wanted the bus route changed. The shaking and noise would not allow her to sleep. After many phone calls and complaints, the bus company sent out a brainless fellow from lower management to investigate.

She told him, "The most shaking is the bed area. If you lie on the bed and wait for the   next bus, you will see."

The fellow thinks this is a sexually depraved housewife. He lays down on the bed and waits. She lay down on the other side of the bed. He laughed inside and thought that soon she would make a move to encourage my confidence to go all in. And today, he was just in the right mood to play in Sin City.

The husband came home and softly walked to the bedroom to get out of his business suit.

On the bed lay his wife and the inspector. They were not touching, but the wife had her skirt pulled up too high and was wearing no panties. The inspector, in anticipation of some play, had slid his pants zipper open and was waiting for her advance.

4867 (2/2) ==> I dare not write what happened next.

******

4868 ==> Of all people's misery, the most bitter is to know so much but have no way, place, or use for what one knows.

******

4869 ==> The decrepit, haggard homeless woman spread a blanket on a busy tourist beach by the fast-food sales area. She put up a cardboard sign. "Gypsy Fortune Teller," "$20.00 for two questions."

A smart-ass young business skeptic walks by and says to her, "Isn't that rather expensive?"

She says, "Yes, now what is your second question?"

******

4870 ==> The fellow woke up with a bad hangover and realized he was in jail. He asked the guard why he had been put in jail.

Guard, "For drinking."

Prisoner, "Great, let's get started."

******

4871 ==> The brighter, shinier, fresher-faced and cleaner you are, the more the slime and dirt will seek to find you.

******

4872 ==> Why do volcanoes never blow up in oil drilling areas?

******

4873 ==> The Man was the oldest man in the village. One day, a passing news crew asked him if you could live all those years over again.

He replied, "Of course, only I would have started a few centuries sooner."

******

4874 ==> The sneaky thinker was the flag's best Politician. He started out not knowing where he was going. Then when he'd arrived, he knew not where he was, but the party was on and he did not hesitate to taste of the sins available.

When he got back, he could not remember where he'd been and what he'd done, so no secrets were revealed. What an ideal Politician doing all this with other people's money.

******

4875 ==> Never judge the horsepower of the leader by the volume of the exhaust gas.

******

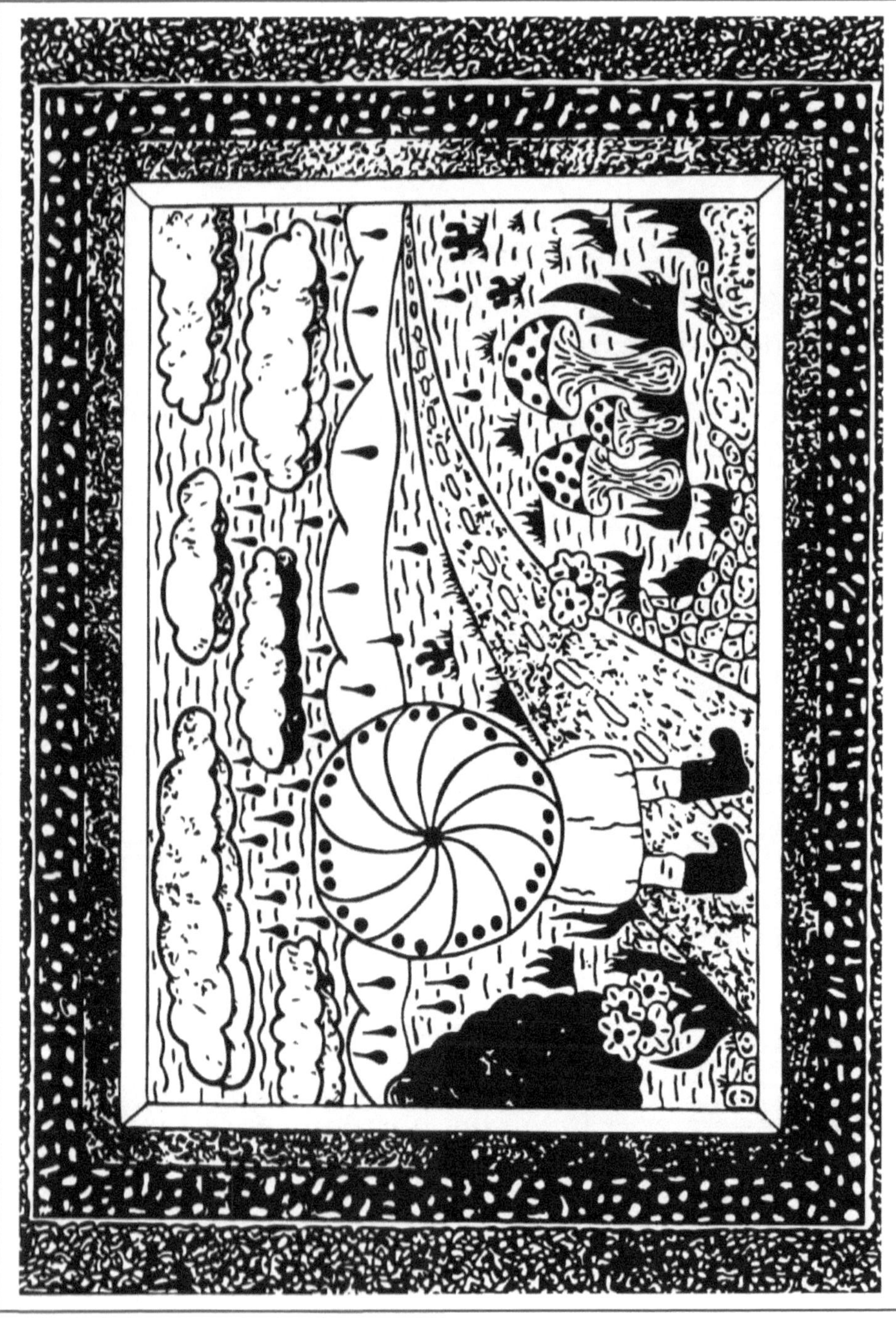

4876 ==> The young, pretty wife had been secretly copulating with the corporation manager where her husband works. She got the manager to promote her husband.

Hubby comes home all happy and full of cheer. He says to his wife, "I got promoted to Vice President of the production floor."

The wife was a little disappointed. She'd wanted something higher than that. She says, "Vice Presidents are by the hundreds. No need for cheer. Even the fast-food place has a dozen Vice Presidents."

The husband phones the fast-food place and asks the speaker on the phone to speak to the Vice President. "Which one and which department? We have twenty-one Vice Presidents. The lettuce Vice President is here beside me, would he do? Oh, I have to go now. The Vice President of cheese just walked in. He's a big stinker around here, and I could lose my job for talking on the phone."

The wife looks sadly at her husband, realizing she will have to copulate with the corporation manager for a few more months until another attempt to promote her simple husband comes along.

******

4877 ==> The student after going to the top schools of education for many years ran out of money. He applied for all sorts of jobs.

Finally, a road crew hired him. He had to hand-paint the center line of a new road. It was hot, but he worked hard at the job.

At the end of the week, the boss said, "I am firing you."

He, "Why?"

Boss, "First day you paint two miles, next day only one, and yesterday you only painted a few paces."

He, "It is not my fault. The paint can keep getting further and further away."

******

4878 ==> Poverty must have great attractions and satisfaction, or there would not be so many poor people.

They realize that with luck, resolution, effort, thought, and good guidance, it is possible to survive wealth, but they seem unmotivated to take the risk.

******

4879 ==> Somewhat frustrating when someone with less intelligence has more sense than we have.

******

4880 ==> 97% of the people are honest, good, hardworking people. The three percent that are not mentioned above have succeeded in getting themselves elected into Politics.

******

4881 ==> The Vice President of the large company had a car accident and became very much dead.

A young junior management fellow approached the big boss and asked if he could take the Vice President's place.

The boss says, "You will have to talk to the funeral director. He has the Vice President now."

******

4882 ==> There is nothing worse than people who think they are right when they are wrong.

******

4883 (1/2) ==> Many of the housewives and female store clerks, and junior female office workers are somewhat frustrated about a new business reality. For many decades, it has been the custom for above mentioned to sometimes secretly solicit and acceptance of a proposal for sex encouraged by a money transaction. It provides meager, exciting entertainment, getting away with a sneaky business cash deal.

4883 (2/2) ==> What has upset the game is the sudden rise of homeless women prowling the streets and who will do anything legal or not legal to get money for food or drugs.

True, they are dirty and smelly, but they are also firm, fresh, unstretched, cheap, and in fair physical condition from so much walking in search of food. Men tired of worn out soft, flabby, stretched-out housewives and others can now buy a half dozen for the price of one.

Renting a girlfriend is now possible even for a poor man. Do anything he wants with his half-hour rental.

******

4884 ==> The manager of the Agriculture Department, who had always lived in apartments, bought a farm and two horses. He had difficulty telling them apart, so he cut the hair off one, but the hair grew back. Then he measured and found that the white horse was a hand's span shorter than the black horse.

******

4885 ==> How many of us work harder and harder but get less and less done, while others work so little and get so much done?

******

4886 ==> The political cheese are always so cautious about tax cuts. They spend weeks and months debating this. But when a political pay raise is considered, they pass this within an hour.

******

4887 ==> So often we pay to research our family tree, then pay double to hush it up.

******

4888 (1/2) ==> The man had lived all his life in big city high-rise apartments. One day, he lost his job, and while out about looking for a new job, he met an old school friend from twenty years ago. This friend was a big stinker in the government. He got the man a job as head of the agriculture department.

The man raced to the library. He scanned through all manner of farming books.

The next day, he entered his new office, sat behind the desk, and waited for the work to arrive. The first week was a hell of frustrations. He knew nothing about farming and agriculture. He was stressed out and overworked by the weekend.

Monday morning, he was back in his office, far too cheerful.

4888 (2/2) ==> Every work, problem, or frustration that came to his desk, he passed to his secretary, instructing her to pass the task to someone in junior management. They would investigate and write a report with possible solutions explained.

So seeing his paycheck larger than the old job, he bought a farm and two horses.

He had difficulty telling the horses apart. He did not wish to insult the horses by calling them the wrong name. He tried cutting the tail hair off one, but it grew back.

Then he made an amazing discovery: the white horse was a hand's span shorter than the black horse.

This discovery led him on to write the great agriculture book, "How to Measure the Height of Horses." All 1,180 pages. You can get a free copy of this book from your local government agriculture depart.

******

4889 ==> A good patient will have faith and loyalty in their doctor until the doc signs the death certificate with a detailed fiction of the illness.

******

4890 ==> Much of the knowledge and insight of the holy one comes from their experience as a sinner.

******

4891 ==> People who throw or blow kisses are often too lazy to take a step or two closer, to real bacteria contact.

******

4892 ==> A zombie political cheese variety is almost brainless, with a mind eager to gain but stay innocent in the shadows. It functions all day, not knowing where it goes or what it does. It slyly pockets any money falling from slippery deals.

This zombie political mutation exists in every planetary government. The mutation grows the fastest where top-secret stuff is active.

******

4893 ==> Where is my hero?

******

4894 ==> Your cash money will always open the door faster than your plastic credit cards.

******

4895 ==> If you plan to do nothing, then is best to wake very early in the morning so you can get a good start, before others clutter up the job.

******

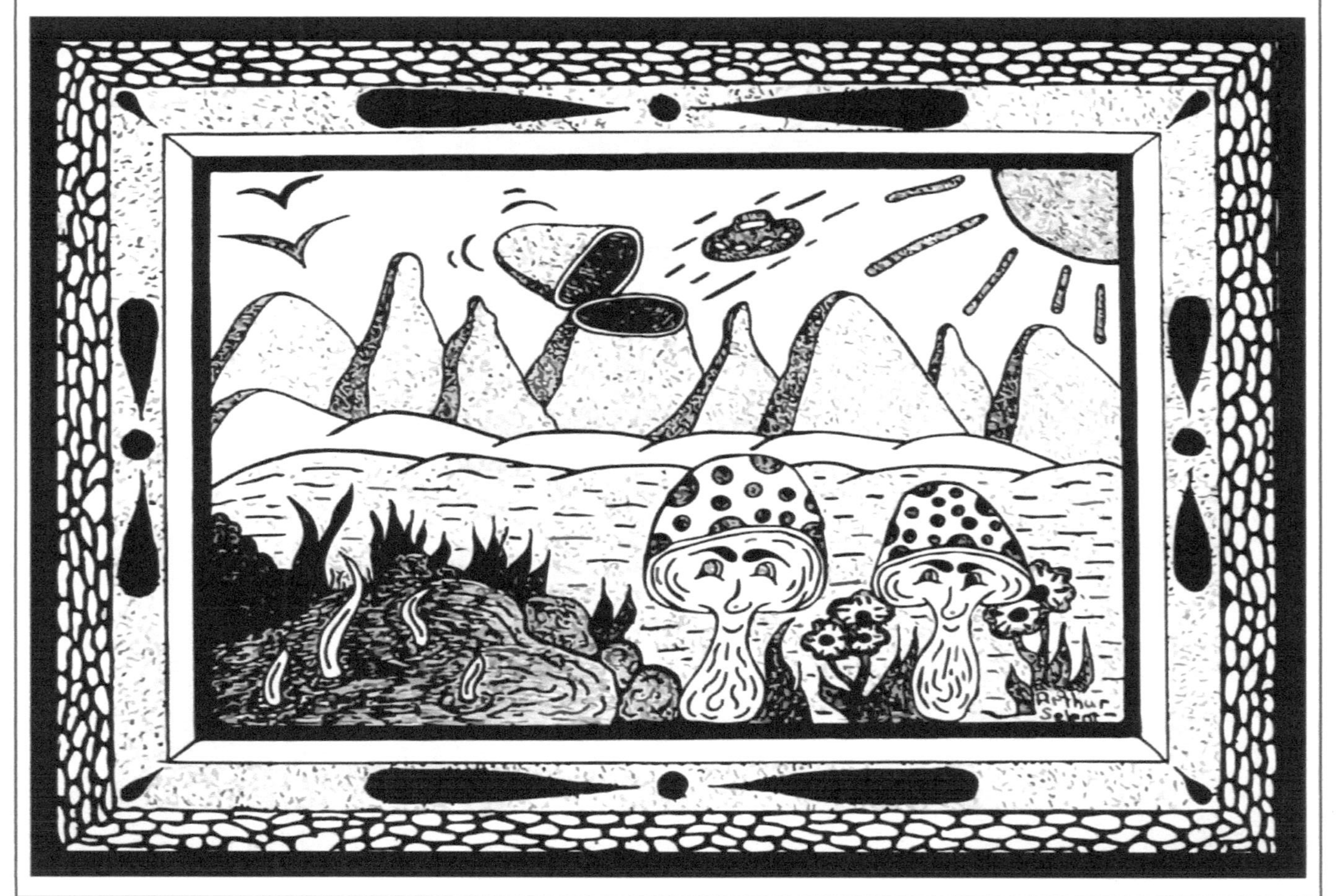

4896 ==> Notice how women who enjoy spending money always seem to marry men who enjoy earning money.

******

4897 ==> Political decay with wandering loose morals always has the highest ideas and ideas for planetary well-being just before elections. It is when they tell the best fairy tales.

******

4898 ==> Just think of how many honest people we save from becoming thieves by locking things away out of sight.

******

4899 ==> To wander into a jungle of troubles, frustrations, and miseries is easily done, but to find one's way out is not easy.

******

4900 ==> The force of two souls who detest each other, even when copulating with atrocious passions, then pushing apart, but still in need of each other. The bondage is gripping ever tighter.

******

4901 ==> They were school lovers who graduated and ended up finding jobs in the same faraway city. They decided to live together and found an economical apartment. He worked nights and she worked days.

One day at the factory there was some equipment breakdown. The factory was shut down and the workers sent home.

Going home, he drove a wandering route ending up in a part of the city he'd never seen before, the red-light district. Hookers and prostitutes lined the street, eager to be rented by perverts and sex crazy men.

There she was, his lover lifting her skirt as a drunk man dressed rather well shuffled by. She was wearing no underwear. The fellow turned and grabbed her; he leaned into her. His arms were around her as he copulated his baby seeds. When finished, the drunk pushed her away and continued his shuffle down the street.

He was in shock, His lover keeping this part of her life hidden from him. He went to her asking for an explanation.

She replies, "We are not married, are we? You here looking for a hooker?"

He went back to the apartment, filled the back seat of the car with his stuff, and went home to his mother.

******

4902 ==> The roads of civilization are land marked by beer cans in the ditch. Follow the cans and you end up at the beer store, the symbol of an advanced civilization.

******

4903 ==> With some effort, you can educate anyone to have a dozen diplomas on their wall. But how are you going to teach them how to think?

******

4904 ==> They will never allow you to escape life with a live body.

******

4905 ==> Of all the people who want a vacation the most, those that just had one are at the front of the line.

******

4906 (1/2) ==> The religion cult in their massive monastery had a profitable business going on with renting darkened rooms to young healthy women who wished to get pregnant. Each room had a large sleeping mat on one side with a lush carpet covering the floor. The carpet made no sound when anyone walked on it. One corner of the carpet hid a secret trap door in the floor.

4906 (2/2) ==> The monks rented these rooms to the women. There in dark solitude the women slept and prayed for a baby. They were given a glass of drugged wine which made them sleep wonderfully. They dreamed of athletic Gods copulating with their woman body, each God eager to make a baby.

Many rich marriages that seemed to be unable to create a baby brought their womenfolk to the monastery.

The trap door raised silently. One by one the monks climbed into the room and copulated. The silent night crept along. The women, drugged had the most real erotic dreams.

Some wealthy women often came to rent a room. Was it the penis they liked or the drugged wine?

******

4907 ==> When one becomes rich and famous or wins the lottery it does not take long for relatives, old school friends, and charity collectors to suddenly show up at the door. Like sneaky salesman selling invisible toilet paper. Like vultures in the desert following a thirsty man crawling to death.

******

4908 ==> Poverty and wealth have both failed to bring happiness to the masses.

******

4909 ==> Nine tenths of the population cannot start a conversation were it not for the changing of the weather.

******

4910 ==> Some cafes now offer local gossip as an attraction. One puts on headphones and via hidden microphones one listens to local people gossip.

******

4911 ==> Those who marry for money often work harder than the average factory worker.

******

4912 ==> Eventually it all comes to an end even though some may stretch their fate doing the devil's work cleaning the gas chambers, sorting, undressing and deliver the bodies to the roasting ovens.

The humans must be fed. Overbreeding has resulted in all meat animals already being eaten. The only meat left is human.

The overseer manager watches the process. Sometimes he would point to a certain human, and armed attendants would load that person into transport and deliver to the overseer's kitchen. The best for management.

******

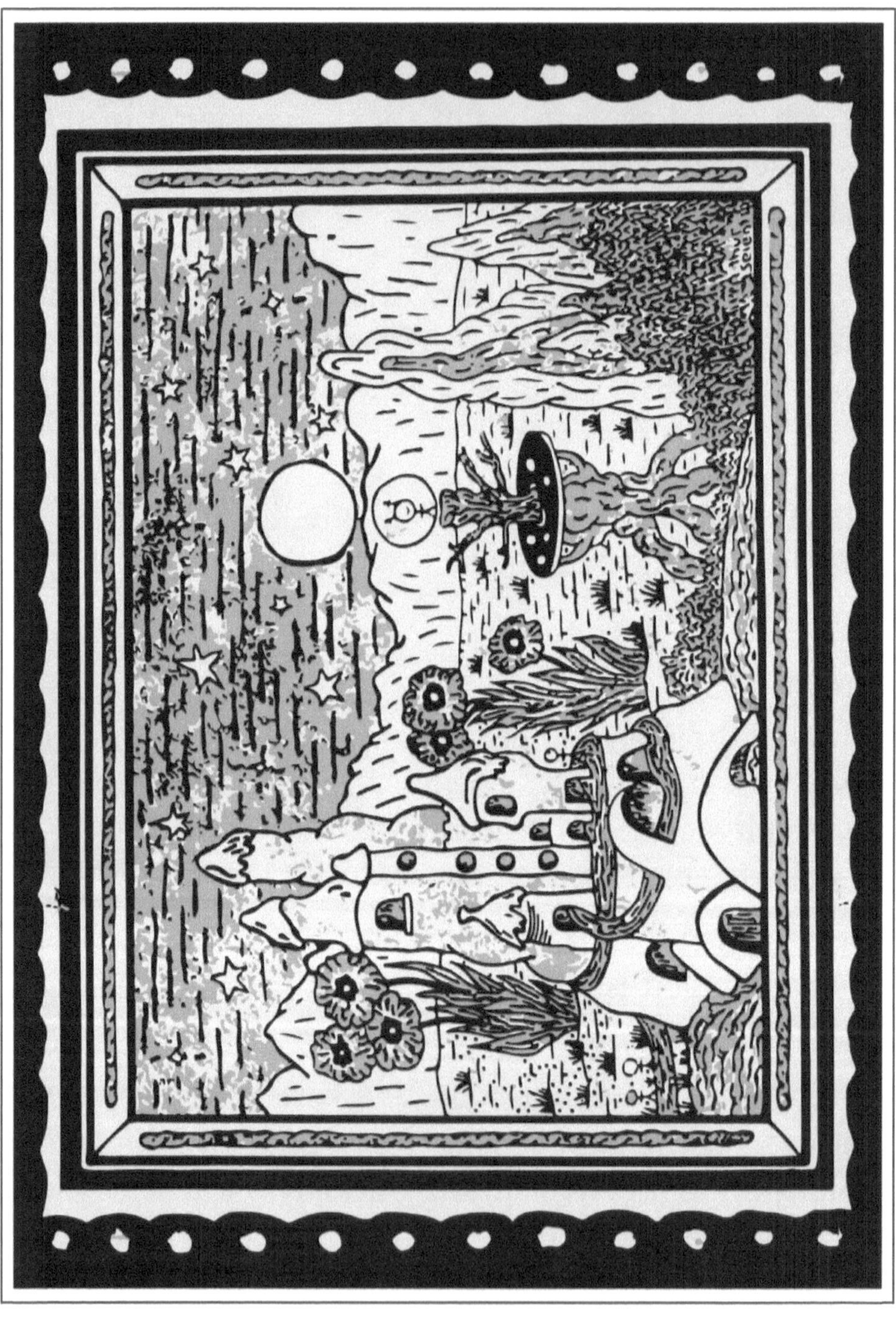

4913 ==> Bragging about our success, skills, gifts or other abilities only results in secret resentment, inner jealously, and often enemies who wish to take down the great trophy so they can feel powerful with destruction.

******

4914 ==> How often does a mental imbalance happen through the kind thoughts and actions of others? Each having a different delusion of the actual needs. They are fed by closed-eye perceptions.

******

4915 ==> His hot sex lover was losing interest in him. At bed time, she referred to his erection as, "Nasty dry old thing getting smaller every day."

He the great man was insulted. Of course this finished the love. The door locks were changed and she was locked out. He was paying for all her needs. She was supposed to build his manly ego not tear it down in mockery.

******

4916 ==> His quick eye had a way of finding out other people's defects and not being concerned about looking for virtues.

Some said he was vicious tongued like a forked serpent.

******

4917 ==> Spiritual light is given to all but some seem not to know how to grab light and carry it about wherever they wander.

******

4918 ==> How much wisdom has died with our ancestors?

******

4919 ==> Every religion has its imagination of God. So many different Gods among the various religions and each supposed to be the only God.

Billions of people searching to find God. The religious and churches making a money industry of the game. But how can they find something that is imagined and has ever been seen in reality as presented by our education systems.

Humans trying to create God.

******

4920 ==> Words without knowledge are best for darkening reality.

******

4921 ==> Wisdom and understanding cannot easily be stolen.

******

4922 ==> The rich and successful are not always wise or smart.

******

4923 ==> Change your belief reality, and gradually your life path will also change.

******

4924 ==> Most people couldn't care less which God or Devil they worship. They only wish to cure their inner insecurity and fears of belonging in the midst of the herd, being crushed by mental delusion pressures. But they feel safe inside the herd as the herd tramples their spirit into mental sewage, making the windows too dirty to see out.

******

4925 ==> "It is useless junk", he says as he haggles the price down, finally buying it for almost nothing. Then the seller having walked away, the buyer brags about what a bargain he got and the useful grand magnificence of his purchase.

******

4926 ==> For many, hope is a tree of life. Our desire leads us onwards where otherwise we would have failed, having the motivation to exert ourselves.

* * * * * *

4927 ==> Can a person be on fire inside, but their clothes not burn?

* * * * * *

4928 ==> She wanted all of him completely and to be completely his. Ownership with passion. She tried to give him everything, both in bed and at the bank. Superficial love or flirting was not her fashion.

But behind the hypnotic happiness lurked suspicion. She was full of it. Many times, he had come to her and been too soft for bed. It often occurred to her that other women were draining his seed. But she needed so much a man that she dared not question for fear of losing him.

As the money in the bank faded away slowly, she looked neither left nor right for a replacement man.

* * * * * *

4929 ==> The sweet taste of stolen drink to wash down the pleasant meal of secret bread.

* * * * * *

4930 ==> We should not laugh at the bad luck of others, for one day will be our turn to have bad luck.

* * * * * *

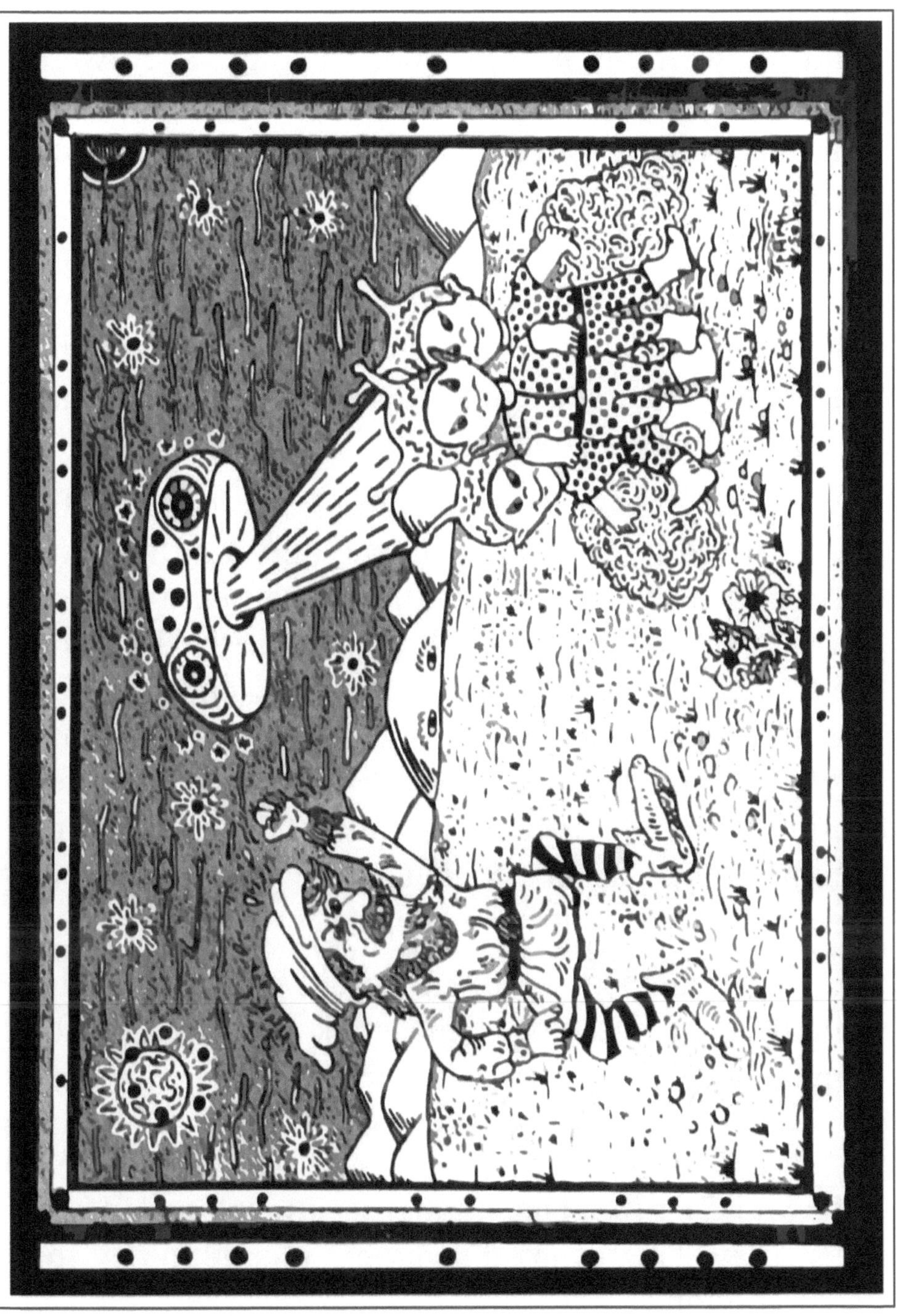

4931 ==> The young man had his arms around her, and the passions in him were cooking. They were behind some shrubs in a dark corner of the mansion's vast backyard. From the bright lights of the mansion issued music and the murmur of activity. It was a party.

"You are going too fast", the girl says. Oh, how she wanted the experience, but she must resist a little or he will think she's just an easy slut. This was her first fling with a young man.

The last few months, she'd secretly approached three church fathers, one at a time, and asked if she could have a little Education to prepare her for marriage. Each felt their fatherly duty and explained the copulation action. Each also felt compelled to demonstrate, so she got laid and from time to time, returned to these old wimpy men for more education. They encouraged her with gifts of money, the usual behavior of married men, providing an incentive to keep a secret.

She fancied she liked the old men better. The young man just took and took not paying for anything.

******

4932 (1/2) ==> The phone scammers called me yesterday. They wanted some big money to pay for some fiction.

4932 (2/2) ==> I told them that they were a day late because I just paid off the police to get out of 144 charges in 28 flags.

I told them to call back next week after I cash my big lottery win. I would like to arrange a visit with them. I have a great business idea and will need to hire some professional phone people.

Oh! They got excited and friendly. They say they will call back next week and make an appointment for the business talks. I told them I would pay cash since it is a slightly secret sort of business. This very much lured on their sneaky little brains.

Then I phoned the crime boss and asked to borrow a half dozen ranchers to help me round up a herd. I mentioned that he'd have some midnight work for the peppered sausage makers.

******

4933 ==> Those who rush and race to become rich are seldom innocent.

******

4934 ==> Better is a simple meal of bread and water with love than a feast of evil will and hate.

******

4935==> Whoever brags about themselves and their grand abilities is like thunder making a noise but not bringing any rain.

******

4936 ==> Good news from a faraway friend is like cool water to a thirsty soul.

******

4937 ==> Do ghosts come from our imagination and longings, or are they a real entity living in an unknown reality?

******

4938 ==> They are too smart for their own ideas. They tried to breed mules but only made assess of themselves.

******

4939 ==> Do you live in a reality of store-bought happiness? Every time life gets gloomy, you go shopping.

******

4940 (1/2) ==> In the evening, when the lamps danced shadows on the walls and ceiling, the ghost sat in warm comfort in front of the fireplace, looking at the young woman make her dinner in the open kitchen area.

4940 (2/2) ==> He yearned so much to have a physical body so he could embrace her in his arms to enjoy a girlfriend experience.

During the day, he followed her about taking special attention to the males she knew. He was looking for a male whose spirit he could evict and replace with his ghostly spirit so that copulation with the young lady could happen.

******

4941 ==> How often do we like to invent scary things for children to believe?

What about the scary stuff we invent for grown-ups to believe?

******

4942 ==> How do I escape the ghost of you?

******

4943 (1/4) ==> She was six years old. Her dad built a small shelter high up in the crowded branches of some trees growing too close together so that the branches were a tangled bird haven. He painted the outside and underneath the shelter to look exactly like the leaves and branches. Invisible for anyone looking up.

She was afraid to climb to the shelter, but her dad kept pushing her mind until she could go up and down with confidence.

4943 (2/4) ==> A few weeks later, her dad brought a floor mat and some blankets up. He also brought a sack of oatmeal, some dried fruit, and a bag of peanuts already shelled. He carried up a massive number of jugs and bottles filled with water. Last to go up were the same plastic buckets for her to pee in.

He told her that tomorrow some bad men were coming and she was to go early at dawn, climb to the shelter, and stay there a few days until the bad men left.

Early in the morning, she climbed high up into the tree and made herself comfortable. Close to noon, the soldiers came. She saw her dad and mom go down into the root cellar, which had a secret little hidden closet just big enough for sitting and sleeping, but room for nothing else. The soldiers wandered about, sitting to rest sometimes. They looked everywhere they savagely ate any food they found.

By nightfall, they had found the dad and mom. They made a large fire in the yard, burning household furniture and any wood that could be carried. By the bright firelight, they tortured the dad for an hour, then shot him. The mother they stripped naked, and various soldiers raped and ravaged her. Finally, they had enough and one soldier bashed her head in with a big hammer. They threw the body into the fire and ambled off to a chosen sleep place.

4943 (3/4) ==> She wanted to scream. To climb down and beat at the soldiers. Her dad's words to make no sound and save herself gave her moral support. She watched and burned inside with emotions.

When she awoke the next day all was quiet.

The soldiers had gone but she stayed up in the tree shelter all day watching just in case they came back. When the next day she climbed down she found the flies buzzing about. The food had all been eaten or scattered about to decay. She was too young to understand. She climbed back into her safe tree shelter and stayed there in shock.

She climbed down the tree and carrying the small sack of oatmeal and one water bottle she started walking down the road. By the start of evening, her water was all gone. It got dark, she blindly shuffled along. By luck she came to a little creek of water trickling along the road, then veering off to get lost in the forest. She slept there on the grass and leaf covered ground. She tossed and turned curling into a little ball. It was a cool night and she had no blanket.

In the morning she saw a well-worn path which followed the creek. She left the road and followed the path.

By the end of the day she came to a small cottage. No one was around and the door was open. The food in the cupboards was untouched and good to eat. She stayed there several days.

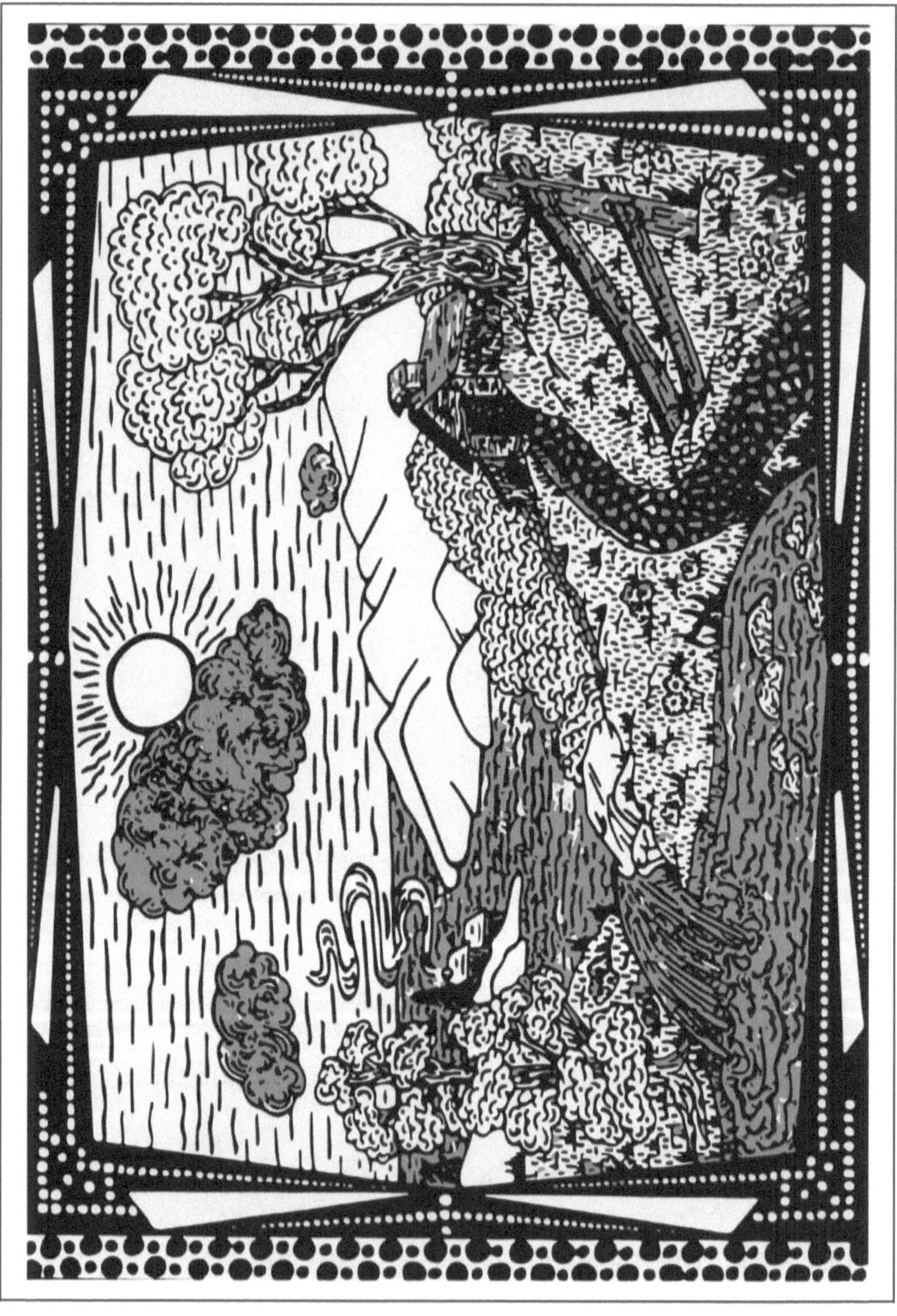

4943 (4/4) ==> On the fourth day a big noise of activity as the soldiers ran past in fast frightened retreat. The Zoomba tribe was chasing them. The soldiers shot their guns but the bullet would not fire. The Zoomba men waved their voodoo sticks chanting some mystic spell. The soldiers dropped their guns and ran faster.

The Zoomba did not touch the guns, they had a superior weapon, the voodoo stick.

At the tail end of the stampede, an old Zoomba man hobbled along. He was too frail to keep up. When he got too far behind, he'd wave his voodoo stick and lift off the ground to instantly fly to the rear of the stampede.

He was more interested in searching looks left and right than in the actual chase. He'd had a dream last night. He'd dreamed he found the future Zoomba queen.

He saw the little girl and knew his dream had come true. He took her home and looked after her. He taught her the most powerful magic he knew.

On his death bed he gave her his voodoo stick and showed her how to used it.

At dinner she waved her voodoo stick and instantly there at the table sat her mom, dad and the old Zoomba man. She had no one else and never allowed herself to become close with anyone. She did not want to be hurt again by losing people she loved.

******

4944 ==> For so long has material society forbidden ghosts and spirits that now they no longer believe in the unseen, even though they try to create it from their fantasy imaginations.

******

4945 ==> Capitalistic society of which most of the planet is a member ticket holder either fully paid up or paid down. The machine of our society works on the platform that those that works on the platform that those that work the hardest get paid the least. Those who work the least get the higher pay.

Now who could find fault with such a perfect system?

******

4946 ==> There goes my hero, running away from me.

******

4947 (1/2) ==> The witch doctor said, "There is a ghost inside this little girl"

The jungle mother frowned, "Is that good or bad?"

Witch doctor, "I don't know, I must study the ghost. Leave the girl with me for a week."

4947 (2/2) ==> The little girl began to kick, jump and move her body about in dramatic fashion trying to get rid of the ghost.

The mother left the girl there. The witch doctor made dinner for them. At bedtime he explained that sleep time is when the ghost is strongest. He would hold her snug all night so the ghost would not walk her body somewhere.

She lay there beside him, nervous and tense. He held her close. After a bit she relaxed and gradually feeling safe went to sleep.

The week flew by. The mother returned.

With doctor, "It seems a harmless ghost. She will come to no harm." Then to the girl he says, "If you feel the ghost then come back to me for more treatment."

******

4948 (1/2) ==> Many months passed then one day the girl told me the mother that she had to see the witch doctor. The ghost was bothering her. Then she began to go visit him more often, spending a few nights here and there, safe in his arms.

The mother was ill at ease, about her daughter spending so much time with that ugly old man. She suspected things but the witch doctor being so powerful in the village always made sure her family got a nice share when the hunters returned each evening.

4948 (2/2) ==> The girl grew older started to bloom into womanhood. Then one night the old witch doctor slid his male part deep inside her. She did not mind. She was under his spell and felt his spirit mingle with her spirit.

The next day the witch doctor explained to the mother that they were married and the daughter would be living with him now.

Now the mother was free. She had seen it coming so the shock was small. A slick-talking safari explorer was passing through the village. She followed him out of the village when he moved on.

******

4949 (1/2) ==> Ten years later the mother returned to find her daughter the richest person in the village. The witch doctor had died and left his massive wealth to his daughter.

The mother dragged wimpy safari explorer about. His talk seemed limited to, "Yes, dear," "Right away, dear."

He saw the situation and a sparkle came to into his eyes. The daughter was rich, young and good-looking. He looked for the keys to her door. His mind already on the path to her seduction.

His sneaky mind cooked, "Let the door get used to me, then gradually we move in."

4949 (2/2) ==> A great purpose arose within him. He puffed up his sagging, wimpy body. He saw himself as a future rich man if he played his cards right.

******

4950 ==> One does not need education or intelligence to live a long time. One just needs good health and a safe place to live.

******

4951 ==> Where there is big money, there are sneaky hands and big secret pockets.

******

4952 (1/2) ==> They were waiting for the rains to wash their floors of insects, food scraps, rats, shoes, and clutter. They made fires and chanted to the rain Gods, but no rain. The dirt piled up on the floors.

They looked to a nearby small hill where a newcomer was building a hut. This fellow must be crazy. He was building on high ground. How could the rains wash the floor?

As if that was not strange enough, he dug about in the soil planting plants and seeds. At first, he used to carry water to water his garden, but one day, he'd made some sort of system where the water came up the hill on its own. The jungle natives were amazed. This must be a strong magic man.

4952 (2/2) ==> They rounded up two of their young women. They marched up the hill to give the women as gifts. It was thought that it would be on good terms with such a crazy magic man.

To their amazement, the floor of the newcomer's hut was clean.

******

4953 ==> Working 27 hours per day and asking the boss for more hours.

Then one day boss is gone, the job is gone, and we sit all day with nothing to do.

******

4954 ==> The hottest spring sales item continues to be lady's invisible swim bikini. One can see right through the fabric as if it were a window.

The moral police patrol the beaches, feeling between the legs of the women to see who is nude or who has a swim bikini on, even if it is see through," Those faking it and not wearing the invisible creation are hauled off the beach and taken to secret locations for a few hours. The moral police enjoy many strange sins doing their modest job.

Don't fake it. Wear the see through thing or better yet get one of those old fashion things that look like lady designer underwear made of visible fabric.

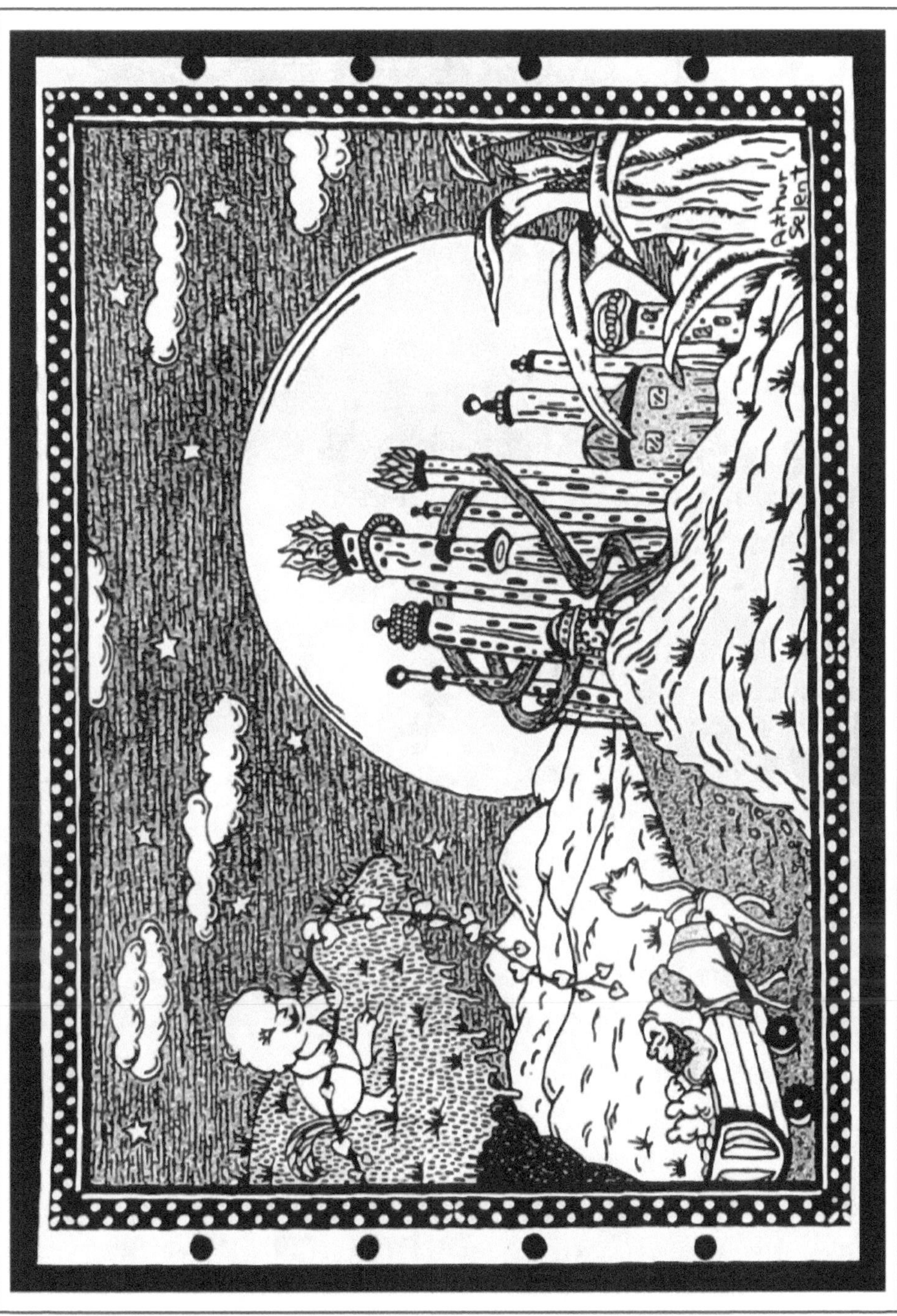

******

4955 ==> The lowest type of people are those who do not try to learn. Even if one is too stupid to learn, the act of trying will at least hopefully teach something if only how to be a better failure next time.

******

4956 ==> Sad indeed will be our future when we make our homes side by side with no space to walk between, when we stack our homes one on top of another, reaching high into the clouds. When we farm the fields, all adjoining other fields, until there is no other space left.

******

4957 ==> Now that X-mas is over, there are discarded X-mas trees on the march. They are not rational. They demand X-mas season be made longer.

Protect yourself by putting a leash on your chainsaw and setting it in clear view on your doorstep.

******

4958 (1/2) ==> Billions of people have faith that they are good people and follow God's path. But they seem to lack a little in investigation.

4958 (2/2) ==> So many Gods, so many paths.

To many only need to be in the herd to feel secure. They shuffle along as the herd moving to slaughter nudges them also to the slaughter.

******

4959 (1/2) ==> He was ugly, one eye lower than the other, a big round ball of a nose, one corner of his lower lip dripping, drooling and hanging loose. He was the newly arrived tramp settling into village society.

The village children thought they'd play a joke with him. They told him of a haunted house where no one lived. He could sleep there and wait out rains and bad weather. They told him the house was in a long legal dispute. Lawyers or others might show up in daylight hours on good weather days.

The old tramp thanked the children and asked if they could guide him to the house so he would be sure of the right location.

Off they set, slinking down the narrow farm road to the outskirts of the village. An hour's walk and they arrived at an ordinary red brick house.

The kids frolicked with mischief and laughter as they made their way back to their homes. The house was haunted. All sorts of stories went about concerning that house. Even the police did not go there at night.

4959 (2/2) ==> The first night was restless. The unease of unfamiliar surroundings had him awakening a few times in the night, thinking he'd heard voices.

By the end of the week, he knew some of the ghosts on a first-name basis. Slowly, they became friends. The ghosts became fond of their human house pet.

They would tell him things. Like one night, the tavern keeper forgot to lock the back door. The tramp walked all night carrying bottles of fine drink to stash in the basement of the house. One day they told where a bank robber had hidden the money. Now the tramp could buy food and did not need to search for each meal.

The ghosts liked their ugly old human house pet. They showed him where the legal deed to ownership of the house was hidden under the stairs. The courts awarded him ownership.

The village children couldn't understand why the tramp did not get scared away by the ghosts. Their joke did not seem like fun anymore.

******

4960 ==> When you're young, they all want you for sex.

When you're old, they all want you for money.

******

4961 ==> Being poor has the advantage that the doctor will cure you faster. But if the government pays the bill, you will be sick until the government runs out of money.

******

4962 ==> It seems that the more useless political cheese is, the more they love the flag.

******

4963 ==> You see this in any large corporation, whether private or government. There are always some who look so busy doing nothing that management simply cannot do without them, so they keep themselves on the payroll.

******

4964 ==> Honesty just doesn't seem to pay enough to suit some people.

******

4965 ==> Some people seem to double their money by folding it in half and putting it in their pocket.

******

4966 (1/2) ==> You notice that the people standing behind the leader should be standing in front, where the leader can watch them.

4966 (2/2) ==> The biggest corruptions always manage to get their puppets close to the leader.

******

4967 ==> They may be wrong and likely are, but should we tell them?

******

4968 ==> It is said that those who have the gift or the curse depend on how the circumstances balance the scales.

******

4969 ==> When one has the weapon is when one is the most eager to find and create the enemy.

******

4970 ==> Everyone likes a nice picture. Even those who cannot read or write.

******

4971 ==> The big truck hauling fruit crashed on the express freeway and created a massive jam pile-up.

******

4972 (1/3) ==> She married him when they were both young. He was a tall, muscular lad, with broad shoulders, trim waist, and nimble feet.

4972 (2/3) ==> Now look what she got. He was fat, four times four fat, flabby-chinned, his gut a sack of soft mush hanging over his shrunken penis. His breath hell pit of rotting meat stench. His eyes were dark, baggy, and bloodshot. His hand is always busy lifting a beer can.

She looked at him and wondered how much longer he would last. The next day, she went shopping for life insurance. She found an overeager, slightly shifty insurance salesman. He set her up with a very big payout contract in the event that her husband dies. She encouraged him to believe he'd get a little secret incentive pay back in a year or two. She even hugged him out of gratitude. She even let him linger his hand on her thigh a little too long.

Then she went home and started reading crime thrillers, having a common topic: "How to get away with murder."

She started cooking fat foods, lots of grease, making his coffee stronger, letting him drink more beer and smoke more.

Then one afternoon when she was out doing the household shopping the house caught on fire. It was a warm day so she'd left a lot windows open. The fresh air blowing through made the fire burn faster and hotter.

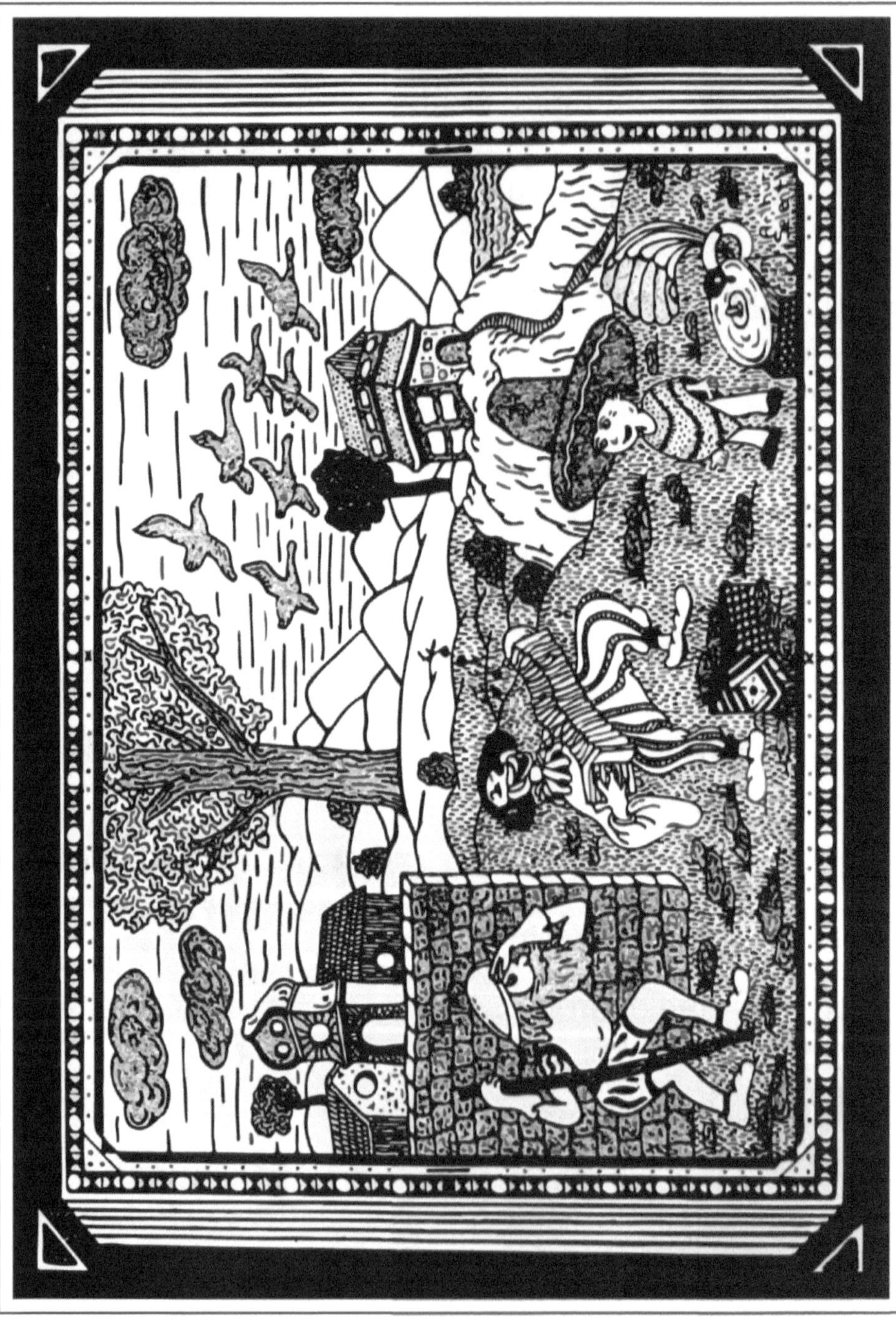

4972 (3/3) ==> By the most strange coincidence she had just six months past put a big fire insurance contract on the house.

So there she sat at the train station, a lonely widow rich with insurance money. The insurance salesman prowling the city looking for her, eager to share his needs. The train arrived, she got on. The train rattled away into the night. She looked at her map.

******

4973 ==> Everyone is looking for the free and easy money, but it seems that corruption and lottery winners are the ones to ever find it.

******

4974 ==> The loyal passions of friendships last for decades until one asks the other to lend one some money.

******

4975 (1/3) ==> The soldiers came, tied her up, and took their time checking the rope knots while feeling their hands about her liquid compost outlet. They knew she would never again return to society. They could do what they wanted.

4975 (2/3) ==> They brought her to the office of the military people-killing corporation. A low-level officer took her into a blood-splattered soundproof room with no windows. He questions her. She told him everything. When she was done, he changed his friendly act and smashed her face with his fist, then removed her clothes and had his pleasure. He wiped her clean with a rag and left the room.

She got dressed and waited.

After a bit a big man with clean uniform came in. He was a captain, he also questioned her but did not attempt to pleasure himself with her. He took her to the top management.

The highest command of the military people killing corporation kept her for many months doing various things to her mind and her body.

They did not bother to question her no more, she was just a toy to be cruel to. One day, after she had gone too soft from lack of exercise and her mind had gone empty, they put her on an airplane. They adorned her with massive amounts of heavy metal jewelry, padlocked to her body. They dropped her from a considerable height into the middle of the vast ocean.

She had seen too much. Little green people flying a spacecraft were regular visitors to a field on her land.

4975 (3/3) ==> The public must not know of this. Established reality must not be stimulated with knowledge of these things. They dare not let her return to society and risk her telling her story.

******

4976 ==> We must understand the mental condition of those who walk a crooked path. A path that goes forever straight has not much entertainment.

******

4977 ==> There are warm-blooded animals and cold-blooded animals. Both eat things and compost the food, within their bodies. But why is it that warm-blooded animals can produce their own heat from the food passing along their intestines, while cold-blooded animals cannot produce their own heat?

******

4978 ==> There may be no future left. The planet may wish to remove the two-legged fleas.

******

4979 (1/2) ==> Would wars stop it if we stopped the profits being made from war? Labor and industry are in full production, paying taxes which are then used to buy the finished product.

4979 (2/2) ==> Would wars stop if we stopped the political cheese from stealing money from the secret war accounts? The bigger the war, the more money racing about in government contracts, many of which exist only on paper long enough to grab some money and transfer to a hidden pocket.

******

4980 ==> Much of writing is often like stealing cars. To take the other fellow's words, remove the steering wheel and attach your own.

I met a fellow who used his steering wheel to steal 183 cars. A very fine upright honest fellow. I have him tied and shackled to the wall beside the bookcase where my collection of dictionaries rest.

I go to him from time to time and torture him a little while asking why he tried to steal car # 184, my car. Sometimes the devil comes to me and I torture him too much. He will not last much longer.

******

4981 ==> After many years of expensive study, it was found that regular breathing is good for people.

******

4982 ==> Patriotism varies from unknown facts to total devotion in belief with mostly moral lunacy and disregard for virtue or ethics. A mental condition pushing passions of being the chosen one defending society from reality.

******

4983 ==> He was a bit rusty on his mental machine. He told me so himself. He claims this machine will soon run smooth as he is actively lubricating his brain with thinking grease.

I mentioned that the best scenery was on the other side of the street. He said he'd have a look. I watched as a car hit him when he crossed the street. It was messy.

He was such a fine fellow, sorry to see him go.

******

4984 ==> The people are oppressed and afflicted yet they open not their mouth. Like the sheep going to slaughter they huddle together going where the herd is moved.

******

4985 ==> It is said that rich people do not own their property but rather the property owns the rich people.

******

4986 ==> The unfortunate are usually the first to help other unfortunate.

******

4987 (1/3) ==> She offered him some drinks and loosened his tongue when the drink began to trickle his brain. She sat beside him and put her arm around pulling him close for a hug. She held him close. She mentioned that he was doing such good work. He felt safe and loved, mother was in his mind. She was saying that some of the women had romantic fantasies that could be used for testing the arousal stimulation induced by the underwear.

He said he also had romantic fantasy but he was afraid to make a move on any of the women. She explained that was normal reaction.

She explained that a small room previously used to store files had been remade into a small office complete with a somewhat oversized sofa for the arousal testing qualities of the underwear. Some of the women employees have volunteered to help him. The women will model the underwear and you will play romance. You will use different ways to remove the underwear, such as tug, pull, slide and etc. Then write a report on how the underwear performed as an arousal stimulation.

How could this be? She knew how to torture him. In his imagination he saw himself alone with semi-nude women who he undressed but could not seduce. But maybe he might also get lucky enough to play. He felt good thinking of the chances.

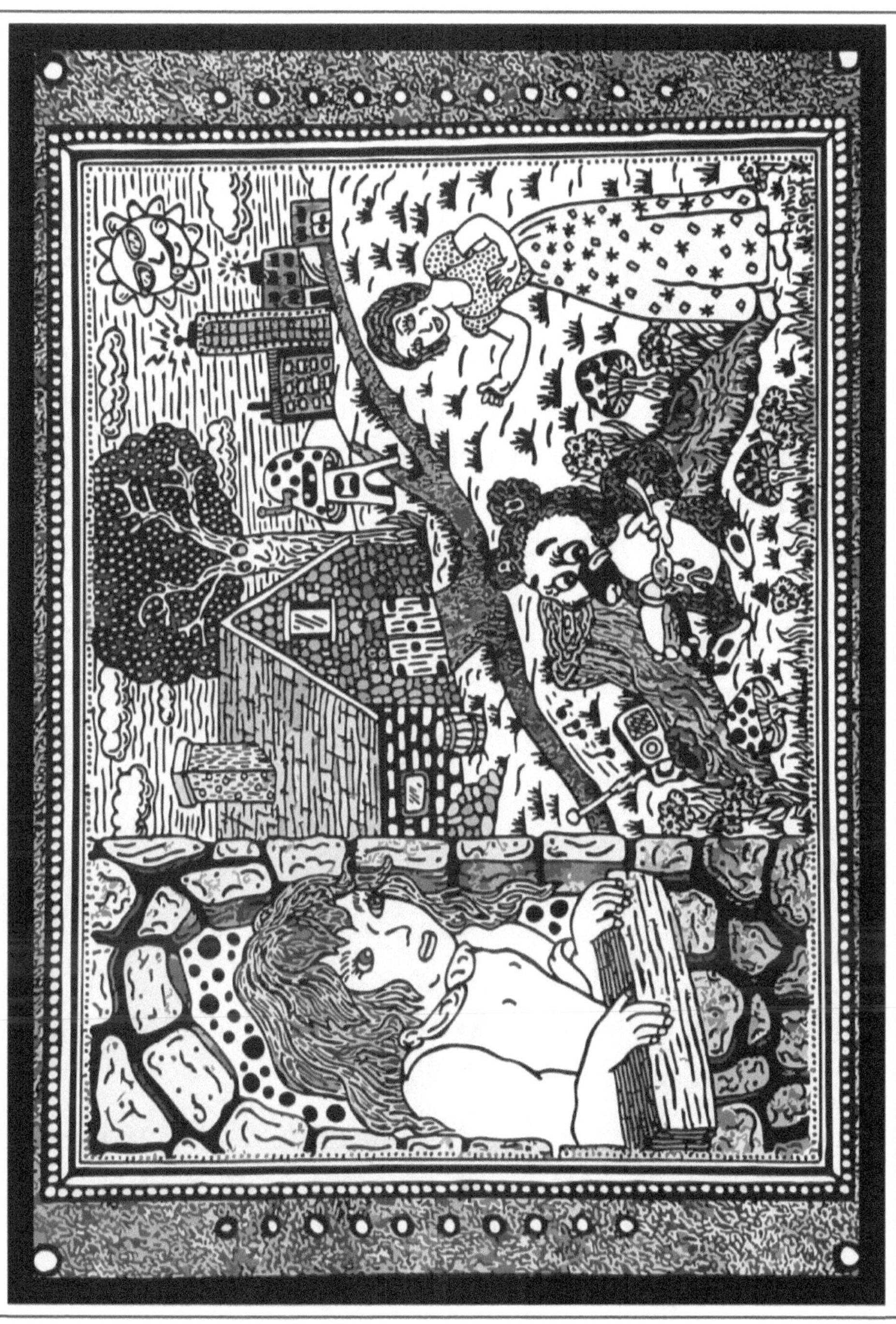

4987 (2/3) ==> The manager was saying that he being better looking than the forklift driver and the repair fellow the women would respond better to arousal experiments.

So a few times each week he and one of the women would lock the door and test the arousal aspects of the underwear. The women were fairly average in appearance, no uglies to stress arousal.

As he undressed the women, he'd use the underwear like a rag to caress the nude woman. He was surprised to see the women actually enjoyed his touch playing about. Slyly, he sneaked his penis closer and finally slowly entered. He was surprised that there was no objection. He went to work acting out his lust fantasy.

Later in his reports, he found ways to describe the erotic stimulation caused by the underwear. The manager read the reports and sent them straight to advertising.

The manager had a hidden camera watching the actions in the room. She did her own arousal inspections by watching, sometimes so overcome that she masturbated.

The secrets of the female underwear business were exposed as told to me by Lenis the Penis, who worked as a quality control inspector for 16 years. He went soft so they replaced him. He's all worn out now and collects a small pension.

******

4988 ==> Maybe it is time to become a responsible member of an established society now, that we are someone we want to spend out future with.

But really, do we have to get a job?

******

4989 ==> The President and Vice-President of the school had both reached an age of retirement. They were cleaning out their desks and saying goodbye to their office. One asks the other what his plans are.

"Maybe I'll start a prison. Those graduating will not hurry to come back for a visit." "What about you?"

"Maybe I'll start an orphanage. I'll never have to listen to advice from parents."

******

4990 ==> As we get richer, we also get better at preaching contentment to the poor, who we can buy and sell by the dozen.

******

4991 ==> There is no person who can endure destruction by ridicule without being overwhelmed by self-doubts.

******

4992 ==> An enemy can destroy a human but it takes a good-natured, injurious friend to do it perfectly.

******

4993 ==> Millions of people fled the northern cities as temperatures cold enough to crack a bottle of drink came upon the land. Week after week. The animals led the way on the march going south.

Millions of people fled the South as temperatures boiled the leaves on trees into brown. Car tires are melting on black pavement. North to the cold lands they marched.

Now the people huddle between the cold and the heat. There is nowhere else to go.

As the cold advances and the heat advances, the area of human life becomes smaller. The human as last survival means will study the technology of the ant.

******

4994 ==> A new theory is often attacked as absurd and insignificant. But after all the ranting, raving and slander are done the adversaries claim they were the original discovers thereof.

******

4995 ==> People are like steam engines. A fire must be started in the heart and brain before thing will go.

******

4996 ==> He is dead now. We will have to stop saying bad things and instead start saying good things about him.

However, that other fellow walking past, well we will see bad things we can exaggerate about him.

******

4997 ==> If you want to find the road to hell, just ask those beside you. Many out of the kindness of their own heart would only be too happy to direct you in the right direction. You can be sure their directions are truthful and not likely to lead astray.

******

4998 ==> A professional person will tell you what everyone knows but they will tell you in a language nobody can understand.

******

4999 ==> Lawyers have the skilled trade to question everything, tell nothing and to talk in circles by the hour as the accounting adds up the costs and forwards them to the client.

******

5000 (1/2) ==> He was a great military armchair commander. With the snap of a finger, he sent millions to hell and death.

5000 (2/2) ==> He himself lived in great luxury back in his rich homeland. He could not understand why the stupid soldiers had to get themselves killed.

The plan was perfect. They should have followed orders.

******

5001 ==> This is an imaginary thought. Do not dare to assume it is true until you have proof.

******

5002 ==> The nest of the political bedroom is too small for them all to cuddle in. The struggle to stay deep inside the inner circle is eternal and constantly in turmoil as to who will be pushed out to make room for a new playmate.

******

5003 ==> To make a mistake is human, but when one wears out a dozen erasers before the pencil needs sharpening, then it is time to contact the eraser company and complain about their product.

******

5004 (1/2) ==> He is a very rich boy, lack of a rich relative passing away. His habits are simple: drink wine from wake to sleep, play with whatever eager playmate the secretary provides, and sign whatever papers his secretary brings to him.

5004 (2/2) ==> The days fly by in mellow drunken trance. The secretary and lawyer work carefully. Little by little, they got him to sign away his wealth. Papers hidden among other papers, all lovingly signed with total faith in the honesty of his secretary and lawyer.

Now they plan to put some big life insurance on him and arrange for him to fall out of an airplane. The paperwork to direct the insurance payout into their own pockets has already been established.

******

5005 ==> We have not yet mastered the machine age, and here we are in the electronic age, fumbling about with our jungle clumsiness.

******

5006 ==> How do you kill the brain but leave the body alive? It is done slowly by simple over education and brainwashing with nonsense.

Today's education is nonsense. This is an imaginary thought. Do not assume this to be true unless you can provide true facts to merit your knowledge of this matter.

******

5007 ==> A good example can be so annoying if we ourselves cannot copy it.

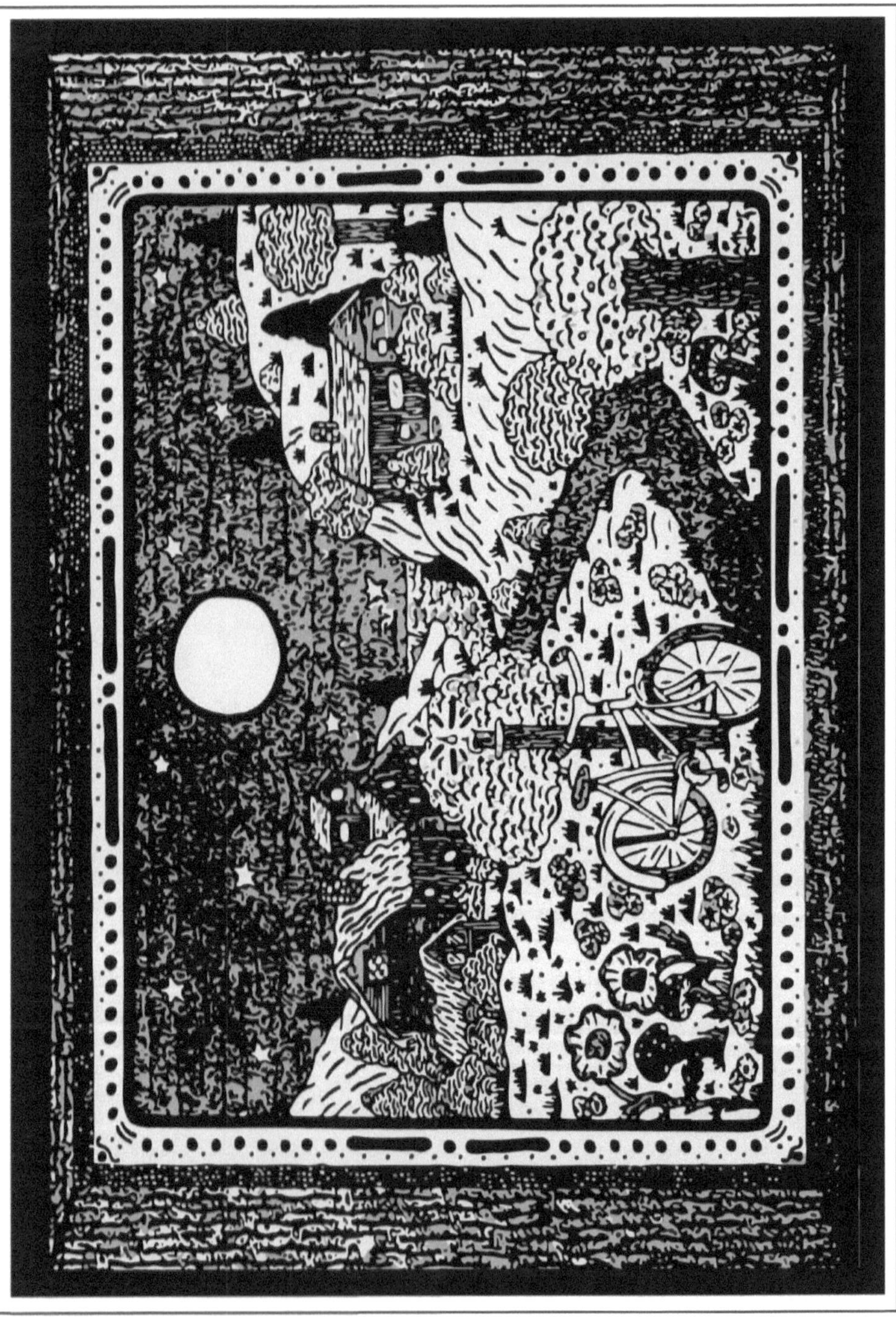

******

5008 ==> Thinking is very important, and don't let the puppet master tell you otherwise.

******

5009 ==> You do not want to dress richer than your client. Your client pays the money, and you are just the humble worker.

******

5010 ==> Truth often has to wait. She has grown used to it.

******

5011 ==> Many of us, though we bitch and complain, actually like work. It fascinates and hypnotizes us all day. We can reflect on our work for days and even years. Just the idea of our work being gone is enough to cause lesser beings to have a complete nervous breakdown

******

5012 ==> How clever we are to find ways to speed up work so we can have more free time then only to discover we have nothing to do in our free time.

******

5013 ==> Only the best of humans would hold an umbrella over a duck in a downpour of rain.

******

5014 ==> When one reads a book, does the reader go through the book or does the book go through the reader?

******

5015 ==> When a war happens, the first to be killed is truth.

******

5016 ==> Too many shut the doors of their minds, fearing visiting thoughts might steal something.

******

5017 ==> The correct orders of the soul lie in the task of successful everyday behavior. Our habits make all the difference, and the more we practice, the more we establish the efficiency of our soul.

******

5018 ==> A rascal and a scoundrel will often find that patriotism is a very safe appearance with which to advertise themselves under.

******

5019 ==> Many raise their voice when they should reinforce their argument.

******

5020 ==> The village gossip ticking away like minutes but never striking the hour.

******

5021 ==> The ultimate purpose of the busy is to one day retire and be idle.

******

5022 ==> The local trucker's group on the night shift had a slow night and was playing poker cards in the warehouse. A big box was the table, and smaller boxes provided seats.

Just when the beer cooler gave up its last can of beer, there was a month's wage sitting in the pot ready to be won.

It was Harry's turn to deal the cards. After the cards were dealt, Harry says, "Now Sam, you play those cards fair. I know what I dealt you."

******

5023 ==> Some are naturally drab and dull, but to consider, they must have made great efforts and pains to become as we see them now. One just does not see such stupidity in nature unless it is helped along.

******

5024 ==> Criticisms cost nothing but often create very important, formidable frustrations.

******

5025 ==> You Wreck Me Baby.

******

5026 (1/3) ==> In the remote, lonely farm lands, there was not much chance to meet new people. She lived a life of romantic fantasy. Visions of the tall, rich prince ravaging her lust-deprived body. Finally realizing there was no hope, she chose a neighbor lad as lover. A few times each week, they'd copulate in the barn or among shrubs bordering fields.

Then one day she won a free trip. Fourteen days, two weeks in some faraway tourist place. She could bring one person with her. She took him.

They got off the airplane and were delivered to their free hotel. She got the keys and did the front desk paperwork. Turning around, she saw him staring at a long-legged woman who had raised her mini skirt just enough to show she was wearing no underwear.

She was smiling and looking him straight in the eye from a distance across the lobby. He seemed spellbound and hypnotized as he stared. She took his hand, breaking the spell as she led him to their room.

The next day, they separated for the afternoon. She wandered the shops and he lay about the swimming pool.

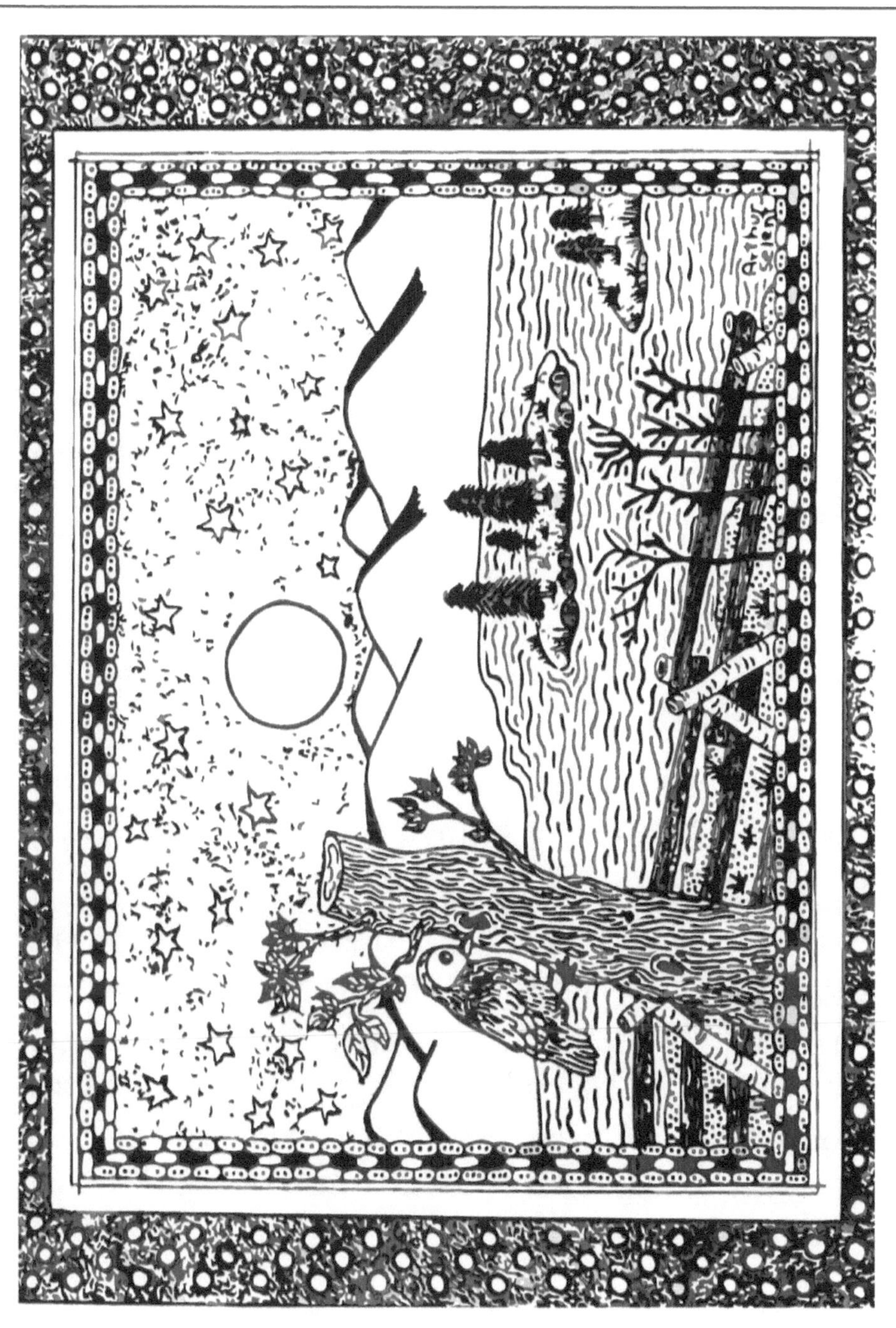

5026 (2/3) ==> The stores were boring. She returned to their room. She looked out the window down to the swimming pool. They lay her lad, and beside him lay that long-legged floosy. She still wore the same mini skirt and no underwear. She was running her hand over his body and sometimes slid her hand under the waistband of his shorts. Then they draped a very large bright colored beach towel over their midsections, and the motions of copulation began.

Jealous, she watched as her lad screwed that trash.

That night, as they lay in bed, he was cold and awkward, too soft to be interested in her desires. In her heart, she knew it was over. She could never love him anymore.

In the morning, her mind was made up. Let that floosy trash have her leftovers. She will find a new lover.

She had twelve days left on her free trip. The shops and streets were full of men. She set out to find her dream vision, a mild-mannered middle-aged man, lonely and secure in money matters. Someone who would be pleased to have a pretty young lady. She was going to run away from home and her childhood life. She will start a new life.

5026 (3/3) ==> She did not have a lot to offer, but she was young and pretty. She could cook and clean the house. She knew how to fake an orgasm and lie there moaning while he fumbles about with his male ego yoga exercise in their lovemaking.

******

5027 ==> Three stupid gardeners were seen at the real estate office. They were looking to buy some land suitable for growing stupid crops.

******

5028 ==> The Great Spirit worked day and night to say there would be obedient women in all corners of the world.

Then he made the world round and laughed.

******

5029 ==> We all want to level others down to our level, but cannot bear to level others up to our level.

******

5030 ==> Many of us use knowledge for sneaky cunning rather than for doing good.

******

5031 (1/2) ==> Why would anyone want a life job of fighting until death? Kill or be killed.

5031 (2/2) ==> They actually pay people to do this kill-or-die job. Political cheese at the rooster fight, replacing the roosters with humans. This heroic job is managed by the military people killing industry.

******

5032 ==> I am moaning and groaning, stiffly creaking and squeaking my body of decaying meat about.

I am practicing so I will have the act perfect when I reach old age.

******

5033 ==> To have imagination without learning is like having wings but no feet.

******

5034 ==> The Rock Star Killed the cowboy gun slinger.

Today, the young people all want to be screaming demons, making metallic wrecking yard noises.

What will tomorrow's hero look like? A guy with a leering grin wearing a white lab coat with pockets overflowing with cash. In his hand, a big needle which he points at as he chases little children in a school yard.

******

5035 ==> The human is a horrible creature. It constantly copulates and breeds, then creates wars and ways to kill its offspring.

******

5036 ==> Friends can change. Sometimes we have to let them go when it is time.

******

5037 ==> Some people are not content to spread gossip. They exert great effort and imagination to improve gossip before passing it along.

******

5038 ==> Conversation always improves if tells the listener a little less than they want to know.

******

5039 ==> Society consists mostly of ambitious, poverty-striving ever harder to entrench themselves in accumulating more and more desires, leading to more complicated frustrations. But to have less and less is not always so nice either.

******

5040 (1/2) ==> Presenting a new history for our new neighbors every time we move to a new place.

5040 (2/2) ==> Presenting a new history to new lovers, new jobs, and so we create our past.

What a great person we were in the past.

******

5041 ==> How much history has never been recorded for the future?

How much history has been changed by the stroke of a writer's pen.

******

5042 ==> Time will reveal if we bloom or wilt.

******

5043 ==> "Want to fly with me in my spaceship?"

So of the five women I asked this I got a date with three, got laid by one. I did better than the other guys.

Oh, look, there is a nice woman. "Hello, there. Would you like to fly with me in my spaceship? We will visit Romance Island."

"X:X//.X??X!!X"

"Oh, sorry to hear that. I thought you were a nice woman."

"Oh, you want to arrest me. Might have guessed, you are the passionate one wanting me all for yourself."

******

5044 ==> What we think upon, that we often become.

******

5045 ==> Shall we set up our lives to be an object of envy?

******

5046 ==> I have interviewed thousands of women in a confidential setting.

This required education for all alien males. So, write my exam report summary, I will venture to say that, in my opinion, at least half the women were telling the truth.

But, oh so boring. Endless hours they cackle and chatter on like park pigeons walking in circles under the clock.

I did my best and graduated from this education.

******

5047 (1/2) ==> Imagine one of those polar bear catching spiders of the tropical jungles translated into human form.

Intelligence sharpened by the hunt.

5047 (2/2) ==> That describes the village mouse catcher, the flea-infested cool cat. Cool cat sitting beside the garbage, drinking his bottle of wine from a brown paper bag. Night after night, he, on watch duty, snores his drunken sleep hidden behind the garbage dumpster. But the mouse never comes.

******

5048 ==> The most important God talking to the news media, looked at all the boxes of gifts piled up. He said, "These are all undelivered because the people lost faith in me before the day of delivery."

Just then, a truck driver in overalls comes close and speaks to God, "We have another load of gift boxes from the Southern Church's charity drive. Where do you want the boxes stacked?"

******

5049 ==> I am stepping out the door of my home. I am boldly going forth to find myself.

******

5050 ==> To maintain reasonable success physically, mentally, and financially, one should not let the body wander too far from the spiritual side of life.

To flip the story, we should also keep our spirit at home in our body.

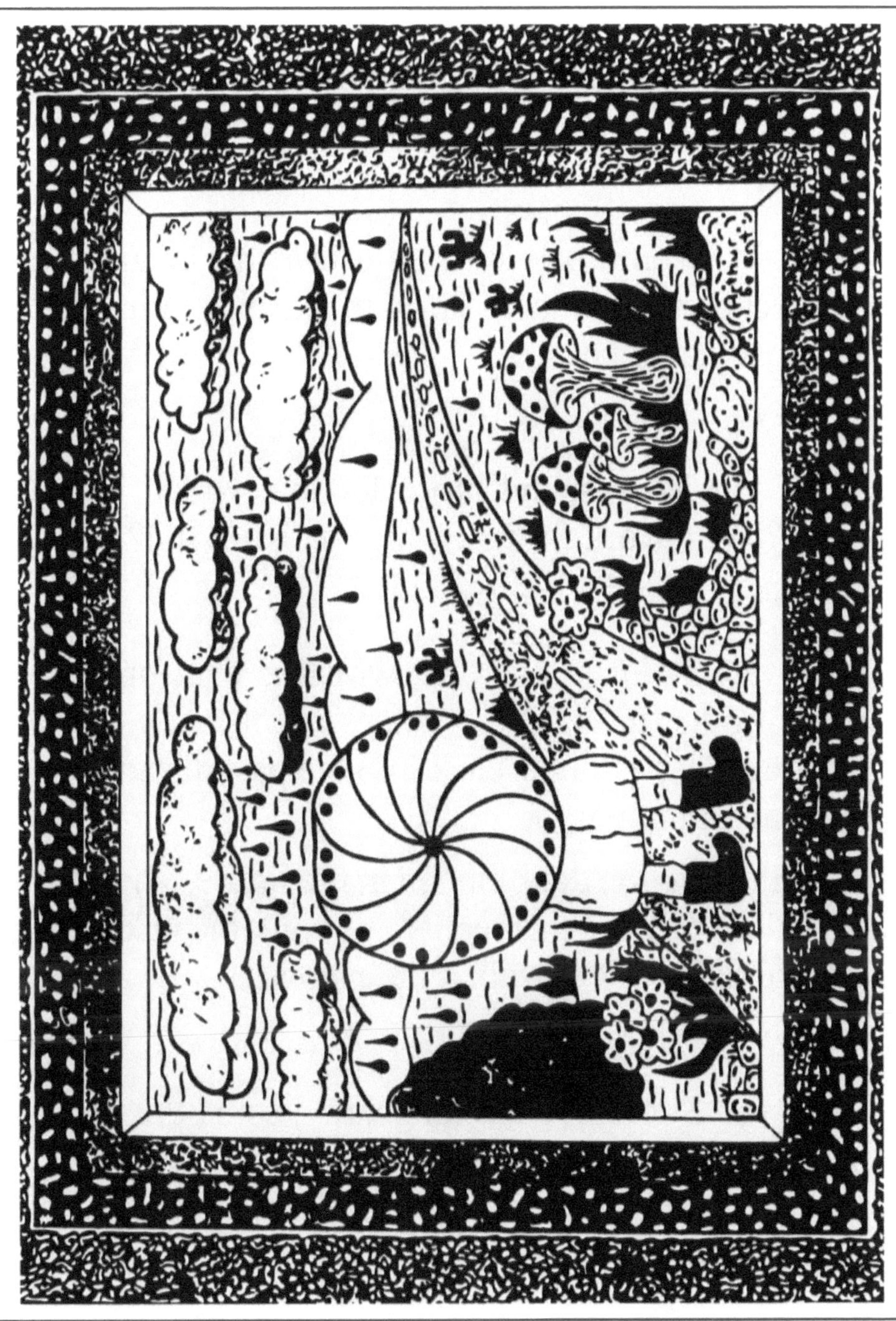

******

5051 ==> Like a leaf falling from a tree, we all one day fade away, no longer seen or remembered.

******

5052 ==> Some people should learn to laugh in a more cheerful manner. They make one think that someone had died.

******

5053 ==> Why spend more for that which is not bread? Why work for that which satisfies not?

******

5054 ==> Point to our end, which is ever present, watching to step into the act. We look back at the footsteps that echo far back into the past distance on the road of memory.

Point to the door hidden in the future. The door by which we leave this reality and enter the unknown beyond. Dare we to walk a little slower?

******

5055 ==> Some live the long story, some the short. Some are exciting page after page, while others drag on, never quite coming to any interesting events.

******

5056 ==> Those bad stories about others are, for the most part, made up by people who would themselves have been doing these bad things.

******

5057 ==> The amount of the same reason, which we total as a just estimate of the universal fears of witches in old times, is rooted in imaginations suitable for scaring the grown-up adults. They actually believed that some people had the power to do paranormal mischief. To counter these delusional fears and group insanity, they tortured with great demonic enjoyment the poor victims accused.

Thus, they turned religion into a mindset of insane mental delusions.

******

5058 ==> The ghost stepped out of the book and looked around the room.

The reader had fallen asleep, and the book lay open on the floor.

******

5059 ==> The longest journey always starts with the first step.

******

5060 ==> She showed up at my door one afternoon with a small suitcase and an old-style backpack, somewhat too large and clumsy. Too much luggage for sure. She was average everywhere, looks, shape, etc. A typical picture of the young drug delusion of the 1960's, "Hippy Chick."

She says, "I have nowhere to call home now. Do you remember me? We met a year ago at the National Festival. You gave me your address and said to visit if I pass by. So here I am."

I had never seen this creature before but I let her in my home. A month later I got her a part-time job at a local cleaning service for whom she cleans offices in high-rise buildings. She took to the job readily enough. It gave her some money.

Now, twenty years later, she still runs off to her job and puts her paycheck in the bank. While I buy the food and provide the shelter. Such a simple mind. She has only two interests, her job and me. She doesn't even seem to care that her bank account could buy up everything I own and have some left over.

The little tramp owns me now. I would have gotten rid of her long ago, but she is such a good cook.

******

5061 ==> Birds sing after a storm, but humans don't seem to be so joyful.

******

5062 ==> A poor person who is unhappy is in a better position than a rich person who is unhappy because the poor person can always hope that money would help.

******

5063 ==> We should be very concerned about the future because we will be spending most of our lives there.

******

5064 ==> The flags make war on each other for dominance and corruption profits. Within each flag, there are ongoing disputes and constant underlying strife, political intrigues, backstabbing, robbery, and deaths. The routine order of the day pulls time along. The political cheese greed and thrive in the stink of corruption.

Before we bring the spaceships down to change the game, we would be wise to have a replacement plan ready. But who wants the game to change?

******

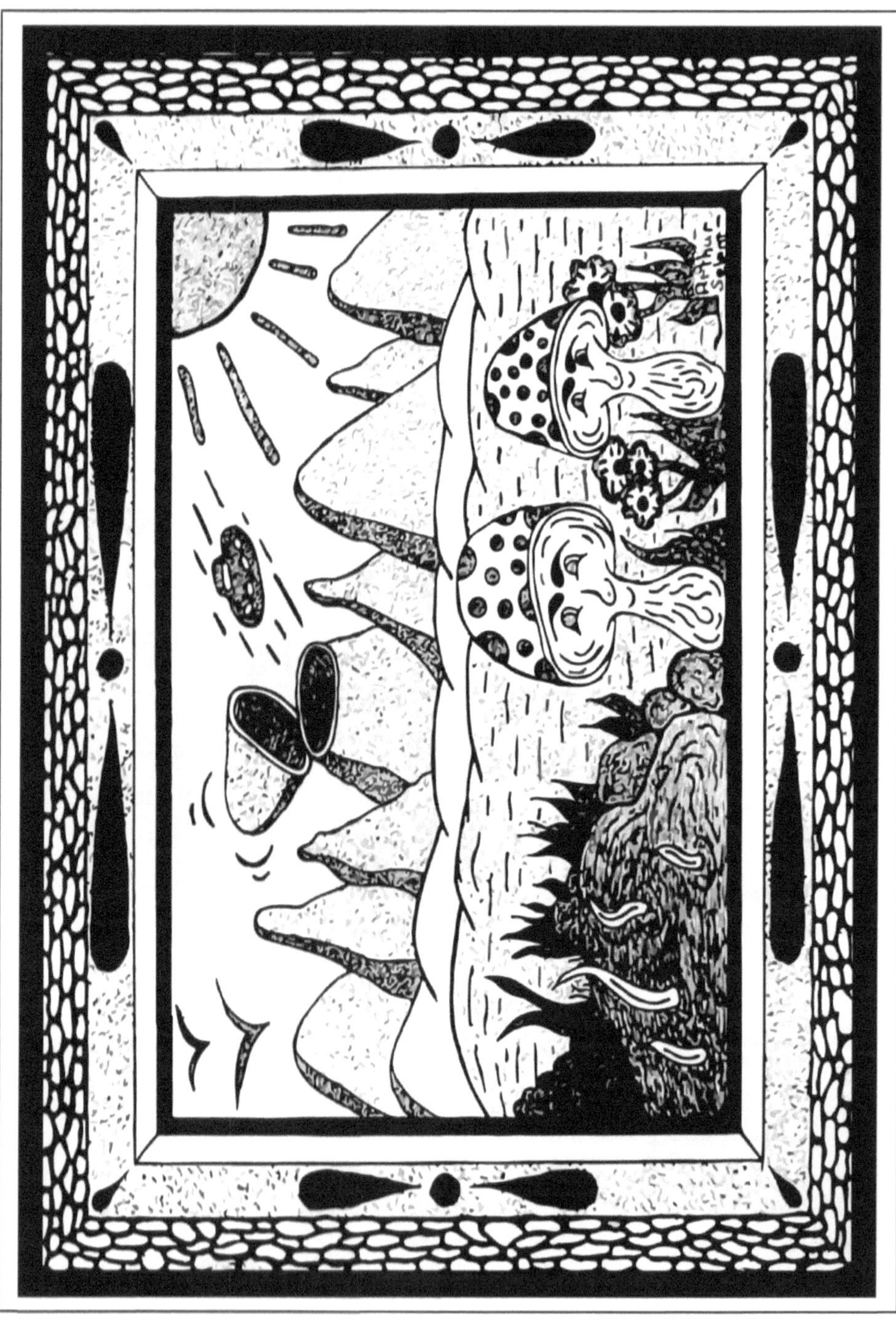

5065 ==> Can you imagine the nervous disgust when the infamous secret they keep from young girls gets found out?

******

5066 ==> Many who are open-minded are so only because they have few holes in their head.

******

5067 ==> Looking down from the mountain top of his ignorance, he hated all the idiots of the planet. He boasted, puffed himself up, and was full of disdain for everyone. He had no greater pleasure than the tavern and night street women. His inflated ignorance gave him ego superiority as he sought to be little all.

******

5068 ==> If you want to confuse the project and get nothing done, then get a committee to work on the situation.

******

5069 ==> A photo snoop is a person with a camera who sneaks about trying to get the picture that will make them sensational heroes when they show off the photo.

******

5070 ==> We must choose our tribe based not on wealth nor family but rather on ability and moral integrity.

******

5071 ==> A flag is at its weakest when the people have no confidence in the government.

******

5072 ==> Humans can do what God cannot do. That is, change the past, rewrite history as a presentation of fiction depending on their imagination delusions or where they wish to direct their emotions for hate and conflict. Or which monster they wish to market as the great hero.

******

5073 ==> Knowledge in the wrong hands is a very dangerous thing.

******

5074 ==> Please excuse my grand mental condition. This was caused by working overtime on the romance production line.

******

5075 (1/2) ==> Anyone who can buy a farm or land is fortunate to be able to grow some kind of food. The long cold dark days of winter have no pity for mere humans.

5075 (2/2) ==> The hardships for food supply demands are starting. The human population doubles every forty years. The big chemical farms will not be able to keep up, no matter how good their chemical growth stimulants are.

Climate change and virus experiments are crimes against humanity that will bring about much anger and destruction. Governments are more motivated to spend insanely on the military people people-killing industry, and weapons industry than they are on the food growing industry. Corruption always takes the fast, sneaky way to skim off percentages of money movement, and military and weapons are secret.

You don't want to be in the corrupt city when the bombs fall, when the roads are closed, and the military takes food shipments and gas. You don't want to live in high population areas when fear, extortion, greed profits conduct virus experiments on the people.

******

5076 ==> Pretty little alien green people are interested in you. They have been sneaking about asking questions. "What did you do?"

******

5077 ==> There will be times of great trouble and hardships. Those who put their trust and faith in the spirit will find conditions somehow and some way to be thankful for reaching another day into the future.

Pulling on time as if pulling on a rope to reach safety.

******

5078 ==> Those who are not very good in their thoughts must one day meet themselves in things that come to their experience.

******

5079 ==> They caught two people who were politically active against the established corruption. The body snatchers drove gleefully with much joy. There will be a bonus paid for this job. The van drove across town to a large warehouse, the doors opened, and the van drove inside.

******

5080 ==> People often begrudge others for that which they cannot enjoy themselves.

******

5081 (1/2) ==> Ad seen in the, "Get Laid," magazine. No woman was ever created so faithful that she could not be seduced.

5081 (2/2) ==> Sooner or later, she will be overcome with the lure of seducing some stranger she will never see again.

An hour of secrets spices up a fantasy desire and boring routine.

******

5082 ==> How often do things go wrong just when we are assured of success?

******

5083 ==> It became a morning ritual. We'd all huddle around the radio like we were a bunch of underground freedom fighter movement awaiting instructions. The weather forecast would finish and we'd all scatter.

******

5084 ==> It is amazing what can be done if one has patience and determination.

******

5085 ==> When Daddy's little baby suddenly becomes Mother's little baby then that is when the little monster has just shit or pissed their diaper.

******

5086 ==> A girl watcher was tabulating the many little luncheon cafes where women seemed to mass migrate to. His beany brain was rolling marbles and cooking cabbage. He invented his history and started going café to café. Always sitting close to the women in hopes of joining the conversation.

Like a big game hunter, he made his move. But she did want him.

******

5087 ==> I wonder how long I would be able to tolerate being a house pet belonging to some rich woman?

******

5088 ==> So much for the hip exercise. No one can fake it. Watch the mirror as a good slap on the bum sagging meat makes the goods quiver. Is your body ready for a bikini this summer? Ready to be the hot beach bunny that all the guys want to copulate with?

******

5089 (1/2) ==> Her innocent beauty was a subtle poison to his well-being. He fancied her with an inner madness of lust and passion. He shivered with weird feelings thinking what their off spring would look like. The fever of his mental condition drove him on. He watched and knew her routines better than he knew his own.

5089 (2/2) ==> He always tried to be near her. He hoped to start a conversation, but always before he said anything, she walked away. The throbbing in his mind was driving him to insane fantasy, night after night of masturbation.

He fumbled about wildly from his inner world back to the real world. Like a criminal, he hid his secret obsession.

Then, one late summer evening after dark had settled in, he seized her as she was unlocking the house side door leading to her room. She did not fight. She did not scream. Like a demonic monster, he ravaged her to his final complete exhaustion.

When he finished, she laughed and said, "What took you so long?

You could have done this months ago?"

She pushed him off, stood up and opened her door. Turning back she said to him, "You going home or you coming inside."

Suddenly he took a dislike to her. She was acting like a slut, an easy prostitute. His hot virgin fantasy was over, a disgusting dirty feeling took over. He had to escape. He ran home back to his mother's warm safe house.

******

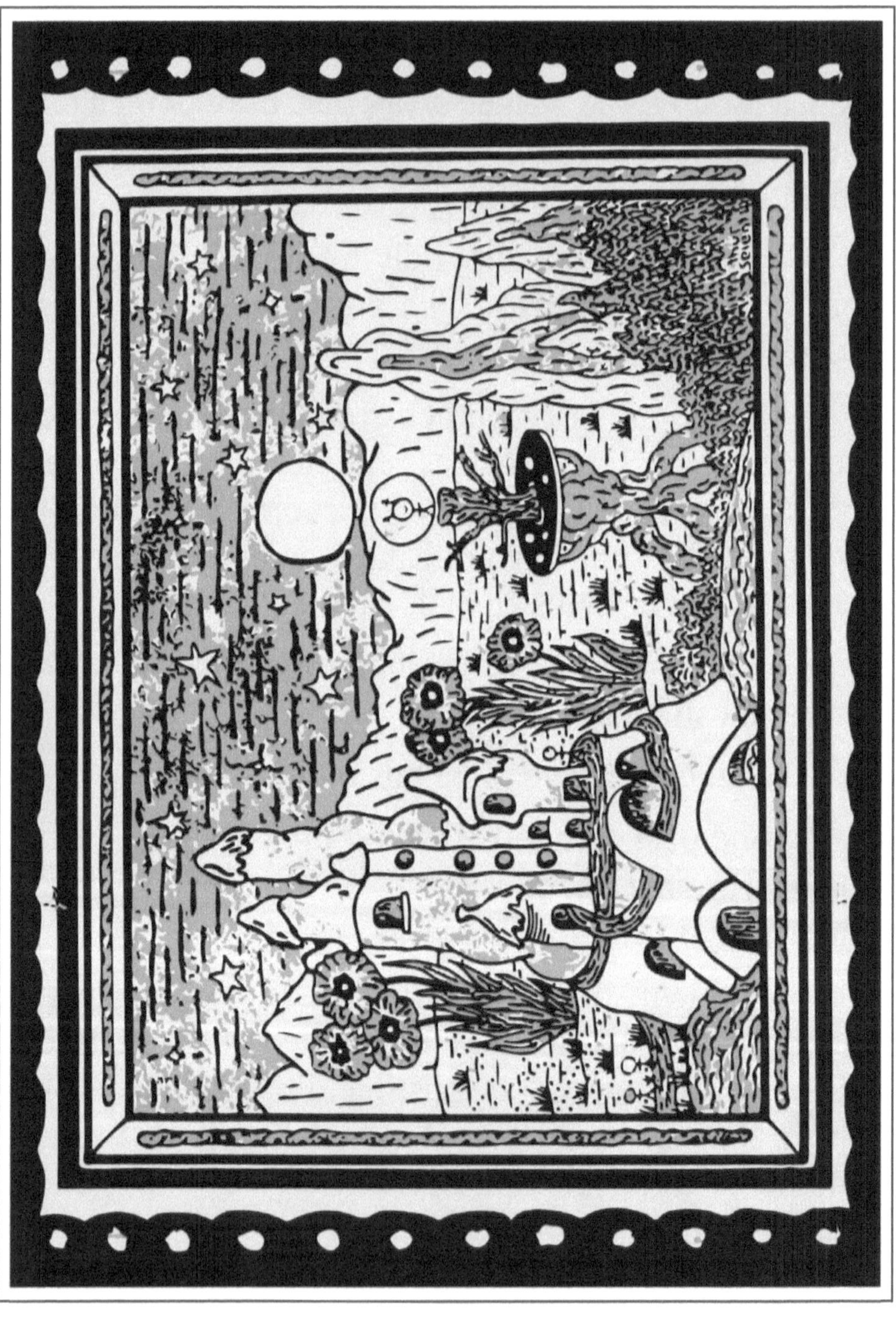

5090 ==> Certain people seem motivated to play with and deceive others. With much suppleness of mind, astuteness, and audacity of thought, they calculate their words and actions.

******

5091 ==> We tend not to comprehend anything beneath us in a variety of subtleties. We divine our own images to divine what we think, what we judge, what we believe, and what we think not to mention what we suspect.

We really are ingenious.

******

5092 (1/2) ==> She'd been looking for just the right man for years, but never could succeed in finding perfection. Each man had something that she could not tolerate.

She was in much despair and turmoil. She was getting old.

So it was when, one afternoon, a nutmeg salesman knocked on her door. He started his sales pitch. She said, "Just a minute, I have to shut the stove off." She left the door open and rushed back inside.

5092 (2/2) ==> She grabbed a woolly blanket, her purse, and stuffed a clean underwear and a pair of clean socks into her purse. Back at the door, she says to the salesman, "You'll do". She closed the door and led him down the garden path as he mumbled his sales talk.

There in the garden shed, sitting on a camping bed, she explained to him his new reality and made him sign on the dotted line. So the nutmeg salesman became domesticated, having a home-cooked supper every night.

✷✷✷✷✷✷

5093 (1/2) ==> The young girl of about 15 looked more like 17. She was rather good-looking in that fresh-faced firmness of a youthful way. But she dressed like a shopping mall sleaze, her mini skirt a little too mini.

With her old, decrepit grandfather, she went to the library. They were quite fond of each other. With little girl innocence, she often put her arm around him to steady his small steps, shuffling along.

They found a table in a remote corner. She scurried about looking for a few picture books. He sat at the table, thankful for the rest. She asked a library attendant which book might be entertaining.

5093 (2/2) ==> Attendant, "Sex with a Senior Citizen, but it is loaned out today. It is very popular among young ladies seeking education. It has very graphic photos of how to do it."

******

5094 ==> Youth is a great habit of ours but seems to always fade away just when we advance enough to start understanding it.

******

5095 ==> Some think there is nothing more amusing than to play a joke on someone. To have a laugh at others surprise and frustrations. Some jokes are merely a trivial thing. Some jokes are very bad and someone gets hurt or dies.

Some jokes go far beyond being nice.

******

5096 ==> He cooked his brain, rolled his marbles and cooked his flowers. Walking back along memory roads to recall all the jokes he'd ever played on others. Using his vast experience to guess what might be in store for him. He was not going to be caught. No, not he.

Oh, if only he knew. There are many strange mental things much too easily picked up.

******

5097 ==> The most delusional woman can manage a clever man but it takes a really clever woman to manage a fool.

******

5098 ==> Two spinster nuns on their way to an overseas jungle missionary camp rented a hotel room for the night. They forgot to lock the door and were awoken by someone searching for something.

Under the covers, one whispers, "I think there is a man in the room."

The other replies, "How exciting. I want him first. You help me hold him so he doesn't run away until we are done. He's not going to talk about it later. It's been three years since I had a man."

******

5099 ==> The rich tell us how wonderful hard work is. Then why don't they do hard work themselves?

******

5100 ==> A smart conversation maker is one who talks to you about yourself.

******

5101 ==> Travel has become an industry of sitting down. Sit in the airplane, bus, taxi, boat, train, or ear, all sitting down while racing away over vast distances.

* * * * * *

5102 ==> We are confronted with signposts at every turn of the path. But we have no place to go and know not which sign to follow.

* * * * * *

5103 ==> Many of us are illegal adults.

* * * * * *

5104 ==> Most of us really should do something to make our day important.

* * * * * *

5105 ==> How many engineers does it take to change a light bulb?

Four, one to hold the light bulb, two to turn the ladder and one to supervise.

* * * * * *

5106 (1/2) ==> The old man was rather pleased with himself in getting a young lady into his bed now and then.

One night after he finished his romantic exercise and lay there limp and soft beside her, he says, "Oh, honey, bunny, I want you to be my wife."

5106 (2/2) ==> She shudders at the thought and says, "I could not do that. I love men and would have to give up my other boyfriends."

******

5107 ==> If the war machine can create an imagined reality saying honest, hard-working people in foreign lands are enemies, then what can we create with our mental delusions?

A storyteller creates an imagined reality that billions suddenly envision as being true. Religions say those other storytellers are all fraud.

So you see, the mind less human, is in dire straits, needing someone to invent an imagined reality in which mental state the human can live and deceive itself.

******

5108 ==> We must make do with what comes our way.

******

5109 ==> The rich wife called the maid in for a talk. She said, "I think my husband is copulating with his office assistant. She's a floosey but likes to call herself a secretary."

Maid replies, "You shock me. He told me, I was his only one."

******

5110 ==> There are too many strange mental conditions, much too easily picked up.

******

5111 ==> The digital world has come along and pulled me into its deep vagina. I, an old man who spent his life in paper and ink is now confused and difficult to retrain into a world of screens and keys to click.

Now what you going to do when no electricity for months. You do not know the wonderful world of paper and ink.

It is too complicated. We are due for things to go wrong one day.

******

5112 ==> The devil has some of the best stories. After all he personally knows the most suspense characters, rascals, scoundrels, and bad guys. The doings of the crook are always more exciting than the routines of the good folks.

******

5113 (1/2) ==> The farmer had a talk with the new hired helper. He says, "I notice you been sneaking off to the hay loft with my daughter. Are your intentions honorable or dishonorable?"

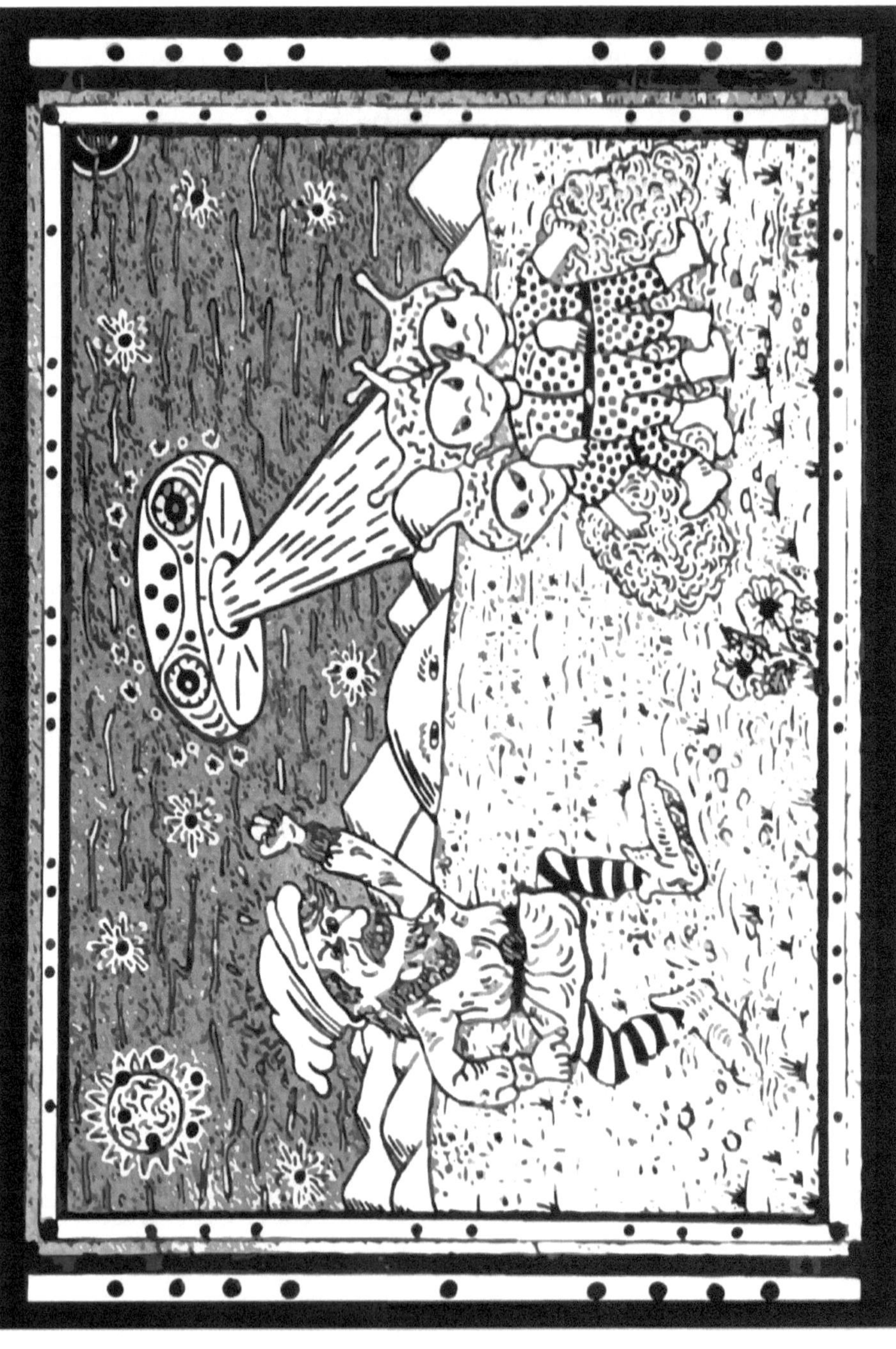

5113 (2/2) ==> Hired helper, "You mean I have a choice?"

******

5114 (1/2) ==> An uneducated farm woman living in a very remote corner of the map had as her only driving experience the trip to the village store once a week. She did this with her clattering tin can on wheels along a narrow muddy bumpy road.

Then one day she got a letter from some big shot lawyer on the coast a thousand lengths away. The lawyer informed her that a long-lost relative had died and put her in his will. She was asked to present herself for the will reading and to transfer her inheritance to herself.

It would mean a three-day drive. She put abundant blankets in the back seat. Also a box of food, a big jug of water, filled the fuel tank and was clattering down the road.

After a bit the road came to a wide paved road with a sign HWY 145. She checked the map. Yes she was on the right direction. She speeded up, her tin can straining at the effort. Faster than she had ever driven before she in a state of nervous panic drove on. Previous she had never driven above 30.

5114 (2/2) ==> A car flashing blue and red lights came up behind her blaring a loud siren. She had the luck to meet a crazy man. She speeded up but her tin can could do no more and the crazy car was too powerful. She slowed down but he did not pass. He drove up beside her and motioned for her to stop.

She was frustrated. This idiot didn't know who he was dealing with. One punch on the nose and he'll soon straighten himself flat on the road.

The crazy man came up to her rolled down window before she could get out. He claimed to be a policeman and flashed all his cereal box tin medals badges. He asked, "Why are you driving so fast?"

She replies, "The sign back there said, HWY 145 so I assume that is the speed limit."

Policeman, "Glad, I stopped you before you got to HWY 401."

******

5115 ==> How many carpenters bite their nails?

******

5116 (1/2) ==> From start to finish, too many workers along the way only means someone is sitting down or standing about doing nothing but wait for the work shift to finish. Certainly not fair for the other workers.

5116 (2/2) ==> However, once a union is created into the game then the time share equal opportunity reality comes into being. Instead of one or two doing nothing all day the situation changes into each worker having one hour of doing nothing.

******

5117 ==> We do what we do to get by although many a time we wish we had something else to do.

******

5118 ==> The depraved old man had a fight with his wife and went for a walk outside of the house to clear his thoughts. He wandered the shopping streets and saw a young lady looking at one of the store window displays, she was wearing a mini skirt a little too mini.

He says hello as he passes her and smiles when she turns to look at him. She smiles and says nice things about the weather.

Encouraged, he says, "If I say you have a beautiful body, would you hold it against me?"

******

5119 (1/2) ==> The doorbell seemed to echo too long, like a church bell and a drunk priest. His imagination roamed, who could be this be? The wind thrown rain slapped off the roof tops. The thunder cracked and ripped the sky tumbling from one direction to another.

5119 (2/2) ==> He opened the door to the dark night. The moon peeked through a small hole in the storm clouds, then closed the curtains and hid.

She stood there dripping wet, shivering and her clothes ripped to rags. Her arms covered in scratches. She said, "I've run away from home and was camping in some shrubs when a bunch of drunk men came by and wanted to take turns on me. I fought and escaped. They were too drunk and clumsy to catch me once I got a few steps away. May I hide in your place until the storm passes?"

He let her in, got some warm blankets, told her to undress and then wrapped the blankets around her. Now ten years later there she is still hiding in his place waiting for the storm to pass. Like old married people they sit on the back porch in the evening.

******

5120 (1/2) ==> The tourist exploring the town for the benefit of his curiosity began to feel a hunger brought on by the exercise of his walk. He saw a run-down, decrepit restaurant with big, greasy windows looking out onto the sidewalk.

He entered and took a window seat to leisurely watch foggy images through the dirt of street actions. The floor didn't seem too clean. The place was a disaster cave, it had the air of an abandoned house long used by tramps.

5120 (2/2) ==> There were only two other folks at a table. They were two middle-aged romantics dressed in fake store-bought beatnik fashions. They were very busy aggressively eating their meal. If those two could eat like that then food must be fairly good, he thought. So he waited for the waitress.

She stepped out of the kitchen door, smoothing down her apron skirt. As if she had been catching spiders in her underwear.

She gave him the menu and said their soup special was the best in the land. He order the soup and other eats.

The soup arrived and he dipped his spoon in stirring. A big ugly fly was floating on top. He yelled and the waitress came running.

She said, "Well done, we have been trying to catch that fly all day and you, a complete stranger did it on your first try." She spooned the fly out of the soup and flicked it onto the floor. Then she went back to hide in the kitchen.

He got up and left, counting six dead fly on the floor before he got to the exit door.

******

5121 (1/2) ==> The mother yell up the stairs, "Is your brother up there?"

5121 (2/2) ==> The son from his bedroom replies, "No, I am up here alone playing with myself."

Mother, "You dirty boy, make sure you wash your hands before you come down for dinner."

******

5122 ==> For many of us, inflation is not a problem because we don't have any money.

******

5123 ==> They parked in a lonely part of the dark lover's road. They were copulating with much passion when a police car pulled up. He asked them what they were doing.

The young couple was in great fear. They had borrowed the family car sort of sneaky-like. The guy says, "We were just petting."

Policeman, "Then put your pet back inside your pants and get out of here. We've had six muggings and two rapes here last night."

The young fellow says to his girl, "That was the best rape fantasy we've ever had. Even a real policeman showed up."

******

5124 (1/2) ==> The workers at the factory sat in the lunch room, chewing on their lunches. Suddenly, one guy starts to laugh. The fellow sitting beside him asks what is so funny.

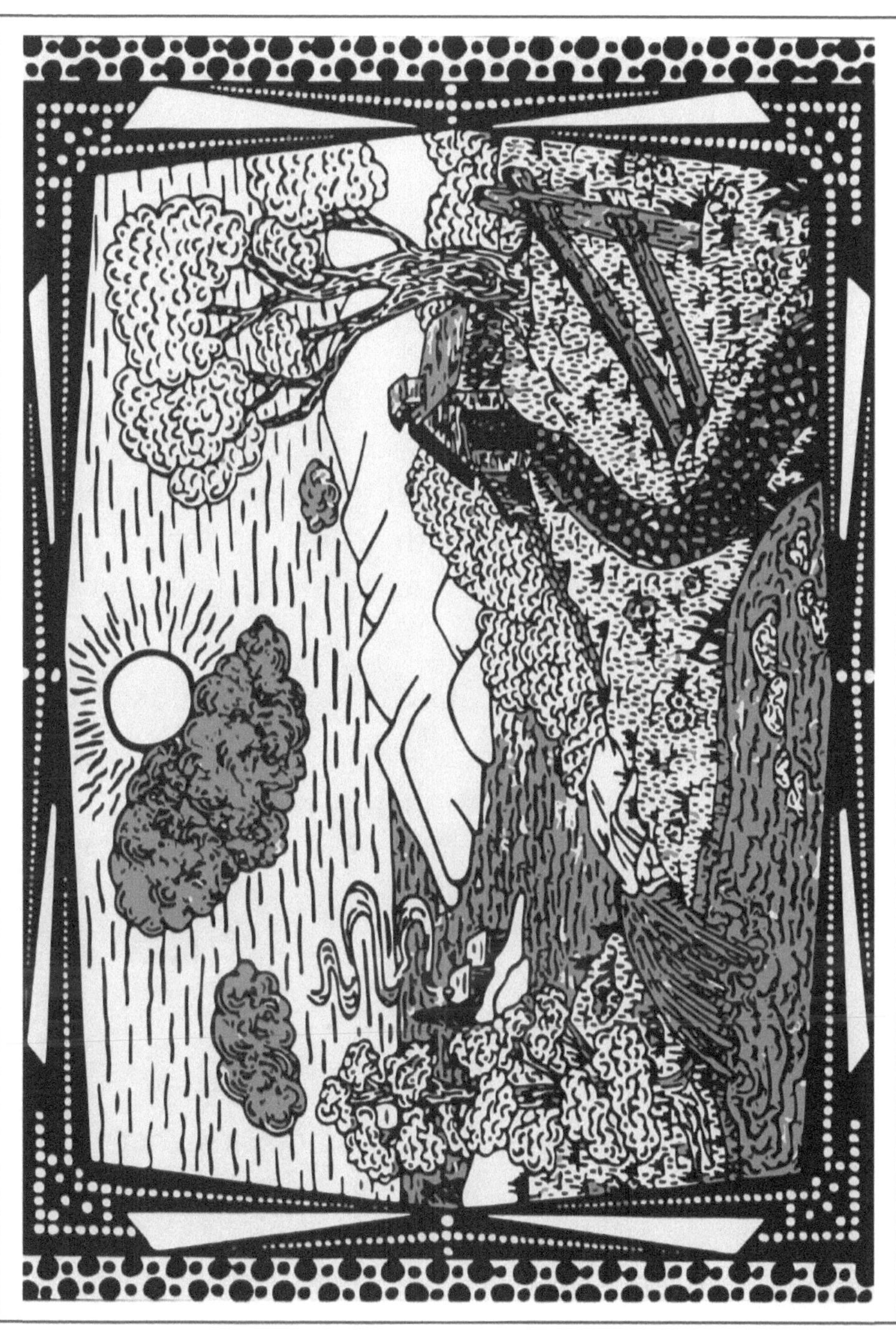

5124 (2/2) ==> "I was just thinking about my wife. The boss pays her every time he has sex with her, and I get to do it for free."

******

5125 ==> A drunk on unsteady feet, being well-pickled and tipsy, suffered much in the summer heat. Passing the church, he noticed the doors open and people walking inside. The priest stood at the door, shaking hands now and then.

The drunk was not religious but thought it would be nice to get out of the sunshine for a while. He stepped up to the door, hiding his bottle under his shirt.

The priest asks what he is hiding. Drunk, "It is holy water to keep the devil away."

The priest reached inside the drunk's shirt before the drunk could react. "This is not holy water, it is wine."

Drunk, "Why, that is a miracle. Holy water turned into wine at God's door."

******

5126 (1/2) ==> The young school teacher was having a few drinks with an older woman in management at the school social night. She was telling how one of the old professors had got her alone one day in the storage room.

5126 (2/2) ==> He had asked for sex saying he could satisfy her beyond her wildest fantasy or he would die trying.

The older woman, is silent a moment then asks, "Where will they bury him?"

******

5127 ==> The wife had invited the priest over for Saturday afternoon tea not realizing that her husband had invited his work buddies over to watch the big sports game on TV.

The priest arrived first while the husband had run to the beer store. She explained that they would have to have tea upstairs because the living room would be too crowded and noisy. She got the tea and cookies on a tray and they went upstairs to the bed room.

The husband returns with a massive load of beer cans. His buddies arrive one by one and they all sit in front of the TV, yelling at the various sport game situations. As they become quite drunk the husband yells upstairs to the wife, "When is the priest coming?"

Wife, "I don't know, he's breathing heavy and moaning a lot right now. He must be close to coming."

******

5128 ==> One of the hazards of self-improvement is that we too often take the task too seriously and attempt to improve others more than ourselves.

******

5129 ==> The young girl fresh out of school applied at the government office for a job. The official asks, "Do you have any religious views?"

She replies, "No, but I have some nice photos of mountains and scenery."

******

5130 ==> An elderly farmer whose wife had died a few years before started getting lonely at night. He went to a dating service. They had him fill out a paper with questions. One asks, "How long at present address?"

He wrote, "Same as at previous address, six inches."

******

5131 ==> Bad publicity is still publicity. It is better to have people talking about you than not talking. Many people have a tender secret loving soft spot for bad rascals.

******

5132 ==> But what human lives long enough to benefit by their faults? Repeating faults all life-long until at last death finds them much improved.

******

5133 ==> That drive to apply for a job was pleasant through pastoral farm lands to the distant big city industrial area. It was the beginning of the end.

There in the factory, the decades flew by. Every day the same routine. Over the years he saved and saved investing here and there now and then. Slowly his fortune increased while he punched the factory clock each morning and again punched the time card each afternoon. By most standards it was a boring life but he found joy in the simple unstressed routine.

Then one day the factory shutdown and the job was no more.

The drive back to the small home stead was pleasant. The home stead had been abandoned and neglected after his parents died. He'd thought of selling it but never got around to it.

He set to work. In the barn he installed a time clock. Each day he punches the clock, works eight hours and then goes home to the house.

The routine established over a life time carried forward. It was the end to the beginning.

******

5134 ==> Untested witch doctor bio-cure for tired feet that also helps a heavy head disturbance and mental unbalance.

Save all your used coffee grounds. Or go to a café and asks for their used coffee grounds, bring a pail or large container, even a wheelbarrow to hold the grounds.

Put these grounds in a tub, add hot water and wash feet, firmly rubbing all parts, even between the toes and higher up towards the knees.

When finished the used coffee grounds can be spread over a lawn or around garden plants for an organic fertilizer.

If the cafe gives you their used coffee grounds you can make a coffee drink. Use more grounds and run the hot water through twice. Enjoy your coffee while your feet soak.

******

5135 ==> You quickly find our who your friends are when you have to beg for food.

However even a friend can take only so much drain on their resources before you have become a pest.

******

5136 ==> An old bush dweller born and raised so far from civilization that his village was not even shown on any maps, decided to see the nearby city sixteen hours' drive from home. A missionary group had discovered the village. They gave him a ride and said they'd give him a ride back next weekend.

He wandered the streets amazed at the cars, buses, people and tall buildings. He wondered what the people ate since he didn't see any place suitable for growing vegetables. The noise, the lights, just like living in an ant colony.

He walked into a high-rise apartment building which had their front door open. He stood facing an elevator with hallways to his left and right lined with doors.

As he stood there, a very old haggard woman all bent over shuffles up and does something on a wall panel with buttons. The elevator door opens, she shuffles inside and doors close. He'd never seen electronic sliding doors before. Soon a the doors slid open and a beautiful young lady steps out.

The old fossil thinks, "I should have brought my wife, make her young again."

******

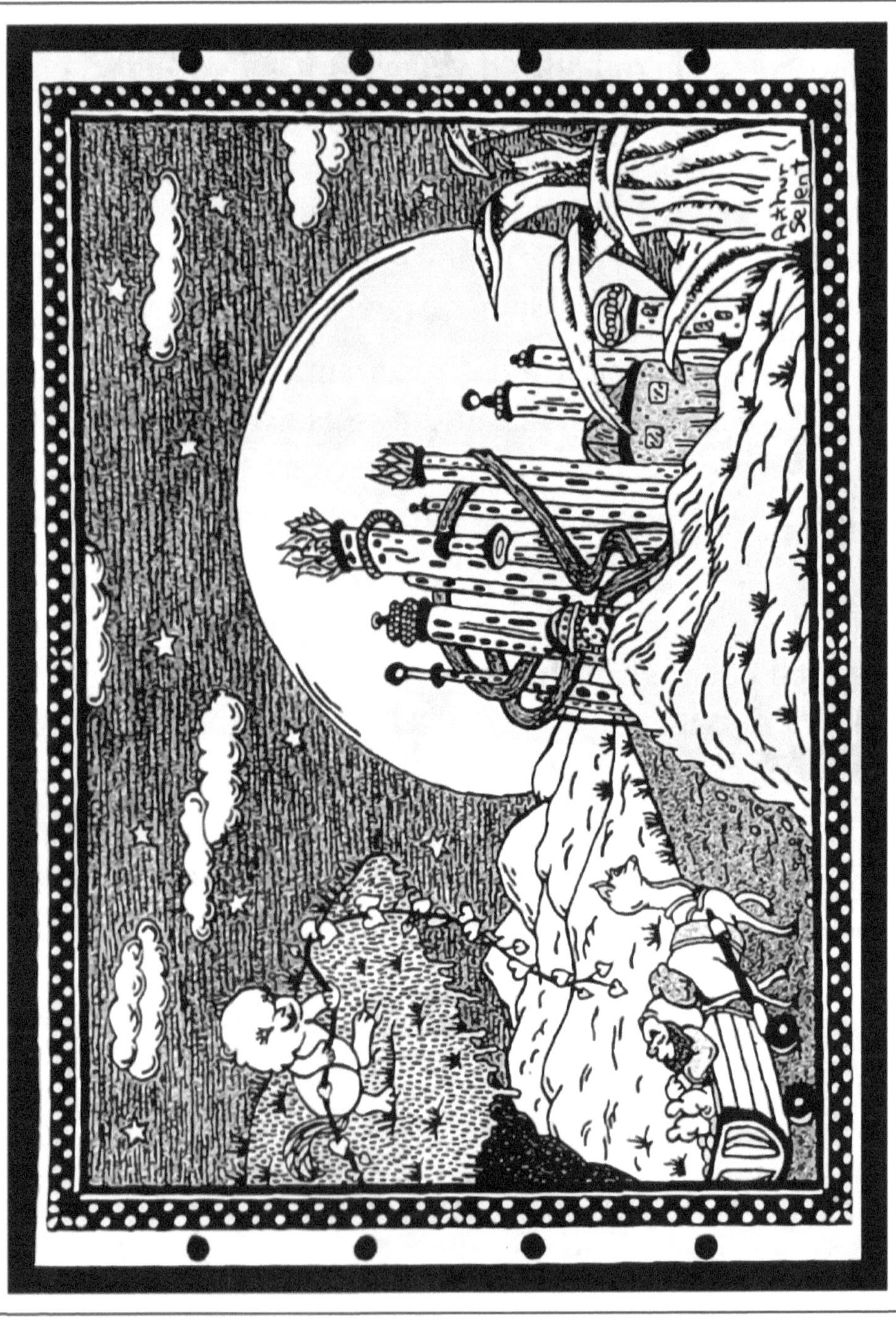

5137 ==> A city fellow during hard times took a job at a horse-riding resort. His job was simple, just clean up after the tourists. One day another worker was sick and he was asked to do his job. He was asked to saddle a horse for rider rental.

One of the other stable workers says, "You are putting the saddle on backwards."

The city fellow thinking he was being made a joke of, defended himself. "How can you say such things? You don't even know what direction they will be going."

******

5138 ==> At the bus stop there were three people huddled under a small umbrella. Why did none of them get wet? Because it was not raining, they were trying to get some shade.

******

5139 (1/2) ==> The rich woman living all her life in city high-rise apartments decided to gather up her investments and retire to the country. She got a farmhouse and some land.

A week later she walks into local garden store and wants to buy some bird seeds.

Clerk, "How many birds do you have?"

5139 (2/2) ==> "None, I want to grow some. Do you have seeds for yellow song birds?"

******

5140 ==> The homeless woman who had not washed in over three centuries was finally becoming upset about searching for food in the garbage every day. She saw on the streets at night all various types of women waving to cars and selling sex. It had been years since she'd had sex.

She thought she'd try it one or two nights a week. She went about the streets doing copycat motions the other women used to lure business.

A middle-aged soft man picked her up. The car was cluttered with wife and baby stuff. He says, "What is that strong smell?"

She replies, "My new perfume, it is called Vagina Sins. The lady at the beauty counter at the shopping mall said it will drive men crazy with desire. I guess I used a little too much."

******

5141 ==> Finishing school he signed up for the navy. He could get paid while seeing the world.

The navy assigned him to a big submarine. He spent the next ten years living underwater.

******

5142 ==> The herds of people migrated, moved, merged, split, multiplied, died and appeared from every compass point only to disappear in a different compass point. The centuries came and went.

But a person might live their entire life in their valley and never see a stranger or foreigner. The cycle of years never been disturbed on their lands which they knew tree by tree, hill by hill.

New people crossed and recrossed the lands yet some places remain quietly unvisited. Every one starting from nowhere and going nowhere. But some never start and still go nowhere.

******

5143 ==> A fellow that was a little too smart started building a house. His friend same by and asked why he was throwing half the nail away.

"Because the heads are on the wrong end."

"Those are for the other side of the house."

******

5144 ==> I do not pretend to be a great person. How can I? It is difficult enough just to pretend to be me.

******

5145 (1/2) ==> A beautiful fresh firm young teen aged girl went to a spring time camp fire in her parent's gigantic back yard. She got a little drunk and smoked some strong drug. She stumbled wandered into hiding behind some dense shrubs. This was her safe haven, where the summer before she had played. She sat there in a confused hypnotic trance.

Then a guy snuck into the hiding place and put his arm around her. It felt like she knew this guy. It was pitch black night among the shrubs and she could not see who the guy was.

But she was not alone now. With his arm around her she felt loved. She snuggled closer into his grasp. She felt the comfort of his warm. He began to play his hands over her body. Passions and urgers began to awaken.

He had sex with her. In her drugged state she clung to him, she felt loved. She put her heart and soul into pleasing him. After he left, she lay there semi naked until the evening coolness caused her to dress and go to her room in the house.

The weather being warm and dry she feeling rest less and unloved went in the dark evening to her shrub hiding place. The illusion memory of her romantic event wishing a replay of action.

5145 (2/2) ==> To her surprise someone was there. She was on him in the dark before she realized she was not alone. She went to escape but he felt familiar so she just lay there where she'd tumbled. He put his arms around her and once again, like in a dream they had sex with her once again putting her heart and soul into pleasing him.

They met in the shrubs whenever the weather was nice all summer long. She was amazed she did not get pregnant. But she needed to be loved.

So far she did not know who her lover was. It was always too dark. Even moon lit nights seemed to be dark because of clouds.

One day she got a red lipstick and as they were copulating she played with his ears, making them red.

Next morning as she walked past her brother's bedroom, the door was slightly open and there lay her brother with his red ears.

She said nothing. A few nights later it rained and was cold outside. She in the middle of the night quietly got up and went to his room to lay beside him.

******

5146 ==> Our ancient ancestors sitting around campfires, living in animal skin tents, always cold, dirty, hot or wet. Only a few sounds, no language yet invented. They feared the spirits and ghosts that drifted in the night. The whispering, moaning, wailing and shrieking, the lost dead seeking to return and belong.

The days of our ancestors where the most insane crazy one, the shaman or witch doctor was the most power to be feared.

******

5147 ==> The uneducated old farmer went to the city to have a look around. He'd never left his small remote farm village before.

He saw a sign, "Fine for Parking." It certainly was a fine place for parking. He parked his old dirty rusty pick-up truck right under the sign. He went sight-seeing.

Three hours later he returned, his legs tired from all the walking and sightseeing. There was a traffic ticket on his truck window fox illegal parking.

******

5148 ==> I plan to get married as soon as I find a rich lady who can tolerate me.

* * * * * *

5149 ==> How easily harmony of life's existence can be struck out of balance at any moment by the actions of other humans.

* * * * * *

5150 ==> I was in a light bulb as it floated as it floated about the space galaxy. It was too bright so I took the last bus out. Now I ride all night in the dark. When will I find a light not so bright?

The doors open and I enter the light bulb. Once again whisked out to space and other planets in other solar systems.

Big magic. Living inside a light bulb flying about the far reaches of space.

Hmmmm??

He's either crazy or he knows something.

* * * * * *

5151 ==> One must play the cards that come to us, the best we know how. The more we know about the game the better we can decide which moves might have the best probability of increasing our chance to succeed and better our chance to win.

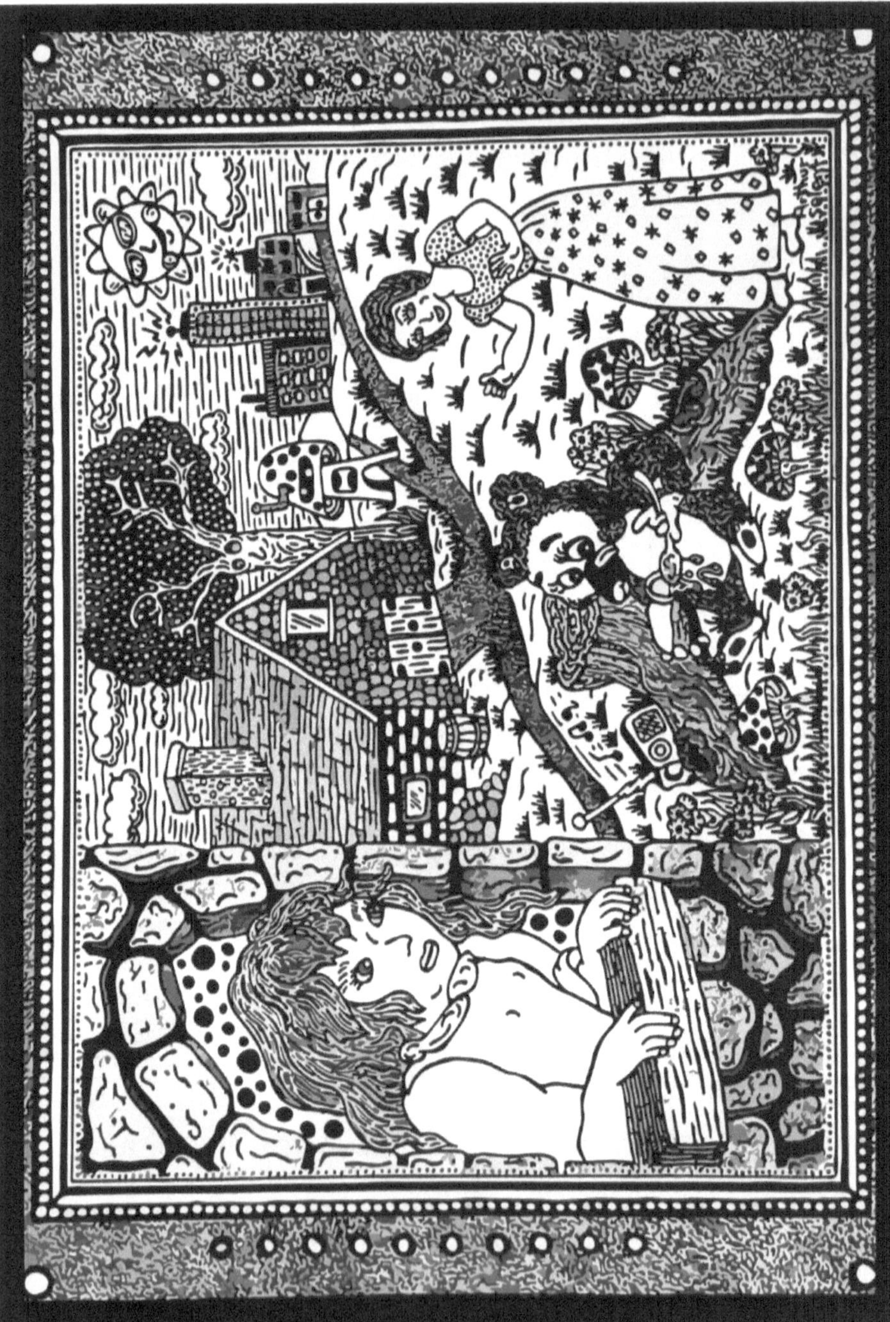

******

5152 ==> The young girl was becoming very interested in boys.

When she went to the library, she saw an impressive massive book laying on a table. The tittle read, "How to Hug." She could not imagine that there were so many different ways to hug that a big book could be filled.

She took the book home and later that night found out she'd taken volume seven of the encyclopedia.

******

5153 ==> When men move to a new city, they are quickly looking over the females abounding about. They seek the grace of bewitching smiles of youthful beguiling bodies. These females' doe eyed with fake innocence running, dancing and prancing with serpentine hypnotic springtime freshness. Every man's fantasy, the seduction.

Then life settles into a routine with very few getting that sneaky secret romance.

******

5154 ==> In the end we all find out that it is better to be rich and happy than being poor and sad.

******

5155 ==> The teacher asked the little children to make up a short story with a moral conclusion. The children made a variety of stories, mostly just repeats of stories heard at church or literature class.

One little rascal-looking kid however, lacking imagination, told a truthful story. "One day my dad was walking in the park and a gang of thugs attacked him. He punched them all on the nose and made their heads fall off. Another time my dad was flying overseas when some terrorists took over the plane. My dad ripped their arms off and threw the terrorists off the plane, but there was a lot of clouds so they had a soft landing."

Teacher, "That is a nice story but what is the moral?"

Kid, "Don't mess with my dad."

******

5156 ==> The mental doctor told the worn out soft middle-aged man, "You should not take your troubles to bed with you."

Man, "That is not possible. My wife refuses to sleep alone."

******

5157 ==> They learned the terror of a storm shouting in their ears and the dread of cold hunger in the bleak, barren winter nights.

They learned the glory of spring dew drops hanging on the branches of morning forests.

Simply by being, they slowly awakened to comprehend the world around them. Living day to day with a belief in personally acquirable magical mental powers. The grand fantasy of spells, curses, and commanding nature with mere thought.

They followed the seasons from the valleys to the hills and from the hills to the valleys. Then one day they learned to garden food. No more chasing hunger and begging ghosts to show where a meal is to be found. Now it is work all day to stockpile food for the cold, bleak, barren winter nights.

******

5158 ==> How many of us stand in front of the mirror for half an hour trying to remember where we have seen ourselves before?

******

5159 (1/2) ==> It was late afternoon, the working people were getting off their jobs and returning home.

5159 (2/2) ==> She stepped out from her modest apartment to go man hunting. She only did this whenever her monthly cycle was infertile. She had a job and did not need extra money but she often pretended that was her motivation. She just liked intimate secrets with different types of men. She strolled along, sometimes waving to a car or looking a man in the eye would smile and try to look encouraging. She was not looking for a ten-minute quickie. She wanted an entire evening romance.

She saw him. He was following her. He was trying not to be seen. He was a fat rubber ball with ornaments hanging from his deformed head and gold flashing teeth. Slowly, he kept up with her.

No way was this her kind of man.

Just then, a car stopped. She had waved to it twice earlier as it drove by. She jumped in and the driver drove on. No one noticed anything.

The fat man, stopped, then turned around going back where he'd come from.

We don't know how the story ends because she disappeared. She was never seen again.

******

5160 (1/2) ==> Think I will write a book, "How to lure women into your arms."

5160 (2/2) ==> But I do not have much experience. Would a few dozen young ladies like to volunteer to help me practice? Sort of pass along their education to me, since my experience is still in the "Grab" mental state.

******

5161 ==> The upper management men all took young women along on out-of-town weekend business meetings. Sometimes a meeting was two weeks long.

One fellow was different; he always brought his extremely ugly wife along. When asked why, he replied, "I cannot bring myself to kiss her goodbye. She holds all the money."

******

5162 ==> A good wine gourmet is one who can sip a glass of wine and tell you not only what year it was bottled but also who pissed on the grapes during harvest.

******

5163 (1/2) ==> Four crude country brothers moved to the big city and decided to share an apartment. All went well for the first month.

5163 (2/2) ==> One day one of the brothers went to the police. He asked them to do something about the toxic smell in his apartment. He explained, one brother had a goat and a pig, another had six cats, and the third had three dogs.

The police chief says, "Have you tried leaving the window open?"

"What? And have all my pigeons and chickens fly away?"

******

5164 ==> He was a soft, round, funny man with a bald head. In summer, the flies bothered him by buzzing around his shiny brain container. He went to a tattoo shop and had them put a spider and a web on his bald head. No more flies.

Now the birds dive to peck at the spider.

******

5165 ==> "God" has become a "brand name" and is marketed through a franchise called religion, which is a program spread through churches. The people giving money to the churches keep the franchise alive. Religion sells an entrance to heaven. Pity those who did not pay the church; they will not be allowed entrance to heaven.

******

5166 ==> The man was from out of town, attending a business meeting at a branch corporation. He went for lunch at a nearby diner. He noticed each item on the menu had a choice of a blue or red plate. The blue plates cost much more.

He asked the waiter why the blue plates cost more when the meal was the same.

Waiter, "Sir, we have to pay a dishwasher to wash the blue plates."

******

5167 ==> Spank the kid often. If you do not know the reason for these punishments, don't worry, the kid knows why it is being spanked.

******

5168 (1/2) ==> The single mother told her little boy that his dad was a big-time gangster. That was why Dad never came home.

The little kid wanted to be like his dad. To see how gangsters behaved, he watched gangster movies on TV and the internet.

Then he found out about the poker game in the back room of the pool hall. He, with his dark sunglasses, came regularly to watch and study the game. On the day he was ready to play, he raided his mother's secret savings stash, intending to return the money from his hoped-for winnings.

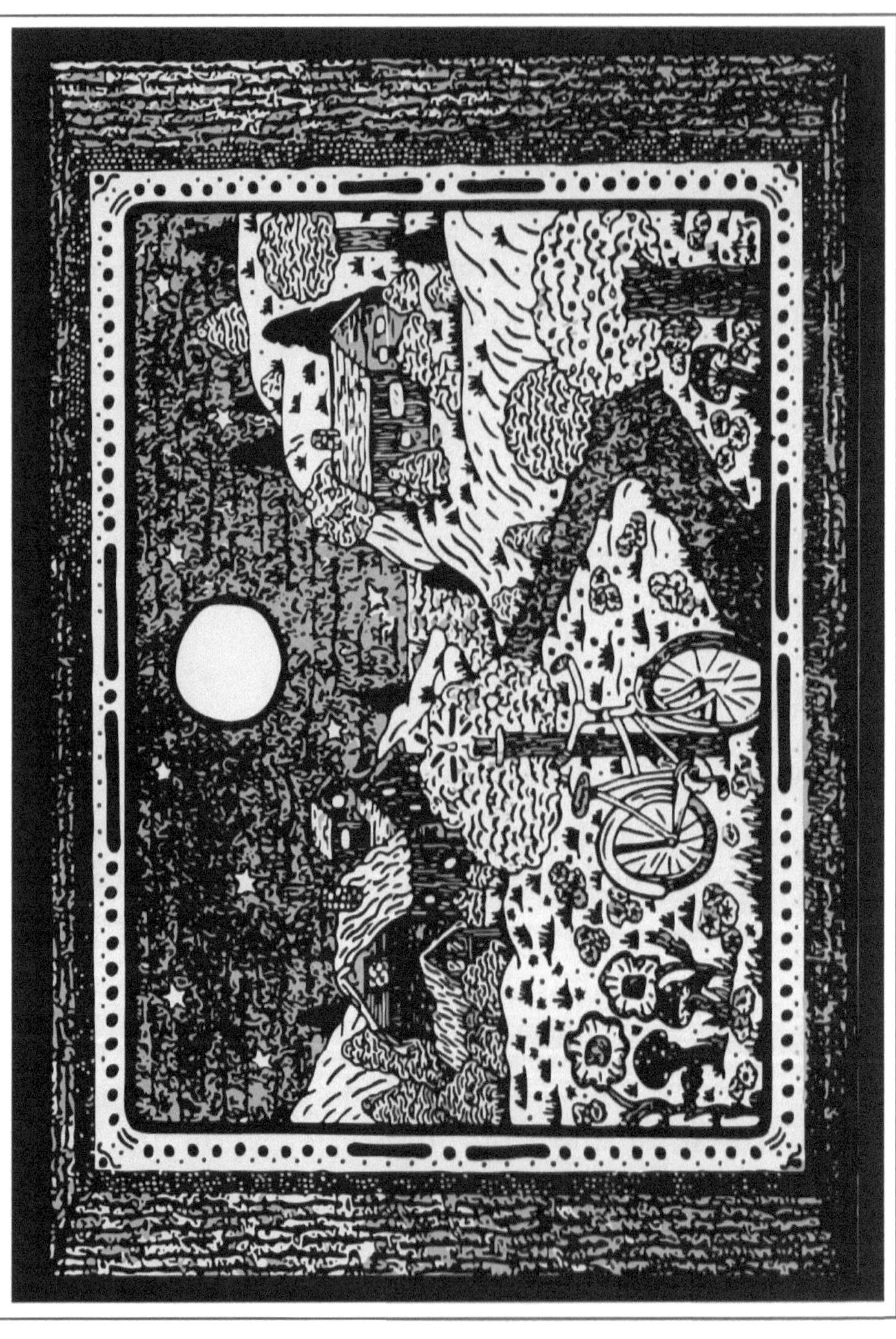

5168 (2/2) ==> A nice-looking looking plump blonde woman was there. She put a fat cigar in his lips and a glass of whiskey on the table. She sits down and lifts him onto her lap. And so he started playing. The cigar and the whiskey tasted terrible but this is what the gangster did so he played along. She made him feel ticklish when she ran her hand here and there as if he was a grown-up romantic flirt.

He placed his bets and was winning. A fellow who has losing said, "why are you not in school?"

Kid, "Because I am not old enough."

******

5169 ==> A fellow going to business school far away decided to go home for the Christmas holidays.

Getting off the train he decides to buy a flower for his girlfriend. There were two flower sellers. One at extreme ends of the crowded train boarding platform.

One seller wanted forty dollars for a flower. He only had three left. Sales had been good that day. So we would assume.

The fellow asks, "Why the flowers so expensive? The fellow at the other end sells his flowers for two dollars each."

Flower seller, "then why don't you buy your flower there?"

"Because he is all sold out"

Flower seller. "Come back in one hour. All my flowers will be sold and I will also lower my price to two dollars a flower."

No one at business school had ever presented this game. He got his meager luggage, a back pack and wandered inside the trin station. On the edge of the eating tables there were a number of potted plants, to give a sense of nature and privacy. There were a variety of blooming flowers in the mix. He pinches one off, no one notices. Business school would be pleased to know he got the deal for free.

******

5170 ==> The fire ring squad marched the prisoner through the pouring rain. The soldiers had umbrellas to keep their guns dry and most of themselves also. They placed the prisoner against the wall.

The prisoner says, "What a terrible day to die."

The soldier, "Lucky for you, you only have to march one way and get carried back but we have to return march in this rain."

******

5171 ==> Dad comes home from work and the little kid says, "Mommy kissed the TV repairman and they went upstairs for an hour."

Dad, "Why does she kiss that bum. We only owe him twenty dollars. She should kiss someone from the electric company. We owe them two thousand dollars."

******

5172 ==> Anyone behind the wheel of a moving car is a potential misguided missile.

******

5173 ==> The relatives went to visit their old, rich grandfather in the hospital. The doctor says, "He's at death's door, but don't worry, we are skilled in our work and feel sure we can push him through."

******

5174 ==> The cute young foolish office helper was fired by the manager's ugly wife. She asked the manager for a letter of recommendation.

He wrote, "To whom it may concern, Lucy was working with our company for six months. I was very much satisfied by her efforts."

******

5175 ==> The prehistoric people of Mexico called Maya, had with the workings of their calendric calculations in used a calendar that was one ten-thousandth of a day per year, more accurate than ours is today.

But they had no electricity or computers. And had not even invented the "wheel" yet.

******

5176 ==> A dangerous, demonic murderer had escaped from jail and was seen moving about in a distant forest. Reports filtered to the law office.

The local sheriff, a soft beef beef-faced sack of sweat and stink, called all the men in the village to the pub for a meeting. All the men who had a gun were given a bottle of whiskey and asked to join the manhunt.

One wimpy hen pecked fellow refused his whiskey bottle. He had an old ball and powder musket that surely took an hour to reload. Asked why he refused the whiskey, he said, "Because it gives me too much courage."

******

5177 (1/2) ==> The education exams were just finishing. The teacher gathered up the exams. She comes to her most unruly rascal and says, "I hope I did not see you peeking at others' papers."

5177 (2/2) ==> Rascal, "With all my heart, I also hope this."

******

5178 ==. The young guys were in police school. The instructor says, "If you are patrolling a lonely dark street and a frightened beauty young, female rushes to you, saying she was ravaged by a man who dragged her behind some shrubs as she walked home from her night shift factory job, what would you do?"

One guy says, "I would calm her and get her to lead me to the shrubs where this happened. I would look about to see if he had dropped something. Then I would ask the young lady to help me re-construct the crime."

******

5179 ==> The pretty teenage wild girl walked into an electronics store, having an elderly male clerk who had been watching internet porn as she walked in. There were no customers in the store. She said, "Can you give me a good screw for this portable radio?"

The leering clerk, not believing his luck, says, "Dear, I'll give you the best screw you ever had and even throw in some new batteries for your radio. Just lay down on the carpet behind the counter and lift your dress. I'll just be a minute to lock the door and put the closed sign in the window."

******

5180 ==> Two old school friends met after many years apart. One asks the other why he looks so run-down.

"I went to the doctor and he charged me a lot of money. He said I would be dead in a month unless I ate ten pills a day. I paid his fee. Even a doctor has to live."

"Then I went to a drug store and paid a lot of money for the pills. Even a store clerk has to live."

"Then I threw the pills away. Even I have to live."

******

5181 ==> It was a night school class on antique furniture. The teacher asks, "Can anyone give an example of period furniture?

One student says, "Electric chair because it ends a sentence."

******

5182 ==> The elephant faces all dressed in their fine clothes venture forth from their shiny new sleek black limousines. With an assured air they shuffle through the doors of the banks to commit legal robbery.

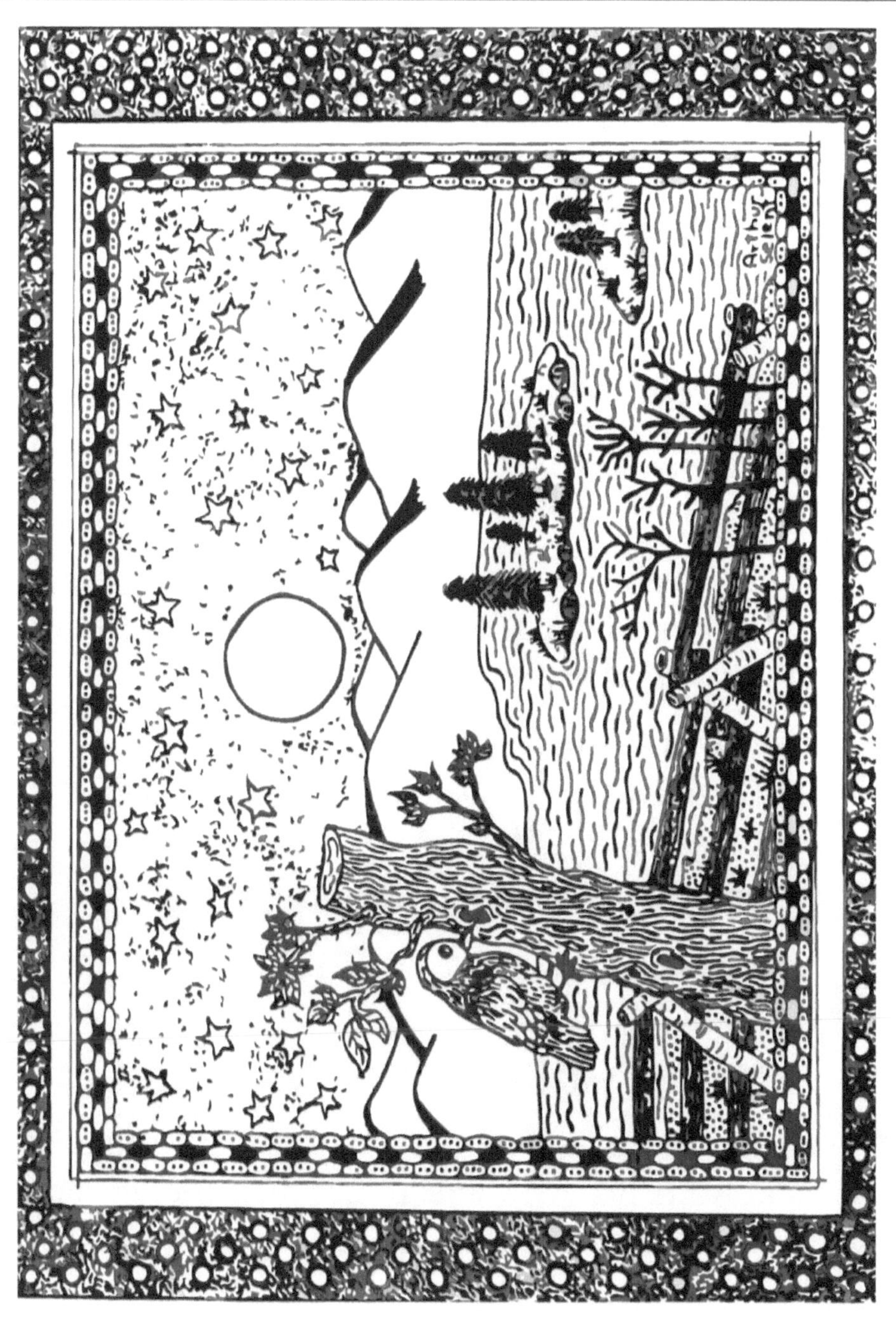

******

5183 ==> The executive management was throwing money around and decided to have lunch at a new restaurant just opened.

The waitress brought the food to their table. One by one the executives said, "We cannot eat this. We demand to see the cook."

Waitress, "What is the use? The cook also refuses to eat this. He brings his own lunch."

******

5184 They were at a church picnic, and the preachers had sneakily provided some wine to relax and loosen the crowd. Make the sins come out to play.

All of a sudden a young female shouts, "What? Twenty dollars. I am not that kind of girl." People looked.

Then man was unnerved and shaken.

She went on, "Make it fifty and you'll get a deal."

The man walked away. People sniggered.

Another man, a married man slowly separated himself from his wife and three kids. Slowly and sneaky like so no one would notice he moved close to her. He showed her his hand holding fifty dollars.

******

5185 ==> The young fellow came home a few days early from a job assignment far away. He entered the house quietly, carrying a small bright cluster of flowers. He heard moaning and the bed creaking upstairs. He quietly sneaks to peek, thinking his wife is doing yoga exercises on the bed. The bedroom door is open, he peeks. There in bed with his wife and a man breeding a family.

His good cheer was smashed. His ego was broken into a mess of jealous defeat. Still carrying his cluster of flowers, he quietly sneaks out of the house.

He goes to his mother's place. Like in his small years, he tells all. "I sent her an email saying I would return early. She was to have everything ready for our long weekend camping adventure."

His mother is silent for a while, hugging her overgrown baby to her breasts. Then she says, "Maybe she did not read the email."

******

5186 ==> She thought he dressed and looked like a thrown-away salad she'd seen in the village garbage dump yesterday.

******

5187 ==> How sad indeed that we are so attached to our own personal virus, which we either hoard at times and at other times spread it among all we meet.

******

5188 ==> The farmer calls up the weather news. "What is the chance for a shower this afternoon?"

Weather office, "That is fine. Just take a shower whenever you think you need one."

******

5189 ==> The workers were all lined up outside the factory. They were on strike and waving their picket signs in a manner suggesting menace.

A news fellow with a video crew came by and asked why they were striking.

They want shorter hours.

The newsman replies, "It is about time someone thought to do something about long hours. Certainly, sixty minutes in one hour is certainly too long."

******

5190 (1/3) ==> The young, uneducated hill billy kid from the remote forests hidden far in the distance had never seen the ocean. He saw a picture and decided to go have a sight see. He talks to the rail workers and finds out which train to jump for a ride to the coast. He takes his sleeping blanket and is on his way.

5190 (2/3) ==> It was high tide and the dusk of evening when he approached a lifeguard on the beach. He asks if he can take a small jar of ocean water home. The lifeguard decides to play along with what he thought was a joke. "Ocean water is selling for one dollar today."

The kid gives the lifeguard a dollar and fills his jar. Then he wanders to higher ground to hide for a night's sleep. He slept late in the shade of nature.

He wanders back down to the beach. The lifeguard was there again but it was low tide today. He says to life guard. "You must have sold a lot of water yesterday. Surprised there is any left."

Lifeguard jokes along, "The government brought big tanker trucks.

They just finished sucking up the water before you came.

They did not pay. They plan to ship the water to the Moon."

Kid, "More secret projects they are hiding from us."

Life guard, "Best not to talk about it. There are spies everywhere. See that new white van parked by the fast-food place. That is the body snatchers, having lunch."

5190 (3/3) ==> Hill billy Kid, "Don't worry, I'll keep the jar hidden in the barn. They will never find that I got it from you. I just came by to say goodbye. I jump the train out of town in one hour. Don't let them catch you."

******

5191 ==> A new reality invites us. See how it opens the door for us. But no one ever returns to tell us what this is like.

******

5192 ==> Much wants more and often loses all.

******

5193 ==> He touched her body with his dirty thoughts. Though he stood at the other end of the bus loading area, she could feel his mind groping and fondling her private place.

She took an oversized mousetrap from her purse. She alarms it and holds it over her private place. She hears it snap. At the other end of the loading area, he jumps and holds his hand in pain.

Next, she takes a feather from her purse. She holds this in front of herself as she looks at him. She blows the feather as she releases it. The feather is pushed along by her breath. He tumbles and is swept from the platform by a strong gust of wind.

******

5194 ==> Support the failure pretending importance at the top of the deception mountain. Don't ask any questions.

Leech the money and life out of them, then sell them to the devil as pet food. Kiss the compost hole of the stinkers at the top, then steal something for a memory.

Who would want anything else?

******

5195 ==> They have planted the wind and reaped the storm.

******

5196 ==> It is Friday night. She's all dressed in her best semi-nude fashion. Hey, boyfriend does not know. He's away for a month working overseas for his boss on an assignment.

She gets out of the taxi in front of the nightclub. She walks inside to join the drunks, druggies, perverts, and bored people all seeking a fantasy in the dark, flashing lights, and music that is way too loud.

******

5197 ==> From her early days, she was a painted savage. All her days, she remained a painted savage. A creature hiding behind a mask. The cosmetic companies made a neat profit whenever she went shopping.

******

5198 ==> The letters and words are in conflict. There are more letters than there are words. The words get shuffled and used again. Many letters have no words in them. This is unheard of con-fusion.

******

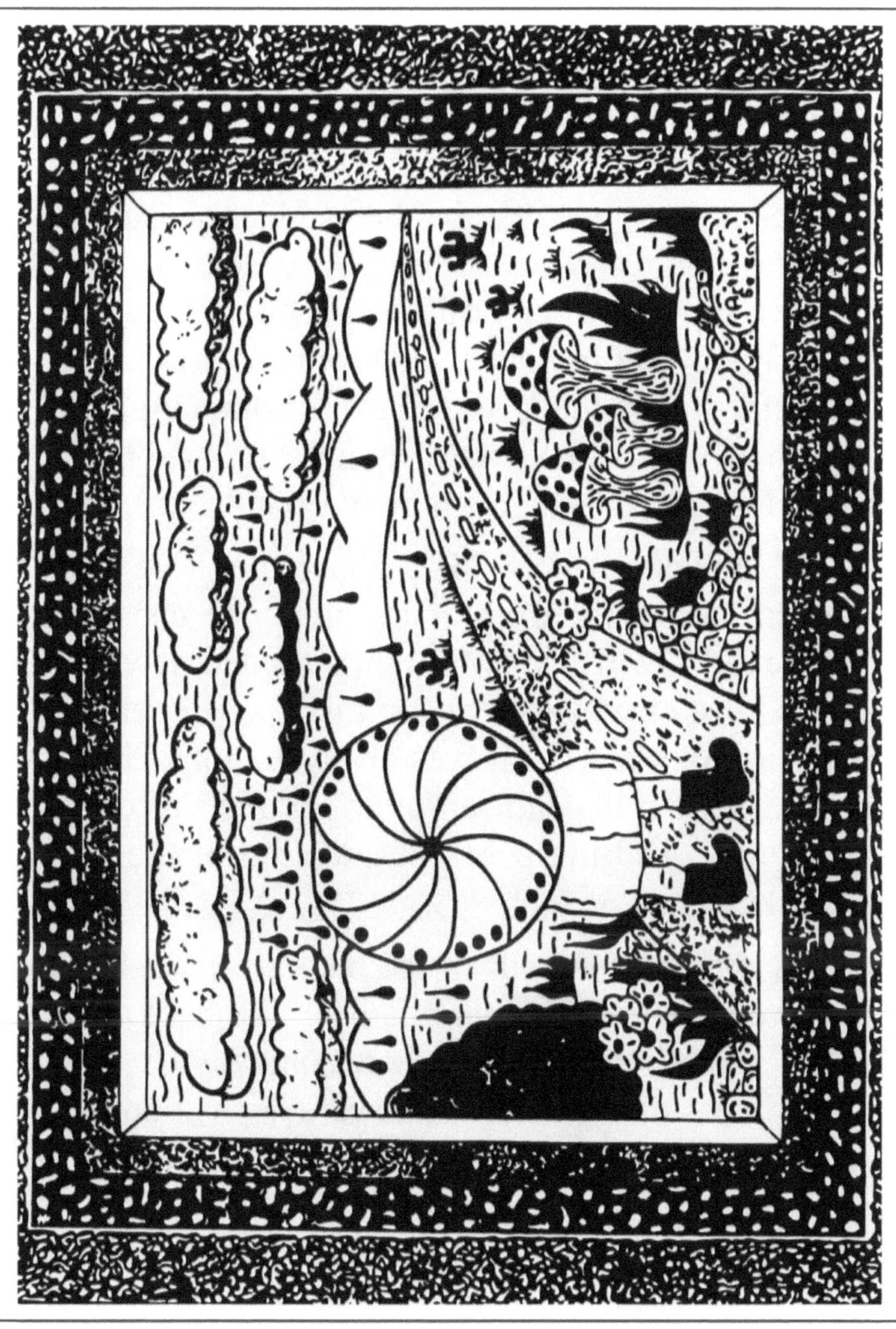

5199 (1/4) ==> It is curious how when one walks a familiar path one had been on many times before, how one's thoughts engross one to the exclusion of surrounding scenery.

So thinking deeply he suddenly stopped walking not really knowing why except his ear's heard a child's voice softly say, "Stop." Looking down at his feet he saw a shiny brass key laying on the path. It was the kind of key for opening locks. Attached was a small tag saying, "Box #49." He should have left it there but he put it in his pocket.

He being single liked the ladies. He liked women who worked around money. He chose his bank carefully. It was where they trained new bank clerks most of which were just his type. He rented a deposit box there but it was always empty. He had no treasure but liked the air of importance in coming and going. And the personal attention of the bank clerks.

Next day he went to the bank to trade smiles and pretense with the bank ladies. The bank had a policy that a bank clerk would accompany the client and witness the opening of the safe deposit box and then wait outside the vault while the client added or removed stuff from the box. This was his chance to be alone and private with one of the young ladies.

5199 (2/4) ==> Only once in four years had he scored a romance. It was a short and ended after the third sex copulation. A bank employee witnessed the opening and closing of the box so if some later incident happened there was protection for the bank.

He was alone, his box open and empty. He looked at his watch, waiting for his usual four minutes before calling the clerk in to witness the locking of the box. Then his eye saw box #49. He laughed thinking it would be impossible.

He tried the found key and box #49 opened. It was packed with large cash notes. He was a very honest fellow but other spirits took over his mind. He filled his box and pockets then locked box #49. He called the bank clerk to witness the closing of the box.

She was cute, just his type and seemed to find ways to be a little too close to him. But he could not even think of romance at a time like this. His mind raced like a bank robber making a getaway.

Back in his apartment he was in shock. What had he done? He was rich. He could not sleep all night. His brain burned with hot fever thinking of all the money still left in box #49. He took his old brief case and removed his important papers hiding them under his bed mattress.

5199 (3/4) ==> An hour before lunch next day, he was back at the bank with his briefcase and wearing clothes that had a lot of big pockets. He thought he looked like a rich eccentric nut as he saw himself reflected on the glass bank doors.

The same cute clerk accompanied him to the vault. He filled his pockets and briefcase. Box #49 was now empty. The clerk witnessed the locking of the box. He felt powerful, naughty, sneaky and invincible. He says to the cute clerk, "Today is my birthday, may I hug you," he does not wait for a reply but grabs her in his arms. She is limp and does not respond. He lets her go. She looks him in the face and says, "I get off work at four this afternoon. Meet me around the corner at the Café."

He raced home, stashed the money and put on his romance clothes. He still had two hours so he decided he'd nap an hour. He slept and missed his hot date.

The morning Sun was peeking in the window when he in his waking moments heard a child laugh and a voice whispered in his ear, "Go to the market and meet the woman in the yellow dress."

Later that afternoon he went to the market and there at the bakery was a woman wearing a yellow dress. He got close and began to make talk. It was love at first sight.

5199 (4/4) ==> Three nights later when they'd finished copulating and she was sleeping he heard the child's voice again, "Daddy, you will soon meet me and see me, I am your daughter."

******

5200 ==> Welcome to Funny Farm Earth.

Are you taking your medication?

Are you making babies for the military people killing industry?

******

5201 ==> After the New Moon as the edge of the Moon becomes visible starting towards the full Moon it looks like a bowl standing on edge. If bowl shape is learning forward like contents being poured out then it will be a wet month. If bowl shape is leaning backward then month will be dry.

This is fairy tale an old man told me when I was a kid, but in all these years I have never studied if this is true.

******

5202 ==> Is your ego so big that it closes the doors of your mental perception?

******

5203 ==> The priests mumbled behind their crossed sticks day and night. The noble's noble day and night. Neither ever did anything useful.

******

5204 ==> You are excuses for yourself but you are not correcting yourself.

******

5205 (1/3) ==> They were little children who sometimes played together in the school yard. She in her rags and he in his fine clothes. She, the daughter of the village beggar and he the son of the richest family.

One day as she in the park looking for treasure in garbage cans, she saw him sitting on a bench crying. She sat beside him and asked what was wrong.

He says, "I lost two money units that my parents gave me last night."

She had that morning found four money units outside the tavern. A drunk had lost this the night before. She gave him this and gave him a comforting hug.

He was just at the stage where his male urges in females were starting to bloom.

5205 (2/3) ==> He took her hand and led her a short distance to some bushy shrubs bordering a wall. Behind the shrubs was a little hideaway where someone had laid some clean cardboard.

She was in heaven. She was alone with him. She was also curious about boys and romance.

He was inexperienced, and so was she. They soon educated themselves.

Often, she would return to the bench and wait for him. If they came by, she would give him what money she had, and he would lead her to some place hidden where they would copulate.

At school, he avoided her and pretended he did not know her. She was hurt in her feelings, but went about looking for money to give to him. He was her secret boyfriend. In her mind danced the fantasy that she would have his baby and be his wife. He was her first love.

Then the family sent him to military officer school, so he could learn the trade of killing people. When he came home, he looked so grand with his uniform and all the hero medals his father had bought for him.

She saw him here and there, but he never sought her out again.

5205 (3/3) ==> Then one day, a big wedding in town. He was getting married to another woman, the daughter of another rich family. She watched with tears but said nothing.

Forty years later she died, alone and unloved. A lawyer came to see the rich guy. He said that she had left her life savings to him. This amounted to almost a half million.

His wife was greatly disturbed but he said he did not know this crazy woman. Eventually the wife said, "She's dead now and half million should not be wasted. We could fill our wine cellar and take a vacation. After all we need it after the evil mind trip she played on us."

He says, "I wonder who this crazy woman was. If I had known she had such mental delusions I would have pulled strings to put her in jail." In his mind he relived all the secret copulations he'd had with her in his teen years.

******

5206 ==> It is easier to walk together if we agree.

******

5207 (1/2) ==> If one has ever watched porn, one cannot help but be amazed at the different sizes of the male penis. Though porn prefers extra-large. Is easier to see by feeble-sighted viewers.

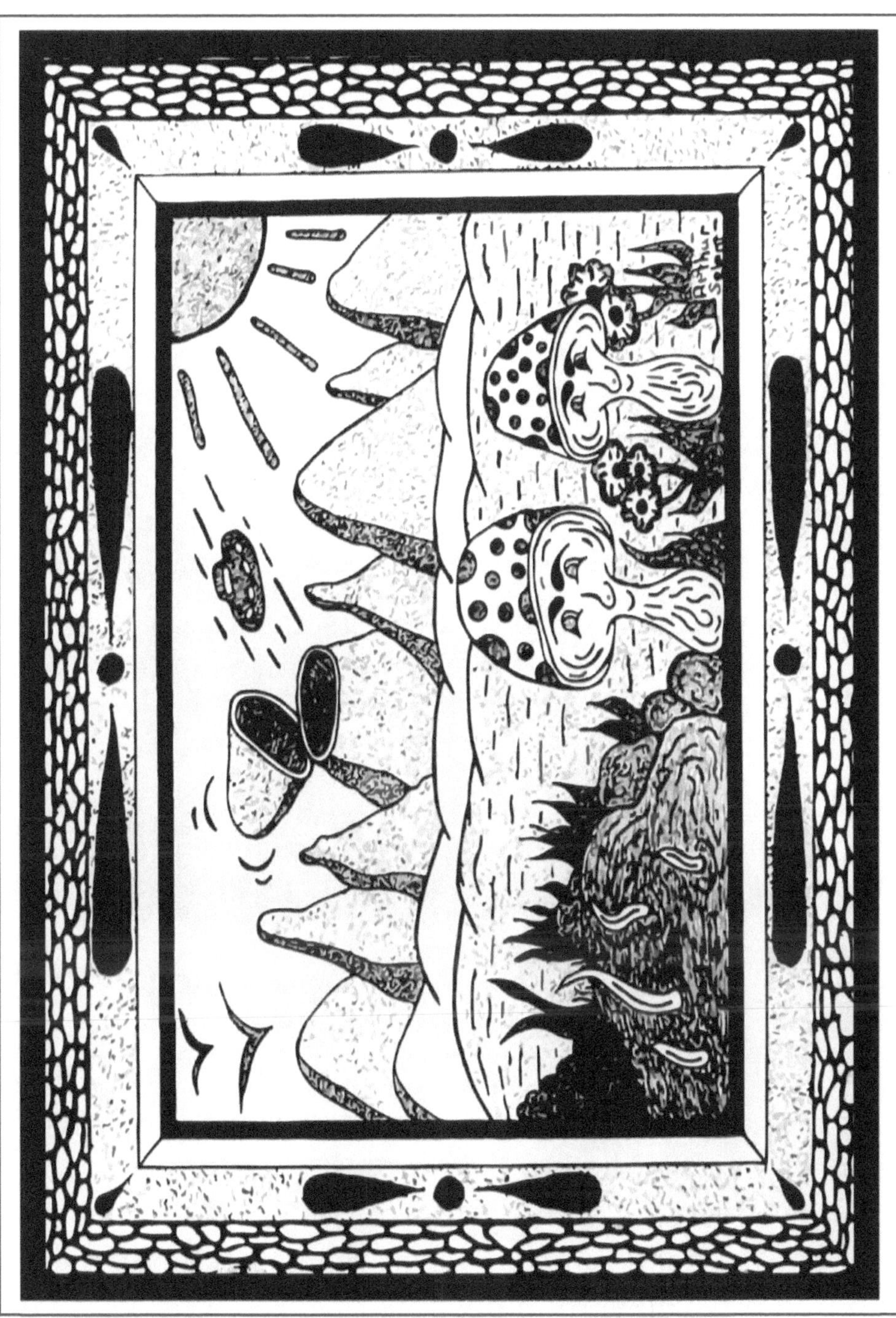

5207 (2/2) ==> Now what about old-fashioned romance, date and hold hands forever, then on the wedding night she finds his penis too large or too small.

People should show each other their private area before romance moves to marriage.

******

5208 ==> How many of us need our past left in peace so time can do its work.

******

5209 ==> Many people who suffer from an uncontrolled obsession with personal integrity are not mentally balanced by a healthy love of money.

******

5210 ==> Being polite is what is left after all else has failed. Politeness is a poor person's virtue. No skill, money or education is needed to be polite or nice.

******

5211 (1/2) ==> When the occasion came to play my hidden card as wildcard, I seized it. It was a sneaky honest move. I had to get rid of the hidden cards, to be discovered with hidden cards would take the fun out of the game. I usually start the game with a half dozen aces, cleverly hidden up my sleeve.

5211 (2/2) ==> Now that I have learned to cheat I must l must learn how to win.

******

5212 ==> Ambition-driven people don't care what others think about them, they do what they want when they want. They get very frustrated when the large rock rolls down the mountain and blocks the road.

******

5213 ==> You have rich, old and sick grandparents slowly ready to die. What do you get? You get a story that ends at the lawyers office where the relatives fight for the best seat for the reading of the will.

******

5214 ==> To many who earn wages put their wages in bags that have holes.

******

5215 ==> Happy people seem to have no history interesting enough for anyone to remember decades later.

******

5216 ==> More things are revealed to humans than the human can understand and not understanding the human closes its eyes and sees not what is revealed.

******

5217 ==> Many kings have lost the royal bloodline because the Queen slept with a different man.

******

5218 ==> Almost anyone can be tricked and have something bad done to them. But a few people have invisible ghost friends. Those doing bad will certainly not enjoy dealing with invisible ghosts.

******

5219 ==> You can see the male chase the female. You see them get married.

You see how the male now on a rope follows the female about.

******

5220 ==> He felt a sense of urgency about this newly met woman. Some twist of fate had put her in his path. He had to know everything, her tastes, her family, her friends, anything about her little secrets. This curious magical unknown young woman that so aroused his male desires.

The less he knew, the more fascinated he was with his desire fantasy.

The more he knew, the more drab and ordinary she became until one day he threw her out.

******

5221 ==> The teen girl was bringing her new gangster boyfriend to the house to have dinner with the family. She stopped him in the hallway leading to the feeding room. She says softly, "You will behave yourself like a reasonably normal, civilized person. Daddy has a lot of connections and can pull strings for you. So be nice to him."

******

5222 ==> How would you feel if I were standing beside you?

******

5223 ==> They called her, "The Sperm Bank." Men coming into her arms made vast deposits. Strange, they never came back to make a withdrawal.

******

5224 ==> The lips were full and fleshy, puckered up to look like the round hole of the ass. The smile was a flat circle, looking like it would fart. The nose grew too high on the head, dividing the eyes. A nose flat and wide textured as if placed there by a concrete trowel and then forgotten before it could be sculptured to look normal.

Her face expressed delightful anticipation as she undressed the drugged, drunk man she had found and brought home. He was now passed out in an unconscious deep sleep.

******

5225 ==> She could have killed him, but she felt sudden sympathy. What if his mother is fond of him? It would hurt forever.

******

5226 ==> An enemy can do many bad things, but only a fake friend can destroy completely and perfectly.

******

5227 ==> A nervous odd bird rumpled by on a motor scooter. People on bright yellow rented bicycles wobbled along, perfecting their balance. The beach landscape was full of young females and young men, all showing off their brainless flesh with the most meager of semi-nude fashions. The ocean waters frothed white, reaching up the beach and then retreating again.

In the distance, tall trees and scattered mansions covered the high rolling hills.

A heaven painted by playful desires seeking happiness.

******

5228 ==> Beautiful expensive cars and women are like gambling. You never realize what a rotten deal you got until all the money is used up.

******

5229 ==> Sitting idle, we explain that we are too busy juggling many projects in our work schedule.

Later, when the projects come to naught, lying about in broken fragments, we can explain that we are overworked.

******

5230 ==> We are alone on this Earth, surrounded by vague dangers and terrible unknown things. We are frightfully alone. Our inner solitude seeks warmth from the evening fire.

Then the building creaks, a night bird flutters against the window seeking the inner light. Then it is gone away, frustrated by its failure.

The wind whispers in the trees and around the building corners. Ghosts telling secrets in a language we cannot understand.

We lock the doors and close the curtains. We are alone. Our soul is silent but yearns and yearns for something we just cannot grasp in reality.

******

5231 ==> Best job to be retired.

Many at this job don't know if it is Monday or Friday. Every day is Sunday afternoon.

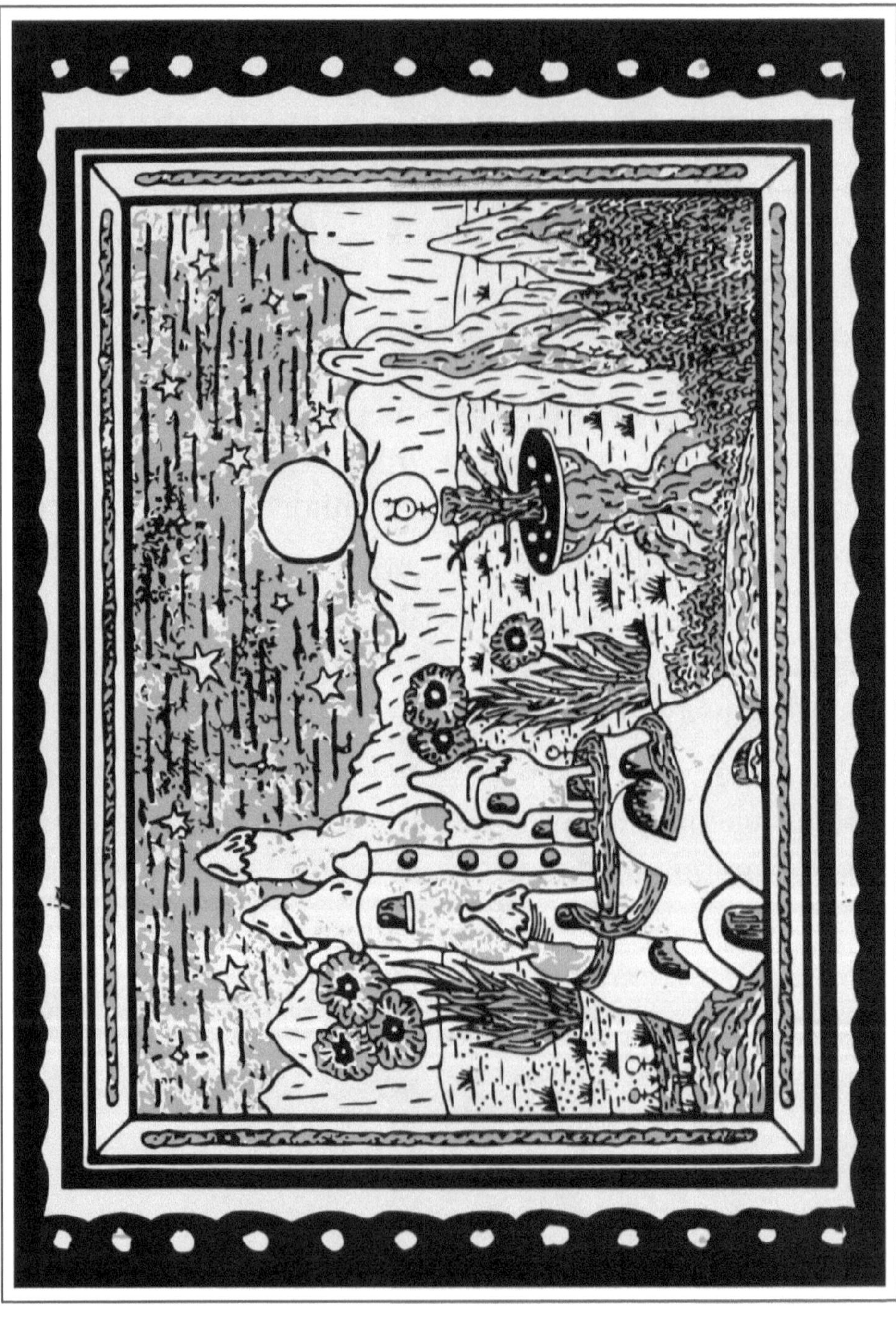

******

5232 ==> Snore and you sleep alone.

******

5233 ==> Go with joy, and the world joys with you.

******

5234 ==> A very frightening thing to talk to one's self in a haunted house or haunted place.

The voice seems as if coming from another; we are the listener. A voice without reason or cause. Our radar finds signals in the hollow space of our minds. Echo's off the wall, and we find not where the voice starts from.

Then the building creaks. We hear the sound of an intruder going into our minds. The wind pulls the curtains from the window. The intruder takes command, and we are deceived into going away from reality and sanity.

******

5235 (1/2) ==> The morning Sun blushed fire red, sneaking quietly over the horizon. The alarm clock had not clanged. The battery was worn out.

She was found still asleep in an adulterous bed. She was not pleased. The wife was not pleased, and the husband certainly was not pleased.

5235 (2/2) ==> Looks like they all had a bad day.

******

5236 ==> A thought came. It sneaked in through a door carelessly left open. This thought entered and roamed about in my higher rooms. It began to pester me like a demonic mischief flea. A little tickle here, a little tickle there.

I tried to chase it away. I opened windows to let in fresh thoughts, but the thought did not wish to leave. How can I express this persistent frustration?

I stepped out the door. The thought also stepped out and stood beside me. We both looked at the path leading to the road. Quickly, I jumped back inside, locked the door, leaving the thought outside. Quickly, I locked the windows and closed the curtains.

Finally feeling inner peace, I turned to look at my lazy chair. There, sipping my finest drink was the thought, its obsessive grip reaching towards me.

******

5237 ==> Far, far away on the other side of time hides our future, hidden it surprises us when we arrive.

******

5238 (1/2) ==> Returning from the wars, we were reckless and eager to use the skills the government had taught us.

With heavy overcoats and ski masks, we sweated. We waited in the dark, hidden by cardboard, junk, and the corners of buildings.

The metal wrecking yard music, the shrieks of women pretending delight, the raised voices of drunk men oozed out of the "Sin City" bar.

We saw the two riot vans pull up. They were half an hour late. A team of oversized goons jumped out. Their uniforms are clean and radiate scary power. They mustered their forces and stormed through the front door of "Sin City" to get their share of some action.

We rushed the van, and with our combat training, we soon had the drivers tied up and left in one of the vans. We took the other van.

In a frenzy, we drove to our selected bank. We took off our warm winter disguise clothes, and underneath emerged our fake police uniforms. We were nervous. Everything had been timed and planned. We were slightly late.

But our luck held good. At the bank, the cleaner was just arriving. He was some migrant from a foreign land who knew not so well the spoken words.

5238 (2/2) ==> He let himself in side door, turned off the alarms and turned to lock the door. We rushed him. The security cameras showed two police men.

We worked fast. This was an inside job and we followed our instructions. We ignored the safe and broke the manager's door in. We could have used the cleaner's keys but we did not think of that.

We moved his desk, raised the carpet and pried the loose floor tiles. Hidden in the floor were stacks of large-denomination money bills. We filled our sacks. It took two trips to the van to remove all the money. Who would have thought that simple paper and ink could be so heavy?

We did not bother locking the door as we left. The security cameras showed the riot van and two police officers carrying sacks from the bank.

We parked the van at a fast-food place where he had earlier parked a car. We drove home.

The next day, nothing in the news. Neither the bank nor the police wanted the public to know.

******

5239 (1/2) ==> Little boys throw rocks at frogs and cats for fun, but the frogs and cats do not die for fun.

Bigger boys shoot birds for fun, but the birds do not die for fun.

5239 (2/2) ==> Grown men go to war to murder people for fun, but the people do not die for fun.

******

5240 ==> She went to the very limit. It had to be done. It was the only way to graduate with honors.

She often took the privilege of bending over the window to watch the boys play athletics down below. She exercised her authority with all kinds of cleverness. she would at these occasions' let down her sincerity and cunningly let the school master use her for his pleasure.

******

5241 ==> So vividly the rather empty landscape of life being a full-time tourist. This thought played in his mind.

There was no need to struggle for any need. Money took care of every need.

Always moving to another place when routines became boring in the previous place. Meeting new people and then leaving them behind before one knows anything about them.

A sort of high comedy with the fun lines hidden and out of each. An untarnished picture of fake happiness sitting at sidewalk cafes and making up fake histories about one's self. The table littered with paper cups holding liquids to sip, slurp and guzzle.

******

5242 ==> Although she has a beautiful face and color with cheeks like vibrant flowers, it is not clear why the Great Spirit has tricked her out of a lifetime of popularity.

******

5243 ==> We must try to be good people but it sure makes us jealous to see the devil having all the fun.

******

5244 (1/3) ==> He could have originated there. His keen hunter's observation saw that he had room and freedom to play. It would be risky but he was in a fever of inner needs. Like a predator he watched left and right looking for the easy reward to satisfy his inner needs.

It was a lucky day. She was fresh, shapely and self-assured. She was his perfect fantasy dream. Was she waiting for someone or was she waiting of the train.

He slowly came close to her, pretending to walk to the end of the loading platform. He looked at her surrounding area. It was good enough. A wide doorway was set deep into a wall. He walked to the end of the loading platform looked around for a bit then turned to walk back to where he came from.

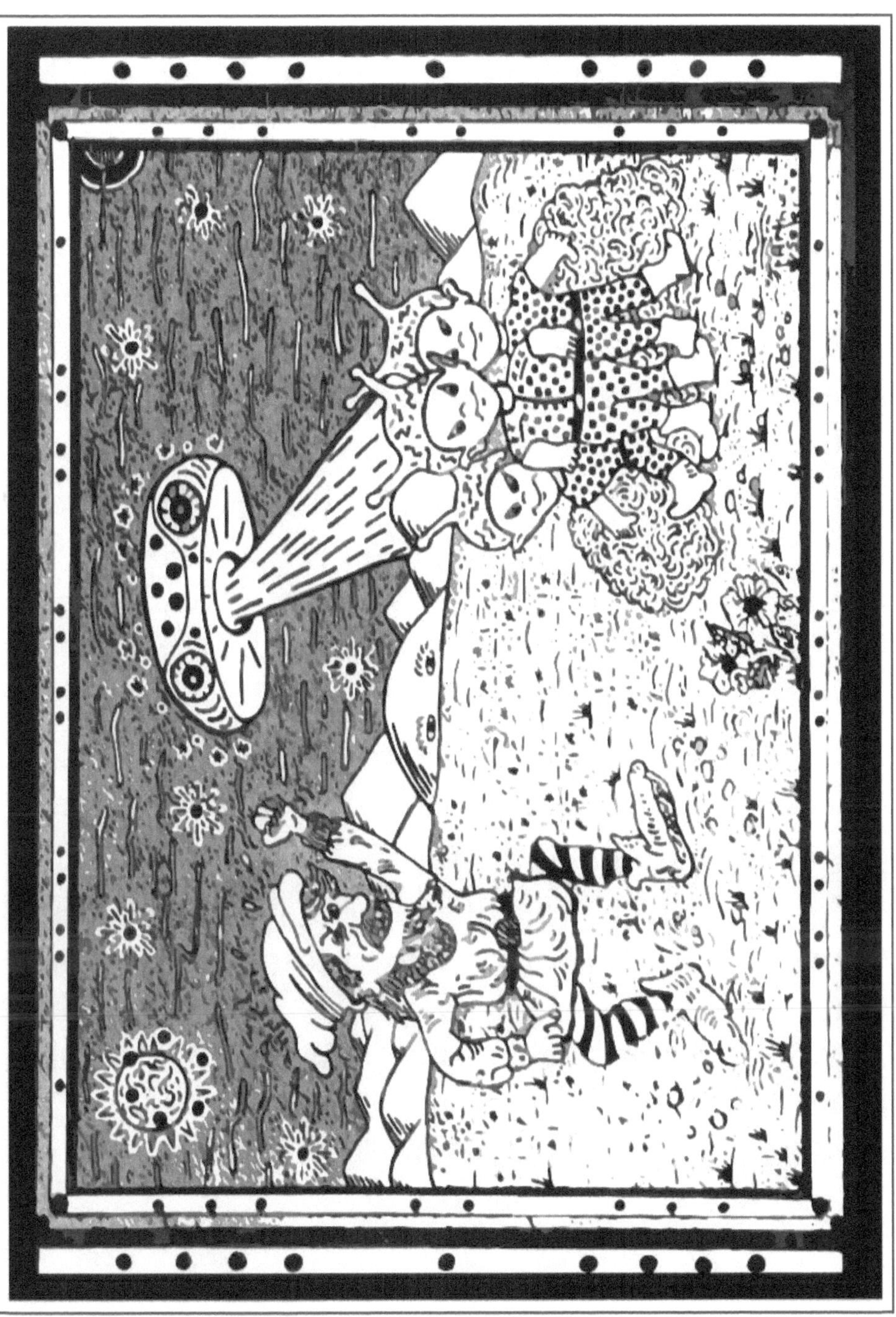

5244 (2/3) ==> She had been a little nervous when he'd walked by the first time but now relaxed and ignored him. He made his move. His hand clasped over her mouth and he had her muscled into the doorway within seconds. His mouth covered hers, she could not scream. She was in shock. He grabbed her arms and with one of big hands he held them firm. With his other hand, he slid her dress up and her underwear down. He entered her secret warmth and with great satisfaction, enjoyed and release of his inner urges.

Anyone walking by the doorway would have thought they were having a goodbye quickie. He finished and quickly ran away to join a few people going inside the station.

She did not see where he ran. She was in shock. Carefully, she made her clothes presentable and stepped out from the doorway.

He watched from the other end of the platform as a thug came along and tried to steal her purse. Apparently, it was not a good day for her. She resisted and struggled, quite mad at this double misfortune. The thug stabbed her over and over before running of with her purse. She fell down, and the blood pooled around her.

5244 (3/3) ==> The train had just stopped and opened its door, so in the rush, no one noticed, and the few who did just wanted to get away from the scene. He was in the crowd pushing to get inside the rain.

From a window seat, he saw her lifeless body lying there, blood all around her. Two police men were just arriving, and one was frantically calling someone on his radio phone.

He sat alone. The train picked up speed, and all was left behind. He thought of his baby seeds deep inside her. Would they come looking for him? No, they would not suspect rape.

Just then, someone sat beside him. He turned to see. It was her. He tried to push her away, but his hand went right through her. She covered his mouth with hers. He felt her cold hands undo his pants. He felt the heat fade from his body. She would not release him. He shivered with the cold. His soul left his body to join her in the Spirit world. All his strength could not save him.

******

5245 ==> The lucky few who are clever enough to be lazy and get away with it.

The lucky few who are lazy enough to be clever and get away with it.

******

5246 ==> Without a doubt, his first lover was odious to a degree of simplified pleasure proportional to her mentally undignified sense of humor. Her atmosphere still haunted him at parties and social gatherings as if she could still reach out and torment his thoughts as joyfully as when she had him shackled to herself by his delusions of love.

While he remained true to his loyalty, she slyly carried on with every seduction to come along to hurt and twist the pain deeper into his soul.

******

5247 ==> The strongest poison ever known came from a blob of grey jelly sitting on top shoulders of belonging to a human.

******

5248 ==> The cry of the night whore roaming from street to street is like the wild dog in heat carrying not whose seeds are planted.

******

5249 ==> The romantic fantasy of guys, to have dinky go for a swim in pinky.

******

5250 ==> The little school boy avoided the short way home because that walked him past the home of the school pest. The pest was a large brute with joy of meanness always ready.

The long way was only five minutes longer. If followed a path going through a church field where graves were filled with bodies. During daylight, it was a pleasant walk and birds sang from the few trees spaced along the path. The trees had benches set in their shade.

The school was putting on a theatre play to raise money for a project. Some kids stayed after school to help set up the stage as well as to practice their acting. It was a ghost story show.

Moving through the night on his way home he took from habit the path through the tombstones. He tried whistling softly but it sounded hollow and haunting as he shuffled along. He stopped whistling. To keep his courage up he silently walked faster. It was too scary at night. He'd never walked this path before when it was dark night.

He looked to and fro. He sees a movement among the tombstones.

******

5251 (1/2) ==> A dark shape had just moved from behind a tombstone and hid itself behind another.

5251 (2/2) ==> A He walks faster. He tense. He just reaches the small gate leading out of the graveyard when he sees the dark shape coming fast for him. It looks big. He went to run but tripped and fell to the ground. He was in a panic to get up, but the dark shape rushed through the gate and tripped over him.

The little school boy with his satchel gripped tight, picked himself up, and ran as if his shadow were on fire.

The next day at school, he learned that the bully brute he feared so much had been found dead at the graveyard gate. It appears he had a fall and smashed his head on the stone-paved path.

The little boy relaxed all his tensions. His soul relaxed. So it had not been some fearful ghost, only the dreaded bully up to no good.

******

5252 ==> Pack eternity into each day.

******

5253 (1/2) ==> The homeless tramp was picked up by a middle-aged housewife as he hitchhiked down the road to nowhere. She took him to her home and fed him. He washed himself, the first shower in four years. The dirt almost clogged the pipes.

She had him sleep beside her in bed. He had not had a girl friend experience in years, so he took every liberty he ever desired.

5253 (2/2) ==> She was either a good actor or she really enjoyed his crude passions. She moans and holds his body firmly, eagerly responding. It was a fast weekend of food and frolic in bed.

Monday morning came and she took him back to the road. Her husband was returning that afternoon and she had to make herself ready. It was time for him to go.

Shouldering his pack he slowly walked down the road. His confidence and fresh outlook seemed to have faded away. He felt like a dejected haggard housewife. And so lonely.

******

5254 ==> We can all read the same story but some of us read black when other read white or even red or blue.

******

5255 (1/3) ==> The prisoner was before the court. The law had its hands firmly on him.

The prisoner asks to say something private to the judge. The arm of the law stretches as he comes close to the judge. He whispers to the judge. The judge seems disturbed and in deep thought. Then they both whisper back and forth for a minute.

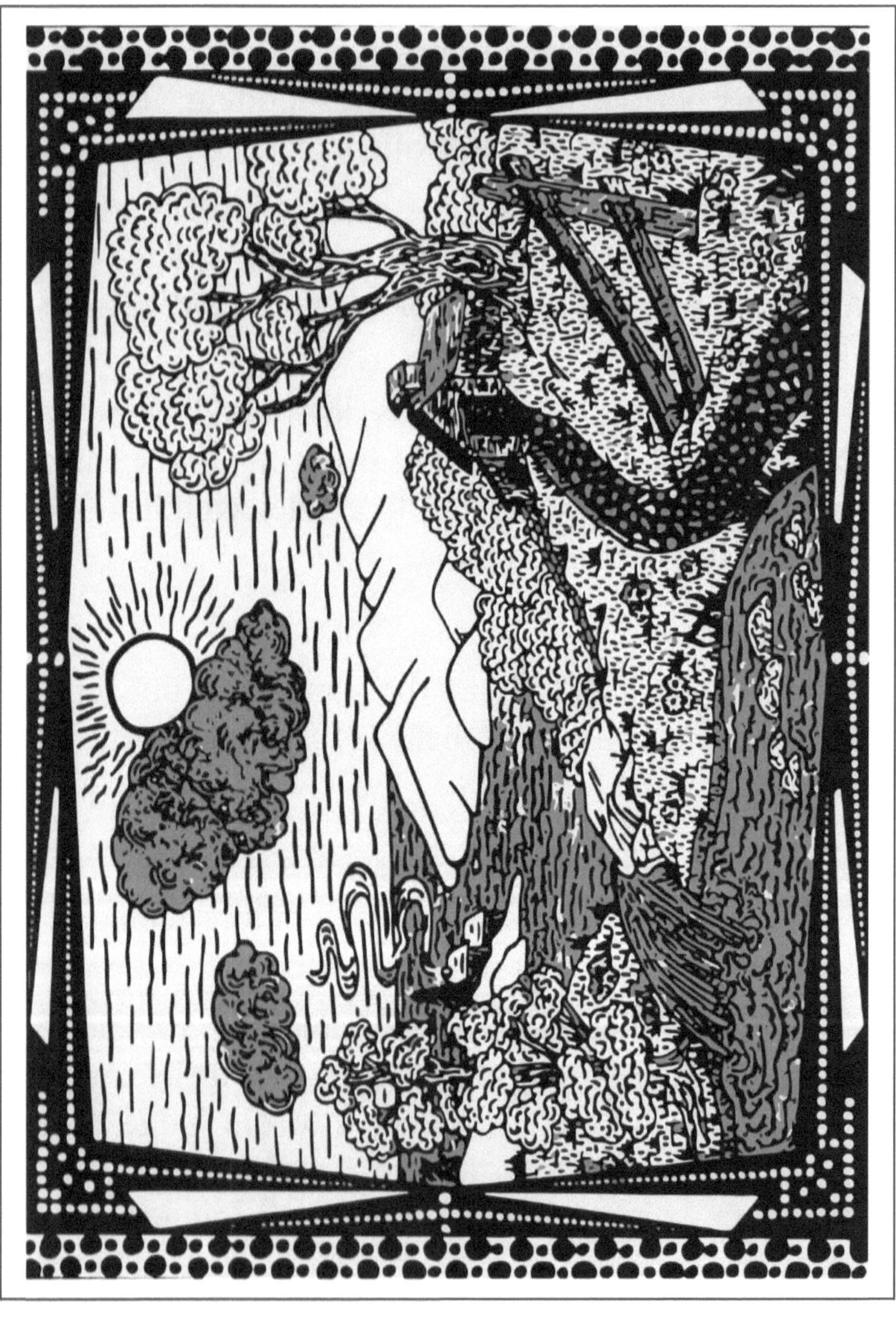

5255 (2/3) ==> Prisoner goes back to his seat. This law on all sides.

Judge in deep thought calls the boss of the law over. He whispers. "The prisoner could not have robbed the bank. He was in bed with your wife at the time and has video evidence of him and your wife in bed. I suggest we keep this private and let the prisoner go free. You can settle with the prisoner at a later date."

Law boss seems shaken, "It could mean my job and our other dealings would be seriously harmed. Ok, let's let the fellow go."

Judge says to court. "Now evidence of a sensitive nature has come up and until we fully investigate, we cannot talk of this case. The new evidence shows that the prisoner did not commit the bank robbery. We the court find the prisoner not guilty."

A week later in the evening, the judge was sitting outside at a sidewalk café. The prisoner comes along carrying a modest-sized canvas pack. He sits at the judge's table. "I've brought one-third of the bank money as we agreed. Thank you for doing business in such a professional manner." He nudges the canvas pack under the table to rest against the judge's feet.

5255 (3/3) ==> As the prisoner stands up to leave, he places a thumb drive chip on the table, "Here is a copy of the law boss wife and me in bed. This video is from our school days before she met the law boss." Then he places another thumb drive chip on the table. "This video is of me and the law boss wife having a quickie at her wedding party."

As soon as the prisoner has faded away down the sidewalk amidst the crowd, the judge picks up the thumb drives and packages. He goes home.

Across the street the law boss secretly watches from a parked car, his brain cooking marbles in cabbage soup.

******

5256 ==> Home, the belonging place. The place we go when we have no other place where we belong. The place where we wait for tomorrow to find us.

******

5257 ==> Doubt often leads to believing a lie just to feel reassured.

******

5258 (1/2) ==> No one has defined this jewel of reality. The wise people's uncertainties make great effort to follow the body's last sleep, dreaming that the grip on the thread of wisdom has been lost.

5258 (2/2) ==> The body has been left, and the soul returns not. We grasp for a grip on the handrail as we enter the spirit world. Our souls are filled with expectations brainwashed into us by religion and people who have never been there.

******

5259 ==> For the most part, we are in our right minds, possession of ourselves, but know very little of the arrangement. Years later, when we leave our bio compost-making body behind, what will we know?

******

5260 ==> Some people who look beautiful and attractive suddenly become very ugly when we see how they think.

******

5261 ==> Every whore was once a virgin.

******

5262 ==> Through both are given the same day of 24 hrs., the fool sees his day different than how the wise person sees their days.

******

5263 (1/2) ==> An addictive woman, wiser, he treated his soft, haggard wife like dirt.

5263 (2/2) ==> Coming home only long enough to wash, eat, and change clothes. Nights spent in other bedrooms scattered here and there in the big city.

The poor wife, all her emotions ripped into fragments of failure, had long ago given up. She was merely content to have a warm, dry, safe roof over her head. She saw herself as a maid to look after the house. She merely existed while waiting for old age to arrive.

******

5264 ==> They say clothes make the person. Then why are there so many well-dressed, stupid people?

******

5265 ==> We must create our life's system or be enslaved by another person's system.

******

5266 ==> Prisons are built with bricks of Law. Soul entrapments are made from stones of religion.

******

5267 ==> We throw our evils into the wind and when the wind blows our evils back to us, we wonder whatever we did to receive such evils.

******

5268 ==> The one who has never forgiven a friend often pretends to forgive his enemies only to prolong the moment of revenge.

******

5269 ==> Oh, brain, you will not find the solution to the riddle. You will not see the road the wise look for.

Why work yourself into a boiled frenzy? Take a day off. Turn the brain off.

******

5270 (1/4) ==> The old lady was crazy. Everyone knew that but she was rich. So rich! She also owned three sections of land. When he died, in her will, she gave each of her three grandchildren a section of land, and a jar filled to the brim of a variety of seeds. At least a hundred different seeds. The old lady was crazy.

Two of the grandchildren sold their section of land and bought a large house on the edge of the city. They worked in industrial factories for a simple existence. Their jar of seeds having gotten lost somewhere, overtime.

One fine early spring with the Sun shining through the window the third grandchild land a bed sheet on the floor and emptied the jar of seeds.

5270 (2/4) ==> She had kept her section of land and restless to work on a project had decided to plant some seeds to see what plants would grow.

To her surprise she found a note inside the jar, hidden by the surrounding seeds. The note was a sort of treasure map showing the location of a spot marked "X" on the map.

Next day under dark storm clouds she got into her car with a shovel. She drove to the back corner of her land. An old crab apple tree had grown there. It was just like grandmother, too old and time to move on. Picking the crab apples each fall had been a fun time for the grandchildren.

The thunder rumbled mean sounds. It seemed to get darker, colder. She went to the crab apple stump. She stepped two steps due North, just as the map said. She started digging. The lightening flashed. She worked faster. She imagined herself digging up a grave. One never knew what crazy grandmother was capable of.

They were not too deep. Three large plastic pails with secure water tight lids. Each pail with secure water tight lids. Each pail had the name of one of the three siblings written on the lid. She fumbled about lifting her pail out and opening the lid.

5270 (3/4) ==> To her surprise, the pail was stuffed full of big bill bank notes. A lot of money. The pails were heavy, but the excitement of the surprise and rain starting had her extra determination. She got all three pails into her car and drove home, grateful to be on the move before the rain turned the farm path into mud. She made up her mind to plant a new crab apple tree on the spot.

Back home, she parked her car close to her house door. The pails were heavy, but she was in an excited, hypnotic trance with determination, she got all three pails inside the house. The lightning flashed, and the rain started as if there were waterfalls high up there somewhere.

Her mind was racing with fever. She made room in a cluttered corner of the cleaning closet. There she placed the pails. In big bold letters, she wrote "Sweeping Compond" on each pail and faced this towards the door. Then she spread clutter all around and on top. The pails are hidden by mops, brooms, rags, and other things that gather in cleaning closets. It looked good. No one would suspect.

Finally, she can sit down and recover from this wild thing that just happened. Outside, the storm released its anger, big thunder flashes. The mind is throwing the rain against the windows. The heavens rumbled from horizon to horizon.

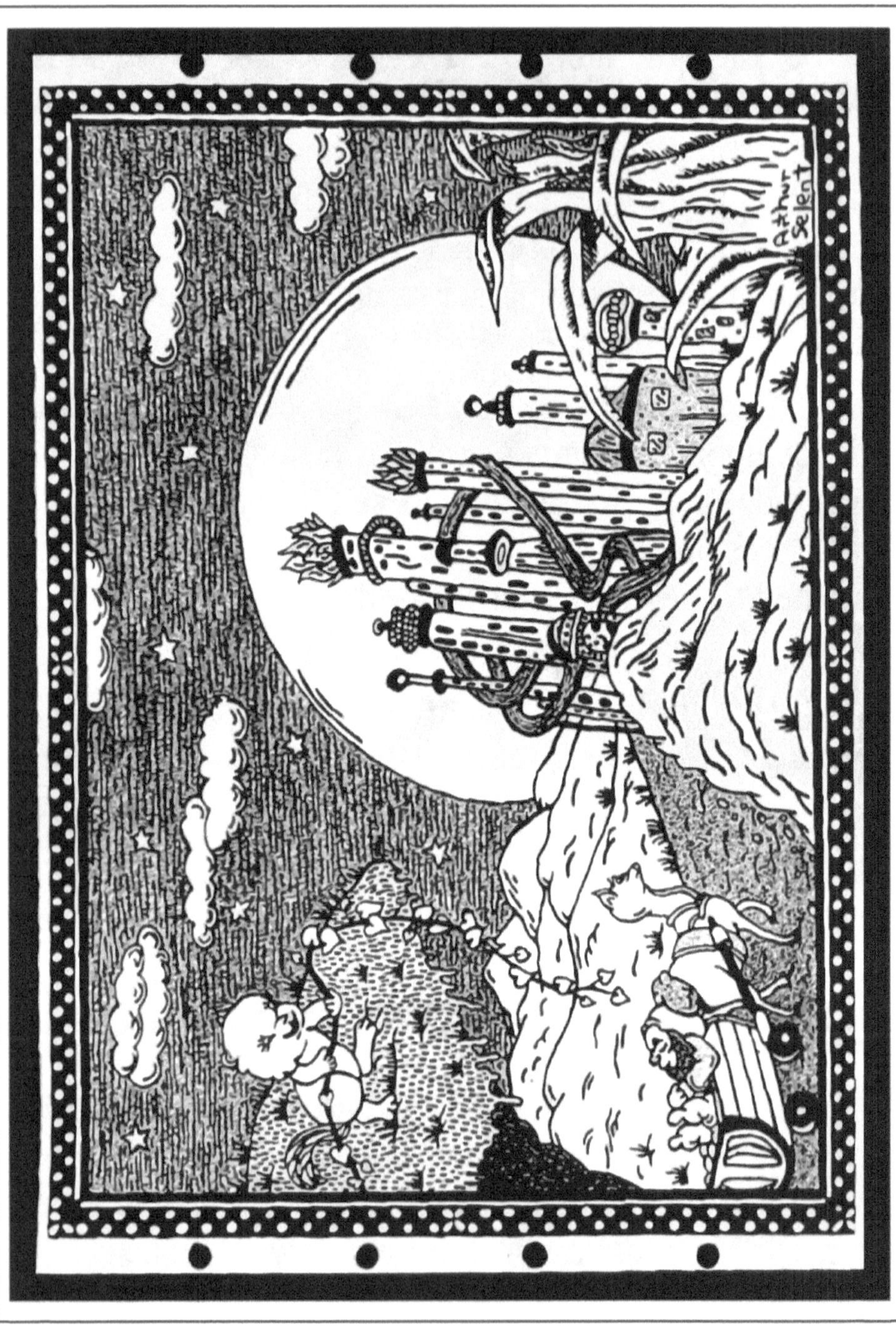

5270 (4/4) ==> Two glasses of wine later, she thinks of crazy old grandmother. It seems each grandchild had received the same treasure map inside their jar of seeds. But what if each had a different map?

She wondered if her siblings would have shared the treasure if they had found it first. She wondered if she would share.

******

5271 ==> Fortune gained nothing from our going and coming. Why do we ourselves often never know if we come or go? Or even why.

******

5272 ==> Let them speak who have been to hell. Let them speak who have been to heaven. Let them tell what they have seen so that we need no longer carry stones of religion when we go for a swim in the seas of civilization.

******

5273 ==> I am one of those nice guys one reads about in the dictionary.

******

5274 ==> The puppet masters peek from behind the curtains. The curtains begin to rise. Oh, look how the puppet masters run, not wishing to be found out.

******

5275 ==> If we embellish material things, then for what reason do we later cast these into decay and neglect?

******

5276 ==> Some people are so grateful for a doctor's attention that they will strive to get whatever sickness the doctor needs this month. Some even take the prescribed medications, believing this will give them the sickness and make the doctor happy, so more appointments can be made.

******

5277 ==> Many are unwanted, unloved, and uncared for. They live in loneliness, despair, and hopelessness. Inside, they yearn for a little love.

******

5278 ==> It is rude to piss on someone's picnic table.

******

5279 (1/2) ==> Two old grey-haired fossils met by chance at the country club. They had been school buddies a century in the past. They had not seen each other in all that time. They were sipping good, expensive wine and already tipsy.

5279 (2/2) ==> One says of his wife, "I don't understand. My wife and I had such a beautiful life for forty years, and then it all fell apart."

"Oh, how did that happen?"

"We met and got married."

******

5280 ==> He found a planet that was flat. In despair after having lived on the planet for years, he one day jumped off the edge of the planet. One wonders how he was able to top the concrete walls holding the oceans from flowing over the edge.

******

5281 ==> They go forth in their airplanes laden with bombs and chemicals. They go forth over the ocean to destroy and murder millions of people they have never seen and know nothing about. They go forth with nervous tension, each with the desire to be the great hero who has killed all the humans.

Why do they do this?

******

5282 (1/2) ==> A prospector made himself a sturdy, simple shelter close to his gold claim creek. He was often gone all day looking for gold. Once a month, he would walk five hours to pick up his government pension check and buy supplies in the village.

5282 (2/2) ==> The walk back was always a trudge since his backpack would be heavy with supplies, and sometimes his hands carried something too big for his pack.

He was disturbed about a few people wandering along the creek. These were city people who camped upstream, a half-hour walk at a tourist camping place. These people seemed to think his shelter was some sort of place to drink, do drugs, and copulate, leaving a mess behind.

Finally, he came upon a solution. He put a modest sign on the entrance to his shelter. "Jack, I've gone to the village to get something to deal with the lice. They are in my clothes, bed, and everywhere. All the time, they bite me. "Just wait nearby. I will be back soon."

******

5283 ==> A mistress is a pussy that is rented on the installment plan.

******

5284 (1/2) ==> We are truth taxed, stamp taxed, gas taxed, life taxed, death taxed, receipt taxed, loan taxed, federal taxed, provincial taxed, neighbor taxed, property taxed, rent taxed, water taxed, electricity taxed, food taxed, and brain taxed.

5284 (2/2) ==> We are inspected, suspected, but never respected. We are cussed, discussed, and disgusted.

We are humans trying our best to complicate life.

******

5285 ==> So many innocent young women on their wedding night already think of their marriage as some sort of sin to be forgiven.

******

5286 ==> This is our planet, yours and mine. But who are those flying between us and the Sun?

******

5287 ==> The rich woman was thinking, would she rather have a man who needs money or money who needs a man.

******

5288 ==> Little girl saying her nighttime prayer.

"Hi, God, it's me, your innocent sweet angel. I told my mother that she must get me a bra next time we go shopping. Please help me grow up. You know where. I would like some big balloons like the tramps have who daddy watches porn."

******

5289==> Can you imagine the honesty some folks have to put up with year after year?

******

5290 ==> The greatest skill of the political cheese is to render their own sins and vice as a service to the cause of virtue.

******

5291 ==> Some people work with a big shovel, some work with a small shovel.

******

5292 ==> The manly man had sixteen children from twenty women that he'd frequently seeded in the last two years. Maybe it was time to retire. But as he got bored and lonely, he noticed so many sad-looking lonely women. He just had to go back to his job at the baby factory.

He looked at himself in the mirror and said, "No use having good equipment go to rust."

******

5293 ==> At the bottom, though some would say the top lies or floats, the ghost of a primitive being covered with hair and fur. A savage wild thing.

******

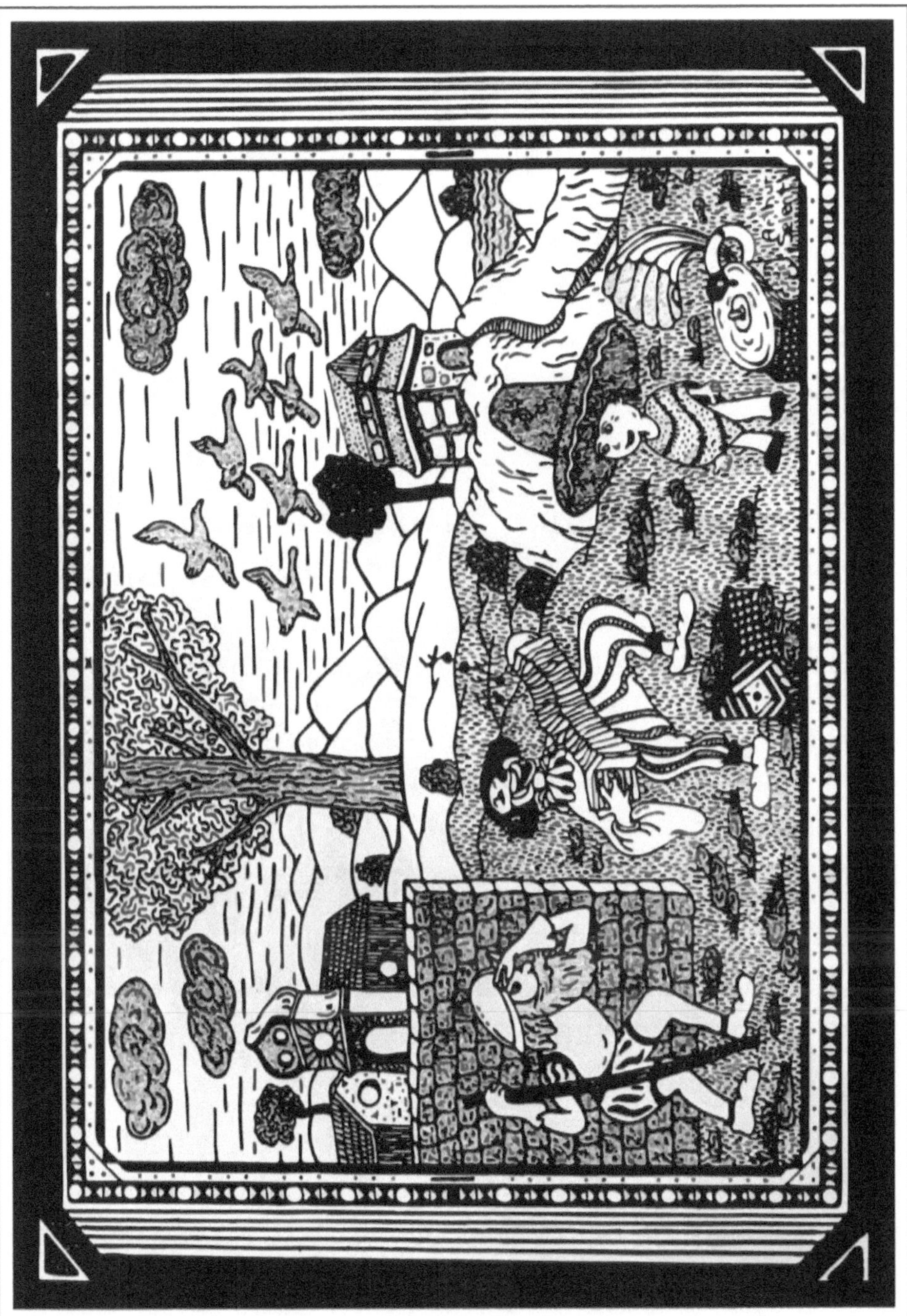

5294 ==> Survival guide for reeking political cheese. When in command, ponder and look intelligent. When lost and in trouble, delegate others to deal with the situation. When in mental doubt, mumble something no one understands.

******

5295 ==> The honest are so few that rarely do two meet.

******

5296 ==> I made her nervous, and she made me nervous also. I felt deep in her the desire to satisfy her urges, lusts, and need for a boyfriend experience. An invisible electrical field radiated from her.

I run my fingers through the hair of her pussy. The electrical pulse runs up my arm to my brain. The brain is overloaded with emotions of heated desires.

She, the most charming and treacherous, cannot easily be thrown off. I fall victim to her reality and splash my seeds. The switch is thrown, and the electrical attraction loses force and becomes inert, soft, and limp.

She, with her clear yet false eyes, has chosen me for her gratification needs and traded delicate cares.

I pay her and go home to my soft, ugly wife.

******

5297 ==> You notice that people often talk about killing time while time is quietly and sneaky, like killing them.

******

5298 ==> Teachers can never tell where their influence wanders.

******

5299 ==> She attacked him like a red neck cop with a water cannon at an anti-nuclear demonstration. She swung the garden hose like a serpent whip. He dodged and escaped extermination. She splashed water on him.

With innocent eyes, he looked at her and walked away. She watched him and went back to watering the flowers.

He was confused. Why had she acted with such hostile fright? All he wanted was to ask for a drink of water from the garden hose.

******

5300 ==> What a person does with what happens to them is experience.

******

5301 ==> Our children are so exposed to the internet and TV media that they are lost to their parents by the time they are ten years old.

* * * * * *

5302 ==> There are devils living here. They are sleeping now.

Does anyone have a devil removal machine available?

* * * * * *

5303 ==> He saved the planet yesterday.

Single-handed with his shiny new gun, he chased out a nest of homeless tramps squatting in a deserted mental home. Now he was a local hero.

The neighborhood rich kids can now once again sneak into the deserted building to do strange, sinister things.

* * * * * *

5304 ==> Sometimes, to push your opinion into the brain of another with no facts of reality, the only defense you have against skepticism and doubt is your own self-assurance and poise. Act confident, and most will believe even if you lie.

* * * * * *

5305 ==> He had a magic paintbrush. Whatever picture he imagined, the brush painted it. His only purpose was to hold the brush and twitch his hand about.

******

5306 ==> How fast the spring of life becomes winter.

******

5307 (1/2) ==> She was at a party that some strange people were having. A friend of a friend had invited her. She knew no one there. The food was lavish and had a great variety. The wine bottles are abundant.

She loitered here and there, but no one seemed interested in talking to her. She went around tasting the wines. She took two bottles that tasted to her liking. They were still full. No one seemed to notice when she carried the bottles into the empty kitchen.

Quickly, she opened the cabinet under the sink and hid her two bottles behind some cardboard boxes of towels. She got a surprise because someone else had already hidden two bottles there.

She mingled a little here and there, but the people were not her kind. The party became a drag of being in everyone's way. People were getting drunk and becoming foolish.

5307 (1/2) ==> She went back to the kitchen. No one was there. She got her two bottles of wine from under the sink. She decided to also take the other two bottles someone else had hidden.

No one seemed to notice or care as she held two bottles in each hand, shuffled along the hallway, and left by the front door.

All week, she nipped a little wine after the evening meal. She drank her two chosen bottles first.

Then she started on the other two that someone else had hidden. She gently sipped away gently fell asleep, never to wake again.

Someone had poisoned the wine.

******

5308 ==> Each person has their own combination of mental insecurity, fears, and questions. Emotions in conflict are confronted with morality, human limitations, and desires. An all-consuming frustration roller coaster ride here and there about our daily lives.

But dare we awaken thought and tell thought what is going on?

******

5309 ==> We must snatch our future when we can before others snatch it away.

******

5310==> She would not take public transportation. One never knew what would happen in those places. In cars, she slammed her foot on the floor every time the driver touched the brakes. Sometimes she'd even open the door, ready to jump.

She refused to leave the house after dark or during rain. One never knew what was out there, hiding. If a draft drifted her incense smoke, then she imagined someone had opened an upstairs bedroom window and was crawling in.

Always around her, vague anxieties buzzed like static electricity, sending little shocks in all directions. The slightest unexpected sound, and she tensed with apprehension and ran to the gun cabinet.

******

5311 ==> No matter whether the worm feeds underground or the wild dog feeds above ground. All our desires come to nothing in the end.

******

5312 ==> So what the master of fortune has written will be before time began will not be unwritten.

******

5313 (1/3) ==> Dark came early in the evening. Dark clouds hid the stars and cooled down the sweating heat of the day.

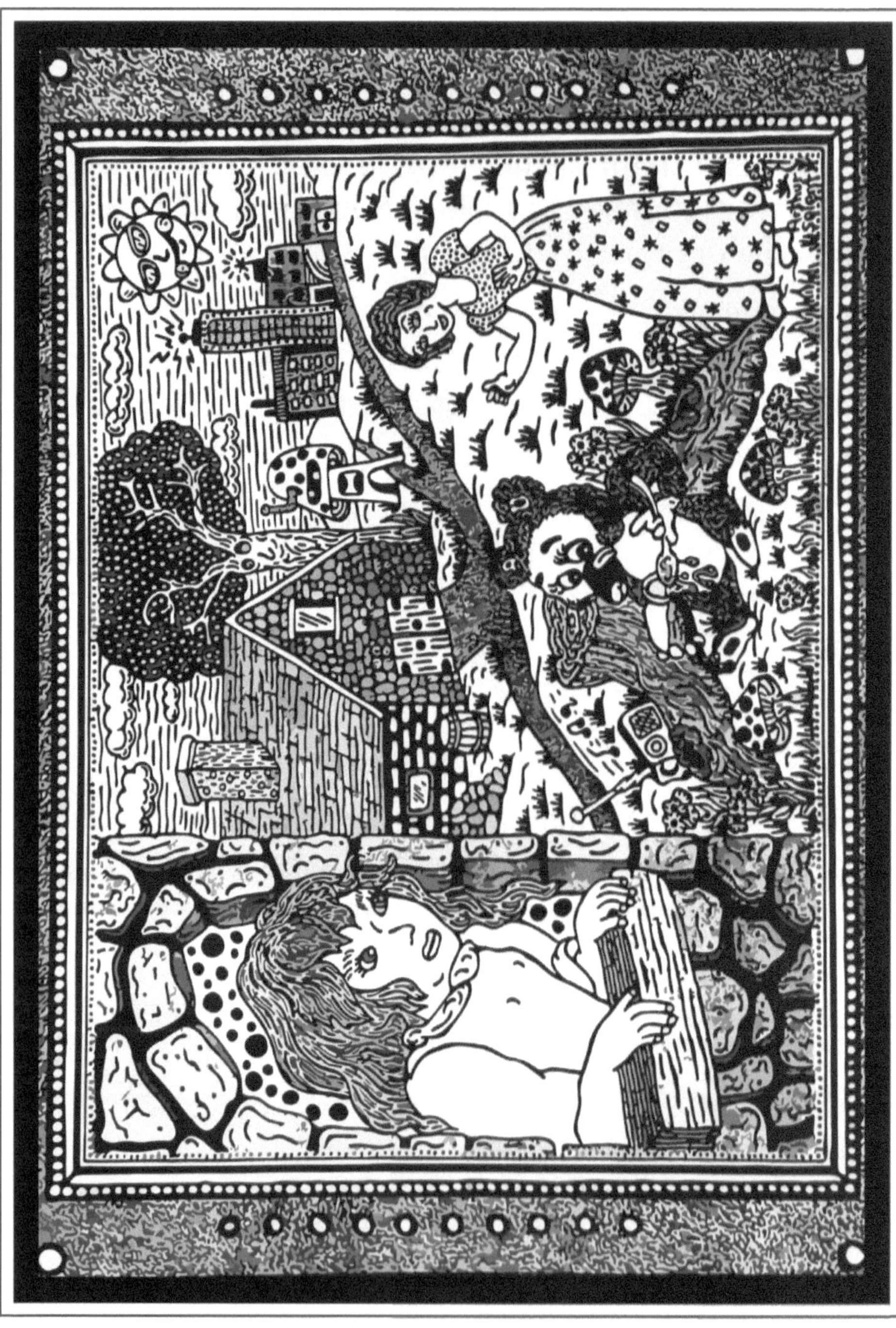

5313 (2/3) ==> It rained hard and soft, seeming to play a slow rhythm on the roofs of tin sheds. The wind was witchy, gusting, then calm, and then to suddenly wail with much strength, bending the tree tops this way and that.

A spaceship silently fluttered down as though it were a feather. It hovered a hand's span above the ground in that lonely cow pasture. In the distance, the lights of a big city lit up the bottoms of low-lying storm clouds. The spaceship shimmered soft metallic grey to match the surrounding darkness. It was hidden. It was silent. It was still.

A sharp crack of thunder and the night lit up with a flash of thunder. The thunder rolled across the sky so loud that one suspected the planet was coming apart.

A door slid open in the side of the spacecraft. I was thrown out. My backpack and camping gear followed.

The door closed, and the spacecraft silently lifted. It started to glow a yellow-orange and zipped out of sight.

There I was all alone in the field. I hoisted my backpack. Two witches flying a boy on their broomstick circled around, cackled, and went their way. I walked until I found a cluster of trees far from any farmhouse and set up an overnight camp.

5313 (3/3) ==> I had seen an alien spaceship hovering over a grass field, and little Aliens descended to look for magic mushrooms. I sneaked onto the craft and hid. They found me and threw me out. Nice of them to return me to Earth.

And I didn't even get any photos to post on social media.

******

5314 ==> A speck of dust joined the soil and was lost. A drop of water joined the ocean and was lost. A human is born and is lost in the population.

A flower blooms and is lost when winter comes.

******

5315 ==> Of all those who leave, where is the one who returns?

******

5316 ==> Much happiness and unhappiness are concerned with the solution of moving colored slips of paper about. Paper and ink are commonly called money.

Now this is odd because the money is neither joyful nor sad.

******

5317 ==> He had just graduated from the best mental school. He set up his office in a humble, rundown part of the city. His first client was a rich society lady, middle-aged and frustrated. Her husband no longer slept with her.

He instructed her to lay on the sofa. To relax and tell her deepest feelings.

He sat at his desk, leafing through a dictionary of the mind, looking for the right malfunction relating to her condition. She rambled and babbled on about her need to have a sex life. He could not find the right condition in the dictionary.

She asked him if he was ready for sex.

******

5318 (1/2) ==> The greasy bar where government workers tried self-destruction by drowning was doing a brisk business. The place was filled with hawk-faced, heavily armed secret agents with delusional hero fantasies in their minds. This caused them to act abnormally, as if they had a mental condition.

Beside the washroom door was a small bulletin board advertising the names and phone numbers of local contract killers in need of employment. The bar provided this public service for free, it being paid for by the Federal Defense Budget.

5318 (2/2) ==> The stripper with the cherry lips wiggled her ass and flashed her tits on stage. Sometimes she'd go on her knees and stick her vagina hair too close to a nose at the front crowd, hooted when she popped ping pong balls out of her liquid compost outlet.

Another Friday night at the National Security Office, keeping our flag safe from those other people.

******

5319 ==> Many of the same as you come and go. Only to be returned to the oblivion from which all came.

******

5320 ==> No flower that wilts will readily bloom.

******

5321 (1/2) ==> The ghost did not believe in supernatural poltergeists. He was too mature, being already four hundred years old. He sat at the slow end of the bar watching the drunks drink. Sometimes, using his supernatural poltergeist's gifts, he dealt murderously with those who behaved badly enough to be murdered.

He had learned the places of pain from an overpriced chiropractor.

5321 (2/2) ==> The fellow playing the Kazzoo was getting on his nerves.

The thugs, pimps, perverts, drug dealers, black market businessmen, men, and low-life political cheese sensed something was about to happen. The Kazzoo player stopped playing, feeling the coldness of the ghost reaching out. He hid his Kazzoo in his clothes and sneaked out of the bar.

The ghost was disappointed; he'd planned to shove the Kazzoo up the hole we don't show polite society.

******

5322 ==> If your reality was shown to you, would you be content to continue as you are, or would you try to change?

******

5323 ==> You are a good person, and you work honestly for the system. You believe in the system. You know nothing different.

Then one day, the system falls apart. You see all the pieces, the dishonesty, the deceptions, the sneaky stealing and killings. Your reality is shocked. You gave your best and were cleverly used.

Now you are lost and must look for a new master.

******

5324 ===> He is of the finest character when in public.

Behind the curtain of his private world, he eats his grand meals and blows his nose off to one side with his fingers plugging one hole. He drools and the wine runs down the sides of his chin as he nosily, beast-like guzzles the wine bottle empty.

Always wanting more.

******

5325 (1/2) ==> He was pleased that luck had brought him a serious goal to achieve. A major unfinished business to attend to. The flight attendant, a new employee eager to do a good job, asked him if he was comfortable. Would he like anything?

"Yes please," he said as he put his hand on her inner thigh and slid it up under her skirt. She did not scream. She just stood beside his seat and let his hand explore.

They were at the back of the plane, and the few others on board had their backs to them. Feeling confident now, he pulled her head down to his lap, where he'd opened his zipper and had his little manly thing ready for his lips.

She took a forceful bite. He screamed in pain.

5325 (2/2) ==> He realized that she did not like him.

She walked to the front of the plane, explaining to passengers who had turned around to see what was going on.

"Everything is fine. He just had a bad dream."

* * * * * *

5326 ==> I gave the devil your address. Please go with him when he comes to get you. I do not want to be alone down here in hell.

* * * * * *

5327 ==> The most virulent laboratory slime ever invented could not compete with the bacteria of her kiss.

* * * * * *

5328 ==> Is there someone inside your head, and it is not you?

Don't despair. It is not the end of the road.

Contact Ghost Removal Services. Millions have already been scammed. Be next to be saved and reborn.

* * * * * *

5329 (1/2) ==> Lawyers may beat over matters and use one thing to prove another, and yet even to illustrate yet another in the game of various legal cases.

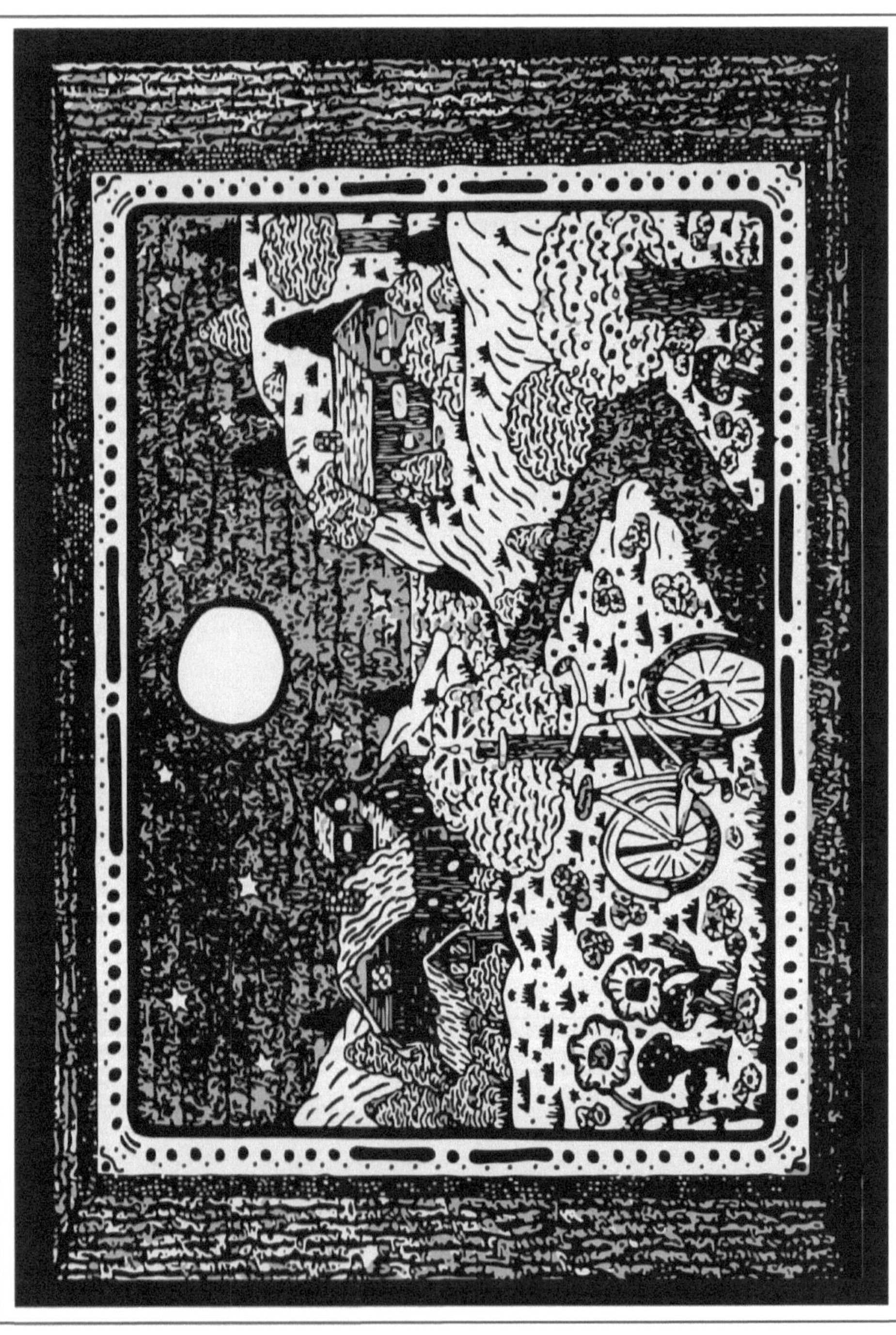

5329 (2/2) ==> So every defect of the soul can be made to look like glowing innocence when confronted with the justice judge, needing a little secret incentive placed in a secret pocket.

******

5330 ==> Always before his wit, his tongue races as though chased by fire. He often tells great fantasy stories about himself. Be they true or false, he knows not but he believes his tongue. He is a smart ass, too intelligent to make a sentence have any truth.

There he is, the grand hero, cluttering up the room.

Yet he knows not that he knows nothing.

******

5331 ==> When failure strikes look to see, if possible, how others succeeded.

******

5332 ==> Encouragement is like a change in the weather suddenly becoming fresh like the warmth of spring.

******

5333 ==> It is Friday night and I am available.

******

5334 ==> It is all bullshit, but it is very fine quality. I make it myself.

******

5335 ==> The summer tourist season at the lake has started. Campers and tents line the shores. Little clearings among the trees.

Canoes glide gracefully following the shore line. Flat bottom row boats powered by undersize out board motors chug slowly along to a spot considered good for fishing. Fast, rich speed boats churn the water racing in demonic circles with silly semi-nude teen age girls shrieking and pretending to enjoy the wild race of going in circles.

In the evening the campfires light up the coming dark. The smell of pan fried fish sizzling over the fires mingles with the wood smoke drifting in the air. Fish fed on sewage, decaying dogs, cats and human bodies, garbage, old tires and people pissing in the lake.

Of course, there are the usual pretenders who pan fry store bought fish because they do not want others to know they did not catch any fish.

******

5336 ==> We have lost the directions back to our youth. We cannot return.

******

5337 ==> The road skimmed along the beach edge. As one moved along, people on rented yellow bicycles cluttered the road, wobbled along nervously.

On the beach, the scene was crowded with show-off people eager to flash their semi-nude bodies for all to see. Some so semi-nude to the point of disturbing society. Women and men lusting for sin and not afraid to take a chance.

They look for the special car, the special motorcycle, the boat, the special person. They use their sexual lure to attract an experience. Their bodies are the currency of exchange.

******

5338 ==> Look at the beautiful flower growing in the garden. If we pull the flower away from the soil, we have created death for the beautiful flower. The flower wilts and dies.

But we have the experience of watching beauty die.

******

5339 ==> A good compliment can put a month's worth of fuel in a downtrodden soul.

******

5340 ==> School books showing hungry elephants pushing a tired, worn-out horse. People armed with burning torches are cruelly forcing the elephants onwards.

A perfect contempt for all business documents displaying any honest transaction. The genuine truth was killed off with the first shot. The deceptions become unintelligent discriminations, twitching mental insanity in the delusions of rich and poor alike.

Religion turned out to be the education factory. Turned upside down and emptied. Every one insolent and hiding weapons as if these were gold. Placing the lust for evil on the shoulders of a God they have never seen or can describe. Slyly, they slink about.

Come, it is a new day, we must awake and go forth to master. Our reward is that when we go to heaven, we sit beside God and eat the Souls of the lost.

******

5341 ==> He looked like something the government would use to scare people.

******

5342 ==> An hour's slow drive from the village, the main road was crossed by a lesser road that ran through a forest and then out of sight, curving around hills and mountainsides. This lesser road got narrower and rougher as we advanced.

We got to a point where large granite rocks border both sides of the narrow road. It became dead end stopping at a sturdy locked gate, stopping the entity on the side of a mountain. A sign on the gate said, "Haunted Mine, Private Property, No Trespassing."

We push a secret button hidden on the gate post. We wait for one minute, then hear a beep-beep sound. We press the secret button again, and the gate opens to let us enter the underground Alien base.

******

5343 ==> They watched the humans buy their fake vaccine poisons. They watched the big fears and even bigger profits manifest. They watched the humans slowly die. How intensely they watched and studied.

They were happy. They felt powerful and important. They were Gods without love. But the only thing they could create was suffering and death.

******

5344 ==> The repulsive ground ape called human smells the stench of death drifting in the air. Over crude campfires, they roast their kills. With full stomachs, they thank a God living in their imagination.

Even the devils hesitate to walk among the repulsive ground ape called humans.

******

5345 ==> He told the entire story to the police. How she had left him on the 12th. They had a big fight because he caught her copulating in the nude with the neighbor. She and the neighbor both left together in her car.

The police listened carefully to his story. They had found the two bodies on the 10^{th,} but it being a big weekend, they were slow to question him.

******

5346 ==> Ghost-like in the dark, familiar sights hide in the dark, unfamiliar confusion of comprehension. One fears the fears ahead and the fears of the past. One is haunted and alone, facing the unknown.

About the Author

I grew up in farming areas up to my late teens. When I was about six our family had some trouble getting along and mother and dad split up. I was brought to grandparents on Dad's side.

They placed me in the storage room where they kept preserves and their wine. It was quite cool but they gave me extra blankets. One day I saw one of the wine bottles was uncorked and a little wine still left in the bottle. I tasted it. Then one by one the wine bottles became empty. I hid the empties best I could but one day coming home from school I noticed all the wine had been taken away, so there I was six years old depraved of my new hobby of drinking.

So my strange life education kept walking. I ended in big city pent house apartments working factories and stock markets. One day everything went wrong and I was homeless.

There followed seventeen years of hitch hiking and sleeping outside. I got money by working tourist places that provided a free bed with the job. Also dis seasonal orchard work. A last social welfare. In seventeen years, I saw all of north America from the sides of roads.

I did three years of bicycle travel in Alberta and British Columbia, Canada. To pay for food I collected aluminum drink cans and traded for money at recycle places. My expenses were small but then also was my income.

Then I started living in vans. I somehow got started doing artwork and making these into post cards which I would trade for spare change or sell for small money. A lot of walking in the big cities for person-to-person sales. The artwork in my books are a selection of these postcards.

One day I got a steady job and shut the artwork down. The spirit seemed to have wandered away. So I spent the next decade plus working one steady boring job after another, working with frustrated people.

The writing of the books started in a sort of sneaky way, I had started a social media account and was looking for something to post. I had a small data plan so videos and pictures used too much data, so I started writing this and that. From the overflow of social Media posts started my book writing new job.

Arthur Selent

June 23-2023

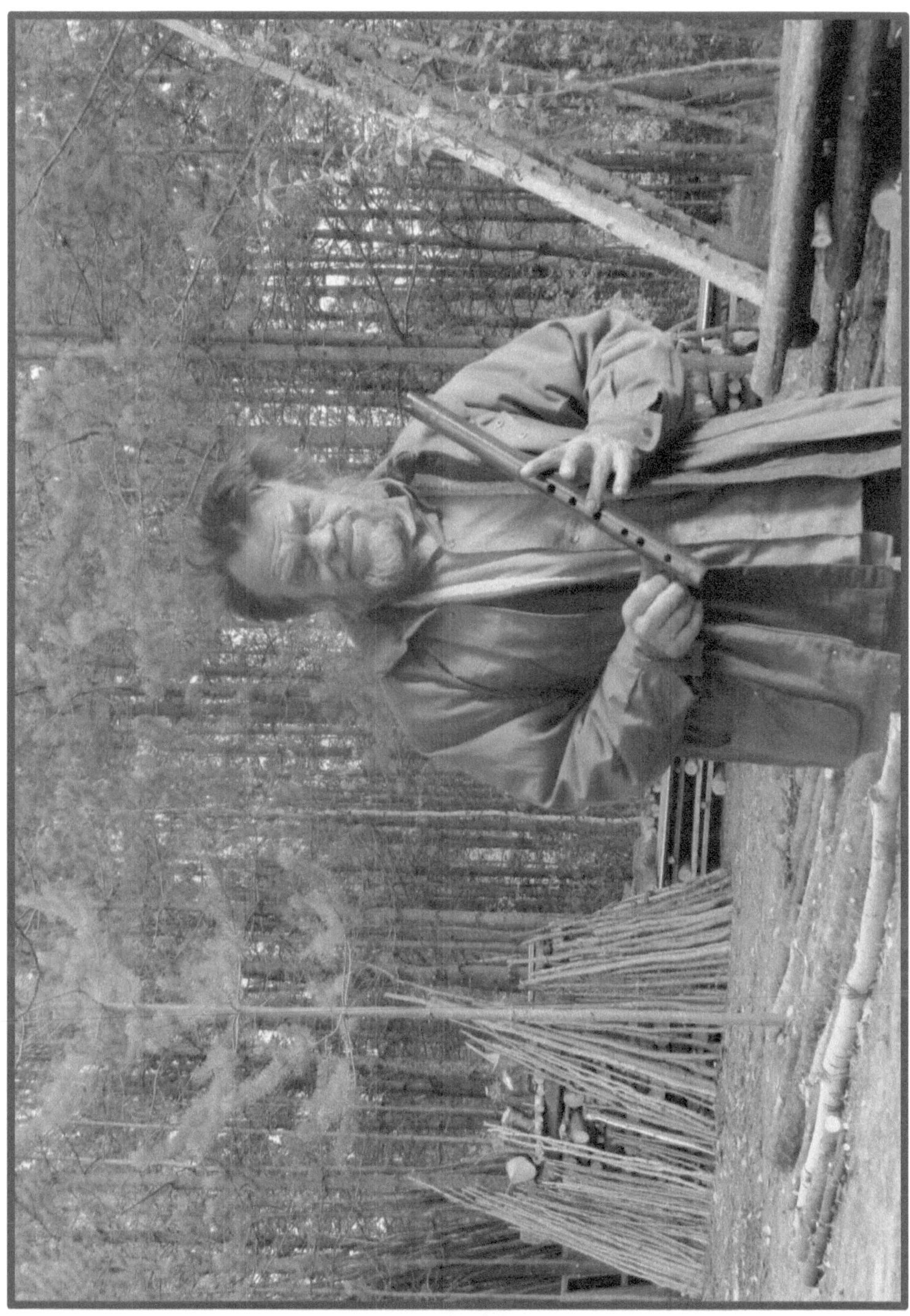

www.ingramcontent.com/pod-product-compliance
Lightning Source LLC
Chambersburg PA
CBHW032139050726
47591CB00001B/28